AF560080

HIDDEN WARFARE

Mangesh Sawant's work examines the various military dimensions from the Second World War to the Cold War that have long remained obscured—the contests waged beyond Europe's main battlefronts. In these operations, conducted through intelligence, deception and maritime manoeuvres, nations sought advantage not through massed armies but through precision, secrecy and influence. Overshadowed by the Allied campaigns in Europe, these efforts reveal the enduring interplay between information, power and influence. Mangesh's analysis reflects rigorous intellect, his narrative is distinguished by remarkable clarity and the stories carry an enduring and timeless appeal. The reader will discern in this work the enduring principles of strategy and the timeless tenets of command that transcend every domain of warfare.

Colonel Ranjit Jha
YSM, Indian Army (Retd),
ex-Commanding Officer, 21 Para (Special Forces),
who planned and led the 2015 surgical strikes in Myanmar

Just as the Napoleonic War against Russia was immortalized in Tolstoy's *War and Peace*, Mangesh Sawant has resurrected some narratives of valour, courage, grit and determination from the Indian Ocean and the Pacific theatre in the last century—from the tumultuous World Wars to the intense contest between the NATO and the Soviet Union. Besides redefining naval strategy, espionage, diplomatic heft and sheer audacity, this is a chronicle of courage, confidence and consequence. The book counters the dominant narrative of Europe being the centre stage of everything!

Sanjeev Chopra
Former Director, Lal Bahadur Shastri National Academy of Administration, Historian and Author

Mangesh Sawant brings forgotten battles out of the shadows and into the strategic spotlight. With the precision of an intelligence analyst and the narrative skill of a field historian, he reveals the covert operations, deception campaigns and geopolitical manoeuvres that have quietly shaped the modern world. Having worked at the intersection of national security, cyber warfare and statecraft, I recognize the same patterns of hidden conflict playing out in today's digital domain. This book isn't just a history—it's a masterclass in how power is wielded in the grey zone between war and peace.

Sachin Deodhar
Former Chief Technology Officer,
Security Establishment, Government of India

Spanning a wide canvas of time from the folds of contemporary history, Mangesh Sawant's *Hidden Warfare* is a mosaic of hidden tales meticulously researched and warmly narrated. *Hidden Warfare* traces the stories of forgotten protagonists who figure in the periphery of wars. Sawant's racy pace and teasing details ensure a riveting read from beginning to end. Each story burns with tension through its twists and turns and reveals the extraordinary circumstances that catapult ordinary beings from the edges into the frontlines of a conflict, shaping forgotten historical outcomes.

Probal DasGupta
Army Veteran, Military Historian,
Author, and Corporate Leader

HIDDEN WARFARE

Unknown Military Operations from **WWII** to the **Cold War**

MANGESH SAWANT

RUPA

First published by
Rupa Publications India Pvt. Ltd 2026
161-B/4, Gulmohar House,
Yusuf Sarai Community Centre,
New Delhi 110049

Sales centres:
Bengaluru Chennai
Hyderabad Kolkata Mumbai

P-ISBN: 978-93-7003-631-4
E-ISBN: 978-93-7003-753-3

First impression 2026

10 9 8 7 6 5 4 3 2 1

Printed in India

Contents

Introduction

Readers have always been fascinated by war stories. Tales of courage, sacrifice, strategy and survival have captivated audiences since ancient times, forming a rich and enduring tradition in military history. Yet, amidst this vast body of work, there remain numerous war stories that are surprisingly unknown or have received only scant attention. This book seeks to bring those hidden narratives into the light—stories that are impactful, adventurous, revelatory and outstanding, but which have largely been overlooked.

Compared to the extensive and robust literature on war, which spans centuries and diverse cultures, these lesser-known stories have been obscured by more famous battles, celebrated leaders or dominant narratives that moulded popular understanding. Many of these stories have been blinded by the fog of battle which captures the confusion, chaos and uncertainty inherent in war. Others have faded into the blur of time, lost amid the passage of generations and the overwhelming scale of historical events.

By uncovering and examining these neglected stories, this book aims to enrich our understanding of war beyond the familiar stories. It reveals the complexity, diversity and humanity that exist within the margins of recorded history. These accounts remind us that war is not just about grand strategy or political outcomes but also about individual experiences—of bravery, hardship and resilience—that deserve recognition. By shining a light on these forgotten narratives, this book offers fresh insights and a deeper appreciation of the operations that shaped the contemporary world.

This book weaves together a rich tapestry of themes and narratives, from the cataclysmic events of World War II to the tense, ideological standoff of the Cold War. It offers readers a fresh perspective through unique and lesser known historical events that unfolded across the twentieth century. By doing so, this book brings a new dimension and invigorates the field of military history, which, despite its breadth, remains dominated by well-trodden stories and widely studied campaigns.

Much of the existing literature on World War II is primarily focused on the European theatre, highlighting landmark moments such as the D-Day landings, the Battle of Britain and the exploits of legendary commanders like Bernard Montgomery, Georgy Zhukov, George Patton and Erwin Rommel. These battles and figures rightly occupy a central place in the narrative of the war; however, they have also contributed to the relative neglect of other theatres that were equally critical to the outcome of the conflict.

In particular, the Pacific and Indian oceans—vast and strategically vital regions—have received comparatively less attention in mainstream military histories. While the European and Atlantic theatres witnessed massive land and naval engagements, the Pacific theatre was the stage for some of the most decisive and technologically advanced naval battles in history. Here, aircraft carriers emerged as the dominant force, revolutionizing naval warfare and surpassing the battleship- and submarine-centred confrontations that had characterized the Atlantic campaigns.

Outstanding naval battles fought in the Pacific—such as Midway, Coral Sea and Leyte Gulf—not only shifted the balance of power in the region but also redefined naval strategy worldwide. These battles underscored the importance of air power and mobility on the seas, marking a turning point that naval historians and enthusiasts cannot overlook.

By highlighting these under-explored regions and events, this book expands our understanding of twentieth-century warfare beyond the familiar landscapes of Europe and Atlantic. It invites readers to explore the vast oceans, remote islands and lesser-known conflicts that played a pivotal role in shaping the global order during and after World War II, extending into the fraught geopolitical tensions of the Cold War.

History is often told in broad strokes—through iconic battles, famous leaders and sweeping declarations of victory or defeat. But beneath the grand narratives lie overlooked moments, obscure operations and quiet battles that shaped the nature of warfare. This collection comprises seven compelling stories extending from the Second World War to the height of the Cold War. Each narrative sheds light on lesser-known but profoundly consequential events that reverberated across continents and nearly altered the course of global history.

Each chapter is rich with detail, interweaving battlefield tactics, clandestine strategies, covert meetings between statesmen and generals, and the murky undercurrents of espionage, sabotage and political intrigue. Through these compelling accounts, the inner workings of prime ministers and presidents are laid bare, revealing the high-stakes decisions and behind-the-scenes manoeuvrings that shaped critical moments in history. Dialogues between key figures offer a rare glimpse into the strategic outlooks of the protagonists who navigate the precarious intersection of diplomacy and warfare. The tension between intelligence and armed conflict pulses through every page, creating a narrative that is both intellectually stimulating and emotionally gripping. Readers are granted a front-row seat to the confidential exchanges and covert operations that defined an era where danger was a constant companion.

The gripping real war stories contained in this book include the two obscure yet perilous conflicts in Europe and Asia that brought the world to the precipice of nuclear confrontation and the daring raid on a German ship—anchored in the Portuguese enclave of Goa—by the British Special Operations Executive during WWII. Witness the dramatic naval battle off the Indian coast, where the largest British fleet ever assembled was unexpectedly decimated by the Japanese Navy. Observe the riveting showdown between a disguised German merchant ship and an Australian naval frigate, culminating in the devastating loss of both. Explore a tense and little-known mutiny aboard one of the Soviet Navy's most advanced frigates. And soar through the skies in one of the most audacious wartime operations ever conceived and witness the violent end of a Japanese admiral—one of the architects of the Pearl Harbor attack—through a calculated assassination plan.

Rich in historical detail, this work offers a vivid tapestry of espionage, strategy and drama—illuminating the shadows behind war and diplomacy. With each turn of the page, the drama escalates—sweeping, suspenseful and unrelenting—until its breathtaking conclusion. Step into a vivid, evocative past and embark on a journey unlike any other across a chronicle of courage and consequence. Though each tale stands alone, together they paint a broader portrait of a world perpetually balanced on a knife's edge; where power is contested not just in open battle but in hushed conversations and hidden manoeuvres. Let us now turn the page and begin.

ONE

A Duel at Close Quarters

The 1919 Treaty of Versailles placed the naval fleets of the Kriegsmarine (German Navy) at a disadvantage in comparison to the continental powers.[1] The treaty imposed restrictions on the manufacturing of German warships, preventing the production of destroyers, frigates, submarines and naval guns. The Germans had no other option but to bypass the same. Kriegsmarine admiral Erich Raeder recognized that commercial ships could be engaged in targeting enemy warships and supply vessels in future wars.[2] On 21 March 1940, Admiral Erich Raeder, chief of Kriegsmarine, issued the Confidential Admiralty Fleet Order (CAFO) 422, 'German Surface Vessels'. The CAFO—which is a printed routine order issued to ships and establishments for information, guidance and action—provided a list of 700 German merchant vessels to be converted into armed raiders. The Kriegsmarine placed an order for merchant vessels and cargo ships to be fitted with armaments and converted into combat ships at the German Naval Yards, Kiel Kaiserliche Werft and the Meyer Werft shipbuilding companies.

The Kriegsmarine admiralty—led by Admiral Raeder and Karl Dönitz—issued instructions for the operations of the raiders. Their task was to destroy or capture enemy merchant ships, and disrupt enemy commerce and logistical supply activities. The strategy of using disguises to launch surprise attacks on unwary ships—which often could not transmit warning signals in time—left the Allied nations unaware of the raiders' exact location.[3] The captains of these ships were instructed to avoid armed clashes with enemy warships, armed convoys and even enemy passenger ships, which were generally superior in speed and armament.[4]

At the start of WWII in 1938, the merchant ship *Steiermark* (named after Styria) was purchased by the Kriegsmarine and converted into an armed cruiser.[5] Fregattenkapitan T.A. Detmers christened it '*Kormoran*' after the bird called 'cormorant'. A bird of prey, the cormorant trains its hawk-like eyes under the water, swooping down swiftly upon noticing a fish and returning with the prey caught in its beak.[6]

Kormoran was the largest and newest of nine raiders, referred to as *hilfskreuzer* (auxiliary cruisers) or *handelsstörkreuzer* (trade disruption cruisers).[7] Raider captains such as Detmers were given the freedom to decide where to operate and which ships to target. Before Fregattenkapitan Detmers left Germany, his instructions from Admiral Erich Raeder were simple: 'The world is your oyster, go where you like, Arctic or Antarctic, but get results.'[8]

The *Kormoran* was an innocuous freighter outfitted with a hidden but lethal arsenal of guns and torpedoes. Its role in the enormous cat-and-mouse game of naval warfare was to ambush and sink Allied merchant shipping.[9] The *Kormoran* could move rapidly across the world's oceans while remaining undetected for long periods. It regularly deceived merchant ships by hoisting the flags of Allied or neutral countries. Once close enough, the *Kormoran* would raise the German flag, reveal its guns and threaten the merchant to surrender. With no defence, the unarmed merchant ship had to surrender as running away was not an option. Thus, *Kormoran* posed a serious threat to any unprepared vessel.[10]

She was the fastest of the Kriegsmarine's commerce raiders. The *Kormoran*'s armament surpassed the weaponry of any warship.[11] It was fitted with six guns, two anti-tank guns, five anti-aircraft autocannons, 360 moored contact mines and 30 magnetic ground mines.[12] The guns were concealed behind false hull plates and cargo-hatch walls which would swing clear when ordered to attack. The secondary weapons sat on hydraulic lifts hidden within the superstructure.[13]

In addition to her guns, four torpedo tubes were positioned on either side of the ship's structure while two secret fixed tubes were located below the waterline. At least two Arado 196 floatplanes and two motor speedboats were always stationed on the raider's deck. Despite this arsenal, the foremost weapon of a raider was surprise. And because many merchant ship victims radioed for help before being captured or sunk, its long-term survival depended on quickly vanishing into the open ocean after each ambush.[14] The *Kormoran* had destroyed 70,000 tons of Allied shipping when it encountered the '*Sydney*'. Fregattenkapitan Detmers's goal had been to reach 100,000 tons and be rewarded with the Knight's Cross of the Iron Cross.[15]

Disguised as the Dutch merchant ship '*Straat Malakka*', the *Kormoran* carried 399 personnel: 36 officers, 359 sailors, and four Chinese sailors hired from the crew of a captured ship to run the laundry.[16] Its capacity of 5,200 tons of fuel-oil gave *Kormoran* a potential action radius of 70,000 miles.[17] To take on the guise of *Straat Malakka*, Detmers had *Kormoran* painted in camouflage colours. He wrote in his *kriegstagebuch* (war diary) for 23 April 1941:

> Stopped. Outboard painted. The painting must take place because the colour had suffered in such a way that the camouflage of the weapons endangered warning. I have now decided to paint the hull black in order to be able to recamouflage quickly in the Indian Ocean as Japanese. The central structure and boats will become brown, the red chimney ring somewhat more yellowish and then we sail as *Straat Malakka* from Rio to Batavia

Kormoran was given a special camouflage coat of paint ranging from white to dark-grey stripes which ran diagonally on the ship's outer steel layer. A grey-brown coat of paint was applied up to six feet above the water line. This was the colour with which the *Kormoran* intended to try to break through—beyond the British blockade—into the outer waters.[18]

Extensive measures were taken to disguise the *Kormoran*'s identity as a raider. All funnels and topmasts were telescopic, and dummy funnels, ventilators and sampson posts were often rigged. This was carefully done so that the raider could be made to resemble a Swedish, Japanese or even British ship as required. In addition, false bulwarks in the well decks, false deck houses, boats and deck cargo helped change the ship's appearance. It was repainted so frequently that reports about the colours of a 'suspicious ship' or raider became quite worthless within 24 hours.[19]

Fregattenkapitan Detmers used his seamanship skills and patience to bring *Kormoran* within gunnery range of enemy ships without attracting suspicion. Once in close range of another vessel, *Kormoran* would decamouflage rapidly—in a matter of seconds—and hoist the German war ensign. Her gun crews could fire rapidly—in the order of four to five salvos a minute. *Kormoran*'s machine guns were accurate and very damaging to personnel and equipment when fired at comparatively close range. However, it did not fire on ships if the orders she gave were obeyed. And it always operated alone.[20]

The victim ship would be located by air reconnaissance or masthead lookouts during daylight. Then the telescopic topmasts and funnel were lowered, and *Kormoran* shadowed its target until the darkness of the night enabled an undetected approach to be made. Alternately, the raider would pass by her victim innocuously during daylight and then—once out of sight—turn and overtake it under the cover of darkness. Another method was for the raider's aircraft—which had British markings—to drop a message to the merchant ship, ordering her to steer a certain course as raiders were in the vicinity. This, of course, brought the victim straight to the raider.[21]

Detmers attached particular importance to effective sea lookouts. An officer was always on station as a lookout.[22] A typical day watch comprised one officer and one petty officer on the forward crosstrees, two lookouts on the gunnery director posts, and two lookouts on the bridge, in addition to the usual sea watch.[23] *Kormoran* also had crew members whose task was to hoist the German war ensign when the vessel decamouflaged. They had been trained in this task throughout the year and could hoist a flag within seconds.[24] Detmers regularly questioned members of the gun crew, whose specific target was the bridge of the opposing vessel.[25] Detmers drilled leading seaman Jakob Fend every week—'Where do you aim at?' He replied, 'At the bridge, Captain.' Once, when they had finished resupplying a U-boat in the Atlantic Ocean, the captain of the U-boat did a rapid dive and ascent and said to Detmers, 'Can you do that?' Detmers asked him to do it again. As the U-boat dived, Detmers gave the order '*entarrnen*' to his men. When the U-boat resurfaced, *Kormoran*'s camouflage was down and all its guns were pointing at the U-boat. Detmers then said to the young U-boat captain, 'Can you do that?'[26]

Kormoran did not know the location or movements of HMAS *Sydney* before the engagement on 19 November 1941. *Kormoran* was not directed to intercept *Sydney*. The German Navy did not know of the engagement between *Sydney* and *Kormoran* until early December 1941. It was late afternoon on that fateful November day, and the two ships were converging at a spot in the Indian Ocean 150 miles off the coast of Western Australia. Thus far into the two-year-old global conflict, this corner of the world had seen little action. All of the war's major naval battles—the River Platte, the hunt for the *Bismarck*, Operation Pedestal—had occurred in the Atlantic or the Mediterranean.

Battle at Close Quarters

In July of 1940, *Sydney* had destroyed an Italian light cruiser—the *Bartolomeo Colleoni*—and damaged another—the *Giovanni Delle Bande Nere*—in what would become known as the Cape Spada action. It was the first cruiser duel of the war and won Captain J.A. Collins and his Royal Australian Navy (RAN) crew national acclaim. The captain and the crew received a hero's welcome when *Sydney* returned home in February 1941.[27]

Sydney—which had become the glory ship of the young RAN due to her famous exploits in the Mediterranean—was headed on an interception course with the *Kormoran*.[28] On 19 November 1941 *Sydney*, under the command of Captain Joseph Burnett, was returning from having escorted HMAS *Zealandia* to a location near the Sunda Strait in Indonesia. When about 200 kilometres from the coast of Western Australia, en route to Fremantle, she sighted a vessel and diverted from her course to investigate.[29]

Sydney was much faster and more powerful than the *Kormoran*. Her top speed was 32 knots as opposed to the *Kormoran*'s 18 knots, and she was fitted with better guns, fire control systems and protective armour. She was exactly the type of deadly warship that Detmers had been ordered to avoid at all costs.[30] The primary objective of a disguised German raider was to disrupt commercial shipping by sinking or capturing merchant vessels. They avoided direct confrontation with enemy warships. Their success depended on remaining undetected and sinking or capturing merchant vessels rather than engaging in combat with heavily armed warships.

It was a sunny day and HSK *Kormoran* was heading in a northerly direction off the Western Australian coast. She had been at sea for 352 days[31] and was proceeding at medium speed on her usual sweep, gradually approaching Shark's Bay.

Detmers walked into the mess for some coffee at 1600 hours after taking the usual look around in all directions. After an afternoon nap other officers were already relaxing in the mess over a cup of coffee and a leisurely smoke. Suddenly the bridge messenger burst in and announced: 'Ship sighted to starboard!' Detmers hurried to the bridge, checked its course and speed, and glanced at the ship on the horizon through his powerful binoculars. He immediately identified it as one of the three Australian cruisers of the 'Perth' class.[32]

Another warning came from Lieutenant Rudolf Jansen, the lookout perched in the crow's nest high up on *Kormoran*'s foremast: 'Enemy heading for us and approaching fast.' Detmers quickly ordered for the crow's nest to be taken down to avoid disclosing the ship's identity. He also ordered Heinz Messerschmidt, a 26-year-old lieutenant commander, to change course.[33] On the ship's intercom system, Detmers wasted no time in giving the standing orders: 'Get into your battle stations. Draw away full speed ahead.'[34] According to Detmer's orders, *Kormoran* altered its course into the sun at maximum achievable speed, which quickly dropped from 15 to 14 knots because of problems in one of her diesel engines. *Sydney* spotted the German ship around the same time and altered from her southward course to intercept at 25 knots.

Barely five minutes had passed since the first alarm was sounded but Detmers already knew that this encounter was going to be far more perilous than anything he and his crew had faced during their previous year operating in the Atlantic and Indian oceans. Detmers had been to Australia in 1933—while serving as an Oberleutenat zur See aboard the German cruiser *Köln*—and had had the pleasure of being entertained on the heavy cruiser HMAS *Canberra* moored in Sydney Harbour. So he had some first-hand knowledge of the fighting power of the RAN ships. He knew all too well that in just a couple of hours his ship would be up against a faster and better-armed opponent. *Kormoran*'s advantage would be to get the cruiser discreetly within its firing range.[35]

Detmers knew that evasion was out of the question as the cruiser coming up could move at 32 knots compared with *Kormoran*'s speed of 18 knots, which could not be achieved on account of the barnacles clinging to her hull. There were three hours until dusk at 1900 hours. Detmers discussed a strategy with his commanders which could get them more time. His plan was to get the cruiser closer than 8,000 yards, so that when the shooting started he would not be able to outrange the *Kormoran* or withdraw to the necessary 10,000 yards distance.[36]

The enemy was coming closer. Detmers could see that the cruiser's guns and torpedo tubes were directed at *Kormoran*. As she closed the gap, the Australian cruiser requested that *Kormoran* identify herself.[37] The *Kormoran* raised 'PKQI'—the call-sign for the Dutch merchant ship *Straat Malakka* and hoisted a Dutch merchant ensign.[38] The call-sign was deliberately obscured by the raider's funnel. This was to create a deception of a civilian ship, a ruse to lure the enemy closer. With *Sydney* barely 26,000 feet away, the malfunctioning engine aboard *Kormoran* was repaired. The cruiser continued approaching at 20 knots and signalled 'What cargo?' *Kormoran* responded, 'Piece goods'.[39]

The warship requested the freighter to re-position the flags. While the German crew slowly complied, the distance between the two ships shrank to a mile. 'Where bound?' came the second signal flashed by the *Sydney*. 'Batavia' was the reply from the *Kormoran*, indicating the capital of the Dutch colony of Java lying over a thousand miles to the north. Detmer saw that the *Sydney*'s crew was preparing to launch their spotter plane from the catapult. The plane, once airborne, would easily spot the hundreds of naval mines strewn about the *Kormoran*'s high deck, giving away its identity as a raider. But the launch crew apparently received new orders and pushed the plane to its storage position. The captain of the *Sydney* seemed to have taken the merchant ship to be completely harmless. The guns seemed to be at half readiness. The only thing that was left out during the reciprocal exchange of signals was the giving of the secret call-sign by the *Kormoran*.[40] Lieutenant Heinz Messerschmidt, Detmers's adjutant, could hear him speaking over the telephone linking the bridge to the gunnery control station and gun positions, 'Ah, it's teatime on board. They'll probably just ask us where we are going and what cargo and then let us go on.'[41]

Detmers cunningly directed his chief signalman, Erich Ahlbach, to respond to the *Sydney*'s searchlight signals slowly by flag as if he was a merchant-navy greenhorn of the type that were often found on ships like *Straat Malakka*.[42] He calmly allowed the signal traffic to develop, during which he either hoisted the flags incompletely or the flag signifying 'not understood' to gain time and allow the *Sydney* to draw closer. The plan was working. By 1715 hours the cruiser had virtually drawn level with *Kormoran* and was stationed at a distance of 900 metres.[43] It had also slowed down to match their speed of 14 knots. The closer she came the easier it would be for the *Kormoran* to destroy *Sydney*.[44]

With escape impossible and surrender out of the question, Detmers knew that he would have to fight the cruiser. But his only chance of survival was to nullify the warship's clear advantage in a long-range gun battle fought at a distance beyond the 12,000-yard range of his own guns but within the 22,000-yard maximum range of the cruiser's. He needed to carefully draw the cruiser closer without raising the slightest suspicion regarding their true identity.[45]

Sydney's searchlight signalled, 'Show your secret sign.' *Kormoran* did not respond because Detmers did not know *Straat Malakka*'s secret call-sign. Since he had rejected the option of scuttling his ship, there was no choice but to fight.[46]

Once *Sydney* received the signal 'PKQI' and consulted her reference books, she realized that the ship before her was not *Straat Malakka*: she had a different bow, stern, superstructure and features. But—having drawn very close to the *Kormoran*—*Sydney* had lost all tactical and weapons advantage. This caused a flurry of activity aboard the cruiser.[47]

Carefully concealed behind special screens and tarps on the *Kormoran*'s decks was an arsenal of naval guns, torpedo tubes and anti-tank guns, all manned, loaded and trained on the oblivious cruiser.[48] Detmers spoke over the intercom informing all stations that they were about to go into action against a small cruiser which they should be well able to dispose of. An answering cheer told Detmers that everything was in order.[49] The range was so close that the *Kormoran*'s crew could see the cruiser's pantrymen—in their white coats—lining the rails to have a look at the supposed Dutchman.

As soon as the *Sydney* came to a standstill, Detmers gave the order—'De-camouflage!' The time was exactly 1730 hours. The Dutch flag was hauled down and signalman Ehrhardt Otte hoisted the German naval war flag.[50] The camouflage screens fell away to reveal the line of gun barrels trained on the *Sydney*.[51]

While the war flag was being hoisted, the armament was cleared for firing.[52] The crew of the *Kormoran* hydraulically raised the guns into position. As soon as the flag became visible, deck railings were folded down; covers over the guns on the bow and stern flew upwards, sprung by counterweights; hatch coamings concealing the two big guns mounted in the centre of the false cargo holds were lowered at the push of a button like guillotine blades; light covers over smaller guns were simply pulled away; the forward machine guns were raised from under the forecastle deck; and the thin plates covering the openings for the twin torpedo mounts on either side of the main deck also flapped upwards. The railings of the *Kormoran* tilted over and two guns dexterously swung out of the hatches and aimed at the enemy. Simultaneously two ack-ack guns rose up on hydraulic hoists.[53] The camouflage was removed in a record time of six seconds.[54]

The *Kormoran* Attacks

There was still no shot from the *Sydney*. The crew didn't seem to have grasped the display of the transformed merchant steamer. Detmers gave permission to 'open fire' ('*feuerlaubnis*').[55] Rapid-fire anti-tank and machine guns roared into action. The bullets soared through the close gap between the two ships and hit the sailors and officers standing on the bridge.[56] One of the *Kormoran*'s heavy guns hit the cruiser's body. A gun aboard it was destroyed. Because the enemy was so close, *Kormoran*'s anti-aircraft machine guns had sufficient range to reach her and they burst into action, raking the cruiser's bridge, port torpedo battery and gun deck.[57] Lieutenant Wilhelm Brinkman, the officer in charge of the anti-aircraft guns, fired directly at the *Sydney*. The shells caused extensive damage and fires, particularly amidships and the engine room.[58] The *Sydney* was unable to reply for a few seconds after the initial salvo. Its forward turrets were out of action.[59]

The firing disabled *Sydney*'s anti-aircraft guns and torpedoes and prevented the crew from using her smaller guns.[60] Not a man could show his face on the upper deck, because the fire of *Kormoran*'s anti-aircraft guns and heavy machine guns were pumping shells into the bridge structure.[61] One destroyed the spotter plane, spilling burning aviation fuel over the decks and black smoke billowing into the sky.[62]

Lieutenant Skeries was the artillery officer who fired the first salvo of the high-explosive and armour-piercing shells which consisted of two shots aimed at the bridge. The first shell struck *Sydney* forward but hit below the point of aim. One or more shells struck near the funnel, carrying away most of her structure. The second three-shell salvo destroyed *Sydney*'s bridge and damaged her upper structure, including the gun direction control tower, wireless office and foremast.[63] Two turrets and the forward engine room were put out of action by the third and fourth salvoes. The fifth was fired at the waterline between *Sydney*'s funnels which started a fire near the torpedo tubes.

Then Lieutenant Greter—the torpedo officer—fired the second torpedo, which struck *Sydney* below the forward turrets. It hit the asdic compartment (the weakest point on the ship's hull) and an enormous column of water shot into the air, ripping a hole in the side and causing the stern to be dipped into the sea up to the flagstaff.[64]

After the torpedo strike, *Sydney* turned hard to port (left side of the ship); Detmer assumed that the she was trying to ram them, but the cruiser passed aft. During the turn, a German salvo tore the roof from a turret and destroyed another.[65] As she swung past the *Kormoran* closely, she could, apparently, fire no more and was blazing fiercely. The action then broke off.[66]

The cruiser's guns had been silent for some time and Detmers sensed that the battle was probably won as he observed his enemy's critical condition. Another single torpedo was fired at the stern of the cruiser—which missed—and they continued firing with their big guns until Detmers finally ordered 'cease fire' at 1825 hours. The final gun range was noted by Skeries to be 10,400 metres.[67] *Kormoran* had fired about 450 of her shells at *Sydney*.[68]

HMAS *Sydney* Responds

Nevertheless, the captain opposite was a determined and courageous man. He returned fire imperturbably—despite the critical damage to his ship—scoring three or four hits on the *Kormoran*.[69] Its wireless communication system and fire-fighting equipment were rendered ineffective. One salvo hit the engine room, smashing the engines and leading to uncontrollable fire. All this happened by about 1840 hours. With the failure of her engines, *Kormoran* came to a halt. Having passed astern of the raider, *Sydney* turned to starboard (right side of the ship) and fired all four of her torpedoes at *Kormoran*. But they missed.[70]

Sydney's first salvo consisted of a full eight-gun fire under director control, shortly after *Kormoran*'s first salvo. The German raider shuddered as a shell hit her. It went through the funnel and exploded, the splinters of its aftermath penetrating the W/T room and killing two sailors.[71] One shell struck *Kormoran*'s funnel, while three passed through the bridge structure without exploding. Another shell, which struck the funnel, exploded and destroyed one of the lifeboats and wounded at least two sailors on the midships.[72] A third shell from the *Sydney* ripped clean through *Kormoran*'s large funnel before harmlessly exploding in the sea. A number of men were wounded and killed by the splinters that had scattered throughout the bridge. The funnel housed pipes that pumped oil up from the engine room to be heated inside it before being sent back to the four diesel electric engines. The flaming oil from the holed funnel cascaded down into the engine room and set it alight.[73]

The radio in the bridge suddenly crackled. It was Lieutenant Commander H. Stehr, the engineering officer who was repairing some of the damage. He roared from the engine room: 'Hit in the engine-room.' An oil bunker had been hit and the burning oil was gushing out from the room.[74] One had torn open the engine room fuel tank and apparently exited the ship without exploding. One had passed straight through the ship without exploding, piercing the firemain on both sides of the engine room on its way. Another had exploded aft the engine room.[75] The results of the hits were catastrophic.[76] *Sydney*'s fourth or fifth salvo hit *Kormoran*'s engine room, causing serious damage and uncontrollable fires.[77]

Smoke bellowed out of the burning engine room and electrical discharges crisscrossed its expanse. At 1735 Detmers hurried to the site to meet H. Stehr. A shell had destroyed the cruiser's boiler room and an oil bunker. The fire extinguishers were put out of action due to the resultant destruction.[78]

Stehr informed Detmers that the fire-fighting equipment in the engine room had been destroyed and the foam equipment was out of action. Neither was there any water pressure in the damaged pipes. The chief plumber's attempt to get pressure in the fire extinguisher pipe from the power unit in the propulsion motor room failed as the pressure in the damaged pipe had dropped immediately.[79]

One shell tore the forward tank bulkhead of the engine room badly open. A thick jet of burning fuel oil poured into the room and filled it with dense smoke. The third demolished the transformers of the main engine installation.[80] The transformers were unserviceable, thereby putting the main generators and propulsion motors out of action. Consequently, the main engines stopped charging and raced furiously.[81] Lieutenant Rudolph Lensch, who was on the bridge relaying messages from the engine room, reported that the 'engines and all fire-fighting equipment are completely out of action'. It seemed inevitable that the *Kormoran* would soon be dead in the water.

The raider was now drifting and swaying in the wind and currents without any electrical or propulsive power. Fregattenkapitan Detmers and the crew of *Kormoran* began to take stock of their situation. The enemy cruiser was no longer a threat as she was badly on fire and slowly limping away in the opposite direction. But the fire in his own engine room concerned him more, which was located dangerously close to the after cargo holds fully stocked with mines.[82]

Detmers was quickly running out of options to save his ship. His second reserve generator room, located just forward of the bridge, had escaped damage but the generators there were not big enough to drive the ship. If they could not put out the midship fires it was just a matter of time before they spread to the nearest mines—separated by only one transverse bulkhead—and trigger an explosion that would simultaneously detonate all of the 340 mines and 106 tons of explosive charges they contained.

Realizing that the *Kormoran*'s uncontrollable fires threatened the hundreds of volatile mines stored on the deck, Detmers knew he had only one realistic option left—to abandon ship and destroy the *Kormoran*. He ordered his crew to set the explosive charges and abandon ship at about 2300 hours.[83] Heinz Messerschmidt lit the charges that had been planted on two of the forward oil tanks. The fuses had been timed for 20 minutes, which would have given Rotzin and Messerschmidt a safe margin to meet Detmers on the forward deck before all three boarded the last lifeboat.[84] Dusk was creeping in from the east over a sea rising with a fresh breeze.[85]

Detmers and his men launched every lifeboat and raft by hand under the constant threat of fire, smoke and the impending explosion of *Kormoran*'s huge cache of mines. These included two steel lifeboats, weighing about a ton each, that had to be manhandled out of the forward hold using conventional block and tackle because the derricks and electric winches were no longer working.[86] The situation for the men trapped on the quarterdeck was far more desperate as they were cut off from all the boats by the fire and had to resort to throwing overboard absolutely anything they felt could support the weight of a man in water, including a green wooden kennel that was home to the ship's pet Alsatian dog named Senta.[87] It took three hours to get lifeboats out of a hatch because of the lack of power.[88] Men jumped overboard and though a number of them were picked up by the lifeboats that had been launched, it would appear that about 80 were lost.[89]

At 2100 the boats left *Kormoran* and the charges exploded at 0035. *Kormoran*'s mines turned the ship into a huge fireball that shot several hundred metres high into the night sky and lit the scene for all the survivors before falling upon them in a shower of debris.[90] The crew watched as the ship began to sink.[91] When the vast flame had died down, the *Kormoran* lifted her bows into the air and slipped backwards under the surface. At daybreak, the survivors checked the supply of water and provisions, and rationed the consumption for eight days.[92]

At about 1900 hours—while disembarking from the *Kormoran* on to the lifeboats—the men who looked in the direction of the *Sydney* could see her in the distance marked only by the glow of the large fire that continued to blaze in several places.[93] From the fore bridge to the stern mast, the cruiser was a mass of flame and she was moving forward very slowly.[94] It was taking water through openings resulting from the penetration of shells and the torpedo strike. The ingress of water caused her rolling to increase until she finally sank rapidly, about 12 nautical miles from the battle site.[95]

The fire from the cruiser was visible until 2100. With darkness, the wind had risen to force five or six.[96] Then the crew saw the flames dart up even higher—as though from an explosion—before the battered hulk of the ship disappeared into the night.[97] Thereafter, the *Sydney* was identifiable only as a glow on the horizon. Around midnight, the glow, which had been decreasing in intensity intermittently, began to fade away. After the *Kormoran* sank at approximately 0135 on 20 November, there was only darkness.[98] With the gathering gloom, the form of *Sydney* disappeared from view.

Detmers murmured to his sailors, 'We have sunk her. What a coincidence! And almost at the spot where the first *Sydney* destroyed the *Emden* in WWI.'[99] In November 1914 the *Emden* had fallen victim to the more powerful *Sydney*; and now, in November 1941, the much more powerful new *Sydney* had been sunk by the re-fitted passenger ship *Kormoran* acting as an auxiliary cruiser.[100]

Kormoran sank stern first. Of her complement of 393 officers and men, 78 lost their lives, about 20 killed in action on-board, and the remainder drowned through the capsizing of an overloaded raft. Two of the four Chinese from *Eurylochus* were also lost. Of *Sydney*'s total complement of 42 officers and 603 ratings, not one survived.[101] The battle between the Perth-class light cruiser and *Kormoran* lasted approximately 55 minutes.[102]

A Warship Lost at Sea

The RAN admiralty at Victoria Barracks in Melbourne was unaware that the *Sydney* had been in action. It was expected to return to Fremantle on the afternoon of 20 November. At 0940 on 21 November, district naval officer of Western Australia (DNOWA), Captain C. Farquhar-Smith, RAN, sent the following signal to the Australian Commonwealth Naval Board (ACNB) in Melbourne: 'FIMAS *SYDNEY* 'O4226 11 HMAS: *SYDNEY* HAS NOT YET ARRIVED?' The signal was received by Lieutenant Commander N.S. Pixley, who took it to the deputy chief of naval staff, Captain R.E. Getting. Captain Getting was not unduly worried by the signal as nothing had been heard from *Sydney* itself. The cruiser was expected to maintain W/T silence unless there was something vital to communicate and its lack of a transmission and non-arrival were not a cause for concern. A late rendezvous with Durban or an unforeseen event on its return passage could have accounted for the delay.

As 22 November dawned there was still no sign of *Sydney*. During the morning, Farquhar-Smith contacted the chief of Naval Staff's office and learned of *Zealandia*'s late arrival in Singapore. DNOWA conferred with the navy office again on the morning of 23 November and it was decided to give *Sydney* another 12 hours before ordering the cruiser to break W/T silence. Accordingly, at 1854 the navy office ordered *Sydney* to report its ETA. On receiving the signal, *Sydney* should have responded. Its continued silence indicated that it had either not heard the signal, could not reply, or did not wish to break W/T silence for operational reasons.[103] *Sydney*, however, was now 72 hours overdue.[104]

The first indication that Sydney may have been involved in

an action should have come on the morning of 23 November. At 0630, *Aquitania* recovered 26 German naval men from two inflatable rubber rafts. The *Aquitania* maintained course and went straight to *Sydney* without informing the navy office. As a result, they remained ignorant of the fact that *Sydney* had been in action.[105] With no report forthcoming, DNOWA contacted Western Area Headquarters, Royal Australian Air Force (RAAF). At 0050 on 24 November, the AOC, RAAF, ordered an air search for *Sydney*. This initial search, conducted on the morning of 24 November, proved fruitless. A second operation was ordered for the following day.

At 1620, the commander-in-chief (C-in-C) of China sent a 'Most Immediate' signal to navy office, relaying a message that had been received from the tanker *Trocas* at 1500: 'PICKED UP 25 GERMAN NAVAL MEN FLOATING RAFT REQUIRE GUARDS IMMEDIATELY. POSITION 024 degrees 06 SOUTH 111 degrees 40 EAST.' Navy office instructed all naval and air force stations to stop calling the ship. At 1957—as a result of the report of Germans recovered off Shark Bay—the merchant vessels *Pan Europe*, *Saidja*, *Herstein*, *Sunetta* and *Centaur* were instructed to pass through *Trocas*'s reported position and keep a lookout for further survivors. Navy office then informed the Coastal Zone Management (CZM) and C-in-C of China that *Sydney* was connected with the rescued Germans.[106]

The tanker captain radioed the Australian navy office to provide the first indication that the *Sydney* might have been involved in a battle. The rescued Germans had come from *Kormoran*. The report from the *Trocas*, and concerns that it might be linked with the overdue *Sydney*, spurred Australia's navy and air force to conduct surface and air sweeps of the waters off Western Australia.[107] Royal RAAF and Dutch aircrew flew 118 sorties in their search for *Sydney*. They were supported 'on the ground' by six naval vessels and 15 merchant ships. Although five boatloads of *Kormoran* survivors were sighted, the aircrews could find no trace of *Sydney* or its crew. A small amount of *Kormoran*-related debris was discovered by search vessels, but the only items recovered that could be identified as having come from *Sydney* were a single life-belt and a single battle-damaged Carley float.[108]

On 29 November the British naval liaison officer at Batavia sent a report to the C-in-C of China, informing that the CZM had come to the same conclusion regarding *Sydney*'s probable connection with the Germans. It was of the opinion 'that due to *Sydney*'s prolonged silence, she was either sunk or so badly damaged that she was unable to make use of any W/T.'[109]

In a briefing minute to the prime minister, secretary of the Department of Defence Co-ordination Frederick Shedden warned that the chief of Naval Staff—Vice-Admiral Sir Guy Royle—feared that *Sydney* had been sunk by the raider. Royle had received a message from the Admiralty stating that the raider might have torpedoed the cruiser.[110]

Another ship called *Centaur* had broken W/T silence to inform navy office that at 2220 it had discovered a lifeboat containing 62 German seamen. Owing to the lack of armed guards, *Centaur* had taken the boat in tow and was heading for Carnarvon. The boat taken in tow by *Centaur* was commanded by Fregattenkapitan T.A. Detmers.[111]

Information received from Carnarvon indicated that the raider had been involved in an action with a Perth-class cruiser on 19 November.[112] At 2300, DNOWA telephoned the navy office to advise that the following information had just been received from Carnarvon: 'Survivors number about 110. Mostly 70 miles north of Carnarvon. The German survivors were from a raider which had commenced an engagement with a Perth class warship on 19th November about 120 miles south west of Fremantle. During an interrogation the German captain mentioned that the Perth class warship was lost at sea.'[113] The ACNB received a sobering signal from the admiralty. It considered that the only logical explanation for *Sydney*'s disappearance was that the cruiser had been torpedoed by the raider.

The survivors were brought ashore and treated for numerous cases of sunburn, sores, swollen feet, conjunctivitis and constipation. Paymaster Lieutenant A.C. Baume, RANR, began questioning the prisoners. At 1335, he informed the navy office that one prisoner said that the cruiser had been struck by a torpedo, and when last seen, was burning amidships.[114] Earlier, Baume had boarded the MV *Trocas* to interview the German officers. The officers revealed that the raider had left Germany in December 1940 and operated in the Atlantic and Indian oceans before being attacked by a cruiser on 19 November. The survivors said three torpedoes had been fired at the cruiser, one of which was seen to hit and explode.[115]

Lieutenant Commander Rycroft—staff officer in intelligence—had found and questioned *Kormoran*'s navigating officer, Kapitanleutnant Henry Meyer, who confirmed the position of the action.[116] Rycroft boarded *Centaur* the same evening, found Detmers among the survivors, and began questioning him. Detmers claimed that the cruiser had been torpedoed forward and struck amidships by salvoes. At 2115, Rycroft reported his findings to Farquhar-Smith.[117]

Rumours of an Australian warship being sunk had begun to circulate in Canberra. The minister for information, Senator William Ashley, instructed the chief publicity censor, Edmund Bonney, to prohibit publication or mention of *Sydney*.[118] This said, 'No reference whatever press or radio to any statements or rumours regarding alleged naval activity in Australian waters.' The press had had an inkling of what happened to HMAS *Sydney*. But *The Herald*'s editor now knew that *Sydney* had been sunk in Australian waters.[119]

The pride of the Australian Navy was gone along with its 645 crew members. In Britain, *Sydney*'s loss was overshadowed by the sinking of the aircraft carrier Ark Royal on 14 November and the battleship *Barham* on 25 November, the latter claiming 862 lives. Both the warships were sunk by German U-boats.

To the people of Australia, however, *Sydney*'s loss was a national disaster. The nation's most famous warship had been sunk with all hands.[120] In Canberra, naval officials prepared for what would become the worst naval disaster in the history of the Australian Navy.[121]

Within a fortnight of Sydney's sinking, the sloop HMAS *Parramatta* was torpedoed and sunk by a German U-boat in the Mediterranean while escorting a convoy to Tobruk. In March 1942, *Sydney*'s sister ship *Perth* was sunk by Imperial Japanese Navy (IJN) cruisers in the Battle of the Sunda Strait. Within days of *Perth*'s loss, the sloop *Yarra* was sunk when her captain valiantly placed her between the small convoy he was escorting and the superior force of Japanese cruisers and destroyers. The frontline warships of the RAN were gone, leaving the Australian population feeling vulnerable and exposed to a very uncertain future.

The tragedy of *Sydney*'s loss was overtaken by far greater events. On 8 December, the United States Pacific Fleet had been attacked at Pearl Harbor by the Japanese. Two days later, the British battleship *Prince of Wales* and the battle cruiser *Repulse* were sunk by the Japanese. Australia had to come to terms with the alarming fact that there were now no Allied capital ships left standing between it and the powerful Japanese Navy.[122]

TWO

A Pearl Harbor on India's Doorstep

It was a chilly, bright and shiny morning in November 1941 in the German town of Berchtesgaden situated in the Bavarian Alps on the Austrian border. A meeting of German military commanders was taking place at an alpine farmhouse—named the 'Berghof'—located in the mountains above the town. In attendance were Wilhelm Keitel (commander of the German Armed Forces), Erwin Rommel (commander of the Afrika Korps), Walther von Brauchitsch (commander-in-chief of the German Army), Heinz Guderian (a prominent commander known for his role in the *blitzkrieg* tactic against Russia), Erich von Manstein (a field marshal known for his strategic planning), Erich Raeder (the commander-in-chief overseeing the entire Kriegsmarine) and Karl Dönitz (admiral of the U-boat arm, a crucial part of the German Navy during the war, particularly in the Battle of the Atlantic). Raeder was running a secret communications operation with the Japanese Military High Command on the possibility of a collaboration between Germany and Japan to defeat the British military in Asia. At the meeting Kriegsmarine admiral Erich Raeder privately handed over a top-secret telegram from the Japanese prime minister Tōjō Hideki to Hitler. The note contained two paras calling for a link-up between the Afrika Korps (The German African Corps) and a Japanese force invading through the Middle East via Ceylon (now Sri Lanka) and India.[1] It further mentioned that 15 Japanese submarines were operating in the Bay of Bengal. The Japanese had hatched a plan to collaborate with the Germans to invade the British territories in the Middle East and Asia through a pincer movement. Defeating the British forces in India and Ceylon was crucial to the plan. India was the crucial bastion where the British political, bureaucratic and military power was concentrated in Asia. Ceylon was a major transit nation from Europe to East Asia for the Royal Navy. The fall of India and Ceylon would disrupt the lines of communication and trade between UK and Far East nations such as Singapore. And once Japanese battleships, aircraft carriers, submarines, and the Japanese Naval Air Force were based in Ceylon, Britain would be forced to resort to heavily escorted convoys[2] if she wanted to maintain communications with India and the Near East.[3] This plan matched the German plan calling for the expansion of the railway line from Hamburg to Basra to transport the German military from a port in Germany to a port on the Persian Gulf.

Hitler read the note and looked at Raeder, who briefed him in detail about the Japanese plan. The secret plan—code-named 'Scorpion'—was unsuccessfully implemented in 1938. The note which Raeder handed over to Hitler was its culmination. Ernst Schaefer, a zoologist, had arranged for a German expedition to Tibet in 1939. British prime minister Neville Chamberlain permitted him to enter Sikkim, a region in India bordering Tibet. In Sikkim's capital of Gangtok, the team assembled a 50-mule caravan and proceeded to Tibet. On 19 January 1939, the team reached Lhasa. One of the expedition's aims was to prepare maps and survey passes for the possible use of Tibet as a staging ground for guerrilla assaults on British India. In 1939, Japanese intelligence agents from the Kwantung Army Base in Xinjiang operated in Tibet to organize infiltrations, sabotage and disturbances in British India in case of a Japanese invasion of India.[4] In the Middle East, the Berlin to Baghdad railway line had been completed in 1940. The German military's plan was to expand the line from Hamburg to Basra to transport the army from a port in Germany to a port on the Persian Gulf.

Strategically, Germany and Japan would devour the British Empire through a pincer movement. Hitler seemed excited about the plan. The Japanese plan would be beneficial for Hitler as the British forces would be cornered by the two nations. He asked Raeder to connect with the Japanese and execute the 'Scorpion' plan. Later both disappeared in the hall room, meeting other generals. While departing Berghof, Admiral Raeder remarked to Hitler: 'When Germany and Japan touch hands in the Indian Ocean, the final victory is not far away.'

By March 1942, Britain had been extinguished as a power in Southeast Asia. A string of military disasters burst across the region following the Pearl Harbor attack in December 1941. Japan overran the British Far Eastern colonies in quick succession. By mid-1942, the Japanese dominated the whole of Southeast Asia, the East Indies and the Western Pacific. Thus, in 1942 the possibility of a German-Japanese link-up in the Middle East was a very real concern to Churchill.

Germany and Italy were steamrolling their way across Africa. Rommel was driving the Eighth Army back towards Egypt. Rommel's plan was to push the British out of Libya, capture key British strongholds along the Mediterranean, and potentially reach Cairo, the Suez Canal and Iran. The Japanese telegram plan of merging at some point between India and the Middle East appeared almost inevitable. The British High Command projected that the Middle East, India and all of Southeast Asia would be under German and Japanese control by September 1942.[5]

Throughout the winter and spring of 1941/42, Japanese naval forces seemed unstoppable, advancing throughout the Central and Western Pacific Ocean following her invasion of Manchuria in 1931 and Korea in 1932. British and Allied forces had been unceasingly pushed back. Japan's well-planned and aggressive military strategy and the Philippines' unpreparedness for a large-scale conflict led to their fall along with the Dutch East Indies. After the fall of Singapore in 1942, the British Eastern Fleet had withdrawn to Ceylon to secure their vantage points.[6]

On 15 February 1942, the Japanese conquered the British stronghold of Singapore. During the brief battle, two Royal Navy warships—HMS *Prince of Wales* and HMS *Repulse*—were sunk off the eastern coast of Malay by Japanese aircraft, making Ceylon and southeast India vulnerable to Japanese advance.[7] Only four months previously, in November 1941, the aircraft carrier HMS *Ark Royal* and the battleship *Barham* had been lost.

In February 1942, the Imperial Japanese Navy launched a raid on the port of Darwin in Australia. The raid was a devastating blow and was the single largest attack ever mounted by a foreign power on the island continent.[8] The raid, popularly remembered as 'Australia's Pearl Harbor', achieved surprise success and—combined with a later attack by land-based naval bombers—killed around 250 people, wounded a further 300–400, and destroyed 30 aircraft. It also sank 11 vessels whilst damaging another 28.[9]

The close of the first quarter of 1942 was among the most critical moments of the war in Southeast Asia, marked by significant Japanese victories and the collapse of British defences in the region. The fall of Singapore—a major British military base and economic port—was a devastating blow, contributing to the end of British power in Southeast Asia. Following the fall of Singapore on 15 February, a rapid series of Japanese successes culminated in the surrender of Dutch forces in Java on 9 March, marking the end of Dutch colonialism on the island. To the east, the defeat at Pearl Harbor had neutralized the Americans, and in the west, the coming land campaign in Burma and Indo-China would threaten India, the crown jewel of the British Empire. Field Marshal William Slim led the

British Army in the Burma campaign. General Archibald Wavell, the commander-in-chief of the American, British, Dutch and Australian command, ordered Slim to withdraw the Burma Corps to India due to the Japanese advance.[10] Burma (now Myanmar) had been occupied and by 25 March the situation in Burma and northeast India had deteriorated.[11] This British retreat brought the war closer to the Indian frontier, particularly the Imphal and Kohima regions, which became strategically vital for both sides. While the Japanese did not occupy significant parts of India, their presence in Burma and the resulting Allied retreat created a tense situation on the Indian border. The battles of Imphal and Kohima in 1944, while not part of the 1942 advance, were a direct consequence of the earlier Japanese campaign and the strategic importance of the region.

During the early years of WWII, Japanese submarines were prowling as far west as the East African coast, torpedoing Allied commercial ships. The Italian Navy menaced the Indian Ocean sea lanes from its base at Massawa in Eritria. After Pearl Harbor, and the loss of territories in the Far East, the Indian Ocean was exposed to Japanese strikes in the west. The fall of Singapore brought the enemy uncomfortably close to Ceylon.[12]

The British military planners focused their attention on the defence of Ceylon.[13] It was strategically important as it commanded the Indian Ocean, controlled access to India and the vital Allied shipping routes from Europe to Southeast Asia, including India, Singapore, South Africa and the oilfields of the Persian Gulf. After the fall of Singapore, Ceylon became a stronghold for the Royal Navy with two bases at Trincomalee and Colombo.[14] Ceylon was now the last significant British naval base in the Indian Ocean, the next link in the chain to the west of Singapore. It was generally felt by the British that Ceylon would be next to fall, providing a springboard into India.[15] And the threat that the Germans might expand east and link up with the Japanese moving westward would become very real.[16] Japan was ready to strike at the very heart of the British Empire. Churchill now expected the Japanese to take full advantage of their naval supremacy from the Pacific to the Indian Ocean.[17]

The US Navy was on the strategic defensive in the Pacific, and with the American, British, Dutch and Australian fleets destroyed in the Battle of the Java Sea, the only remaining Allied naval force of any significance that could counter the Imperial Japanese Navy's onslaught in the region was the Royal Navy's 29-ship Eastern Fleet under the command of Vice Admiral James Somerville.[18]

Japanese War Planning

In January 1942 at the Japanese Navy office in Tokyo, Mr Yosano, the foreign office liaison in Imperial General Headquarters' (IGHQ) army/navy intelligence section, met and handed over a note to Admiral Isoroku Yamamoto, a high-ranking naval officer. He was the marshal admiral of the Imperial Japanese Navy and the commander-in-chief of the Combined Fleet during World War II. It mentioned that since the attack on Pearl Harbor there had been a couple of meetings between Vice Admiral Nomura, the Japanese naval attaché in Berlin and Admiral Fricke, chief of staff of Germany's Maritime Warfare Command. Admiral Fricke had convinced Vice Admiral Nomura to start operations that would assist Germany's own efforts against Britain. The note further mentioned that Fricke stressed the importance of the Indian Ocean to the German Navy and expressed the desire that the Japanese begin operations against sea routes in the northern Indian Ocean. The Scorpion Plan was now being implemented. Fricke also emphasized that Ceylon should have a higher priority for the German and Japanese navies than operations against Australia. The note mentioned that the German naval attaché in Tokyo had even provided the Japanese with particulars of suitable landing sites in Ceylon.[19]

The next day, Yosano and Admiral Yamamoto met Makoto Matsutani who was the military secretary to Prime Minister Tōjō Hideki. After a short discussion, Matsutani spoke to the PM and called for a war cabinet meeting after four days. In the meantime, Admiral Yamamoto spoke to Chuichi Nagumo, commander of the First Naval Air Fleet, and called for a meeting of top naval officers to discuss the note from Admiral Fricke. At the meeting Major General Kiyotomi Okamoto, who was the chief of Second Bureau (intelligence division), passed on a handwritten note across the table to Admiral Yamamoto. It mentioned that in August 1941 the German naval attaché in Tokyo handed over secret British documents to the Japanese obtained in one of the great intelligence coups of the war, which made it clear that Britain could not spare forces to save Ceylon in the event of a Japanese attack.[20] By day two of the meeting, the Japanese naval general staff came up with a plan to strike Ceylon.

The Ceylon plan was composed of two strategies. One was to destroy the British Eastern Fleet, which was reckoned at two carriers, two battleships, three heavy cruisers, four to seven light cruisers, and a number of destroyers. The other was that the Japanese Navy would strike Calcutta (now Kolkata) and Madras (now Chennai), attack the commercial ships in the Bay of Bengal, while the Japanese Army would make a thrust through Burma into Imphal and Kohima.

At 1000 hours on a winter day on 2 January 1942, the war cabinet assembled at PM Tōjō Hideki's residence. According to the protocol, Yoshimichi Hara—the emperor's representative—arrived at 1020 hours after all the Imperial Japanese military officers had taken their respective seats at the high table. Admiral Shigetarō Shimada, chief of Navy General Staff, and his team presented the plan to attack Ceylon. Kaoru Muramatsu who was the official of the Research Section of Ministry of Foreign Affairs started the narration of the Japanese attack plan on Ceylon. He started by remarking that the Pearl Harbor attack was a preventive action in order to keep the US Pacific Fleet from interfering with Japan's thrust in Southeast Asia and the Indian Ocean against Britain. The plan contained the details of the destruction of the British fleet based in Ceylon. Along with keeping the Japanese at bay, the British also had an on-going secondary challenge to deal with—political unrest amongst the populations of Ceylon and India who were demanding independence.[21] If the British Eastern Fleet at Ceylon could be neutralized, the colonial rule of India would be seriously eroded, leading to independence.[22] This will be beneficial to Japanese war plans as an independent India would withdraw their support of the Allies and become a neutral country for the remainder of the conflict.

Captain Kameto Kuroshima, chief of the operations division of the Naval General Staff, got up and said that the Japanese military intended to attack by air and destroy the British naval forces in a single day. It would be a surprise attack similar to the one executed at Pearl Harbor four months before. If all went well, the British presence in the Indian Ocean would be completely annihilated.[23]

Commander Nagumo entered the war room at 1530 hours. He had decided to deploy the zero fighters in the battle of Ceylon. The key to Japan's success at Pearl Harbor had been the extent of her air power—led by fighter aircraft—a secret closely guarded from the outside world. Until the attack on Pearl Harbor, the Americans were completely unaware of the existence of the Zero fighter aircraft that inflicted so much damage. It proved to be one of Japan's best-kept secrets. The Royal Air Force knew only of Japan's older aircraft which might attack Ceylon.[24] Even the Japanese ministers were not aware of it.

Kenji Tomita, Japan's chief cabinet secretary, intervened and enquired about the special feature of the Zero the use of which was being emphasized. Commander Nagumo stated that it was a fast, manoeuvrable aircraft with high firepower, capable of flying over 200 miles, spending 20 minutes in the combat zone, and returning the same distance. The RAF and the Royal Navy did not have a fighter aircraft that could match the Zero. In early combat operations, it gained a legendary reputation as a dogfighter, achieving the outstanding kill ratio of 12 to 1.[25]

Although the British were aware of this aircraft, their assumptions got the better of them. In late-1940, British intelligence had received information about the superior combat performance of the Mitsubishi Type-0 'Zero' fighter. The Chinese, who were on the same page with Britain in their opposition to the Japanese, had provided a detailed report to the British air attaché at Chungking—Wing Commander Warburton—about a dogfight that had taken place at Chengtu between 12 Type-0s and 31 Chinese-piloted I-15-3s. In this battle four Type-0s had been shot down for the loss of 12 I-15-3s. However, instead of treating this as confirmation of the efficiency of Japan's new fighter, both Warburton and British intelligence downplayed the incident from the perspective of the poor training and combat performance of the Chinese pilots.[26] This led to the complacency displayed at several meetings at Whitehall, assuming the operational value of the Japanese Air Force to be less than that of the Italians.[27]

Admiral Yamamoto handed over the task of attacking Ceylon—the heart of British naval power—to Vice Admiral Chuichi Nagumo's First Carrier Fleet of the Imperial Japanese Navy. Admiral Nagumo had earlier overseen the attack on Pearl Harbor.[28] The First Air Fleet contained the five heavy carriers *Akagi*, *Hiryu*, *Soryu*, *Shokaku* and *Zuikaku*—with over 300 aircraft—and supported by four Kongo-class battleships, seven Tone-class cruisers, five submarines and 19 destroyers.[29] These were complimented by two fleet carriers, one light carrier, five battleships, seven cruisers, 15 destroyers, seven submarines and 30 smaller warships, such as corvettes.

After her 1935 refit, the *Akagi* became the first Japanese carrier with a modern, large flight deck. But it was the operational experiences aboard her that forged the Japanese naval airpower doctrine. She participated in every major action in the early part of the war— including Pearl Harbor and the attack against Port Darwin—and would later be a part of the Battle of Midway.[30] Now *Akagi* was a part of the fleet which was deployed to attack Ceylon.

The Japanese strike was planned to be a four-pronged attack led by Vice Admiral Nagumo's larger Second Southern Expeditionary Fleet. Rear Admiral Takeo Kurita took the cruisers *Kumano* and *Suzuya*, and the destroyer *Shirakumo* to sweep north in the upper reaches of the Bay of Bengal. While Jisaburo Ozawa took the carrier *Ryujo* and seven cruisers—such as the *Chokia*, *Yura*, *Assagiri* and *Yugiri*—and 11 destroyers to strike convoys in the centre, Captain Sakiyama took the remaining group of the cruisers *Mikuma* and *Mogami*, and the destroyer *Amagiri*.[31]

The war cabinet adopted the plan to destroy the British Eastern Fleet, take Ceylon and establish contact with the Germans in the Middle East.[32] The plan was to culminate in German and Japanese forces meeting at Suez.[33] The Indian Ocean raid, also known as 'Operation C' or 'Battle of Ceylon', would be carried out by the Imperial Japanese Navy (IJN) just over a month after the raid on Darwin from 31 March to 10 April 1942.[34] The plan was presented to Yoshimichi Hara who got it approved from the Japanese Emperor.

A Flurry of Meetings in London

Britain and the US had signal intelligence SIGINT stations situated in South Asia, Southeast Asia and the Pacific. The key intelligence organization supporting the British Indian Ocean fleet was the Far Eastern Combined Bureau (FECB). The FECB received a steady flow of Japanese radio traffic from intercept stations located throughout the Far East and Pacific, including one based at Esquimalt, British Columbia. The British Wireless Experimental Centre (WEC) worked closely with US intelligence units based at Guam, which is a part of the Mariana Islands archipelago, and Leyte, Philippines. These bases connected the wireless signals, travelling 4,000 miles or more. These, apart from the huge US intelligence gathering network in the Pacific, ran in a great arc from Melbourne, Canberra, Brisbane and Darwin through Ceylon to Calcutta and southern China.[35] Soon after the Japanese attack on Pearl Harbor, the FECB was relocated from Singapore to Ceylon.[36]

In India the WEC was situated in Ramjas College, formerly part of the contemporary Delhi University campus, securely perched atop a hill called Anand Parbat some miles outside the city. There were three other stations which were supporting the FECB—the Wireless Experimental Depot in Abbottabad which monitored Russian transmissions in the interwar period, the Western Wireless sub-centre at Bangalore, and the Eastern Wireless sub-centre at Barrackpore, which is close to Calcutta.[37] WEC at Delhi—the largest Bletchley outpost in the East—had an estimated 1,000 staff.[38] A small Royal Indian Navy W7T and the Cypher Office at Bombay Fort, Colaba, also intercepted Japanese signals. Intercepted traffic from this station was forwarded to Naval HQ in Ceylon.

In 1939 Ian Fleming was recruited by Rear Admiral John Godfrey, director of Naval Intelligence of the Royal Navy, to become his personal assistant. Fleming's code name was '17F', and he worked in Room 39 at the Admiralty Building in London. Fleming also worked with Colonel 'Wild Bill' Donovan—chief of OSS and President Franklin D. Roosevelt's special representative on intelligence cooperation between London and Washington.

Back in London on 1 March 1942, Ian Fleming met Victor Cavendish-Bentinck who was the chairman, Joint Intelligence Committee (JIC), at Whitehall Gardens and presented a file containing two typed pages of paper. The file mentioned that prior to the attack on Pearl Harbor, the US SIGINT station had managed to decode Japanese radio messages sent between Tokyo and Japanese embassies abroad. The intercepted Japanese signals indicated a possible attack on Ceylon.[39]

The file also contained an intelligence note from the FECB, New Delhi station. FECB had also intercepted JN25B message which gave a detailed and broadly accurate breakdown of IJN's southern forces. It further referred specifically to IJN forces likely to be deployed in the Indian Ocean, anticipating at least three fleet carriers, three battle cruisers and a substantial cruiser force. In a brief discussion with the chairman, Ian mentioned that the IJN Task Force could deploy a far superior force as compared to the Eastern Fleet. The two intelligence messages warned the British government and military of Japanese attack on Ceylon.

The chairman called his secretary and asked her to call Admiral Sir James Somerville immediately. Somerville and Fleming met the chairman in a secluded meeting room who handed over the intelligence file to Somerville and discussed the situation. After leaving the JIC office, Somerville dashed to Sir James Grigg's office—secretary of State for War. He summarized the Japanese threat drawn from his discussion with the JIC chairman,[40] which was Sir Grigg briefed to the British prime minister Winston Churchill over the telephone.

The next day, at 0930 hours, Sir James Grigg called for an urgent meeting of the War Cabinet. It consisted of the PM, his key advisors, cabinet ministers, the chiefs of Royal Air Force (RAF), Royal Navy (RN), the army and intelligence, all of whom arrived at the war room located at Whitehall in London. The members of the cabinet dispersed after discussing the status of the RN in the Far East.

Later that day, the War Cabinet Joint Planning Staff submitted an assessment entitled 'Far East Policy' which stated that the fall of Ceylon and the Japanese attacks on India's east coast could raise overwhelming internal security concerns in

India, create a revolt in the British Indian Army and threaten communications with Middle East, Burma and Australia. The British fleet would be denied the use of Trincomalee and Colombo.[41] Agreeing with this assessment, Francis Henry Norman Davidson, director of Military Intelligence, advised immediate military measures to be taken to provide Ceylon with adequate defences. General Sir Archibald Wavell, commander-in-chief, India, warned the cabinet that the immediate danger to Ceylon was from an aircraft carrier fleet attack similar to Pearl Harbor.[42]

The British Admiralty was concerned that Japan could take Ceylon and launch an offensive on India from Bombay and Calcutta which were the two centres of British power. Ceylon could also be the staging base to launch attacks on British outposts in the UAE and the wider Middle East.

After the fall of Singapore—and with the fall of the Andaman and Nicobar Islands and northern Sumatra—the narrow sea lanes to Singapore and Malaysia were severed. An attack on Ceylon was obviously imminent.[43] The chiefs of staff, the heads of the Royal Navy, British Army and Royal Air Force (RAF) sent a joint report to Churchill stating 'We must secure Ceylon…The loss of Ceylon will imperil our whole British War effort in the Middle East and Far East.'[44]

Churchill quickly realized that after the loss of HMS *Prince of Wales* and *Repulse* in 1941, the fall of Singapore and the disaster at Darwin, this was the most dangerous moment of his political career. He had recently survived a 'no-confidence' vote in the parliament. The fall of Ceylon could potentially bring down Churchill's wartime coalition government and compel Britain to concede defeat.[45]

British Prime Minister Winston Churchill retreated to the UK PM's designated country house in Chequers. One Sunday evening he hosted a dinner in honour of John Winant—US ambassador to the Court of St James—together with Averell

Harriman, President Roosevelt's special envoy. Prior to the dinner, Churchill handed over a file in a diplomatic pouch to John and asked him to personally deliver it to US President Roosevelt.

The file outlined the dangers of Japanese dominance in the British Indian Ocean territories resulting in the invasion of eastern India through Madras and Calcutta with incalculable consequences to the war plan.[46] Churchill warned President Roosevelt, 'Immense perils are now threatening Burma and India.'[47]

The note explained that if India allied itself with Japan, or followed a policy of non-cooperation with her, it could close the gap between Japan and Germany by over 2,000 miles. China would also be cut off from all military and commercial supplies and the Allies could lose the Suez Canal—the key transit route for British logistical supplies to India and the Far East.[48]

Early Monday morning, Churchill spoke to the prime ministers of Australia and New Zealand and directed them to position their cruisers and destroyers in Ceylon. He directed General Wavell, who was on his way to Ceylon, to establish a position of a supreme commander who would be overall in-charge of the island in order to prevent a repetition of Singapore. On 5 March, Admiral Sir Geoffrey Layton was promoted to commander-in-chief of Ceylon. Churchill immediately appointed Admiral Somerville as the commander-in-chief of the Eastern Fleet.[49] Admiral Somerville assumed command on 26 March 1942. He was heavily involved in the development of radar for the Royal Navy.[50]

Admiral Sir James Somerville arrived in Ceylon to take command of the newly constituted Eastern Fleet on 24 March 1942, just two days before Vice Admiral Nagumo and the Japanese fleet set sail from Kendari in the Celebes. Somerville ventured the date of the attack might be around 31 March.[51] As opposed to Somerville's assumptions, Kendari was several days sailing time nearer to Ceylon than Singapore and Nagumo's fleet entered the Indian Ocean through the Ombai Straits unopposed.[52]

The British War Preparations

From a naval perspective, Ceylon had two harbours which were Trincomalee and Colombo. On the east coast was the large natural harbour of Trincomalee, entered through a narrow channel from Koddiar Bay, itself well-protected from the open sea and capable of hosting the largest of fleets in its anchorage. It was one of the finest natural harbours in the world. The Royal Navy's East Indies Station was based at Trincomalee, having moved there from Colombo. [53]

The Eastern Fleet had to be strengthened so that it could maintain control of Ceylon.[54] The 16th Brigade of the British 70th Infantry Division in North Africa and the 21st East African Infantry Brigade Group, supported by two batteries of light howitzers, were deployed to Ceylon. At Prime Minister Churchill's request, Canberra also reassigned the 16th and 17th Infantry Brigades of the Australian 6th Division to Ceylon, which were en route from Libya to defend Australia.[55]

Thus, Ceylon was transformed from a military backwater into a key Allied military base. The First Sea Lord, Admiral of the Fleet Sir Dudley Pound decided to immediately withdraw the battleship HMS *Warspite* and the aircraft carrier HMS *Formidable* from the Eastern Mediterranean and move them to Ceylon. They were followed by four Revenge-class battleships and six destroyers.[56]

Seven miles south of Colombo was Ceylon's civilian airport at Ratmalana. The RAF moved in with their Hurricanes of No. 30 Squadron, newly arrived from the North African desert campaign, and the Blenheim medium bombers of No. 11 Squadron, veterans of Greece, Crete and the

Middle East. Another eight Catalinas arrived in Ceylon.[57] The surrounding coconut plantations made excellent camouflage and cooling shade for the air base.

The new Eastern Fleet consisted of the battleship HMS *Warspite*, the aircraft carrier HMS *Hermes*, the destroyer HMAS *Vampire* and the cruisers HMS *Emerald* and *Heemskerck* of the Royal Netherlands Navy, the destroyer *Isaac Sweers*, and eight submarines. All of these vessels were based at Trincomalee

At Colombo, the aircraft carrier HMS *Formidable* was stationed alongside the cruisers HMS *Cornwall*, HMS *Dorsetshire*, HMS *Enterprise*, HMS *Dragon*, HMS *Caledon*, and six destroyers. The battleships HMS *Resolution*, HMS *Ramillies*, HMS *Royal Sovereign*, HMS *Revenge*, the carrier HMS *Indomitable* and eight destroyers were all placed under the command of Vice Admiral A.U. Willis, second-in-command of the Eastern Fleet.[58] The Eastern Fleet was the single largest concentration of warships and aircraft carriers that the Royal Navy would deploy against an active enemy throughout the Second World War.

On 25 March 1942, after having dinner with his officers, Somerville retreated to the captains' quarters on board HMS *Warspite*. He wrote in his diary that the present British naval and land-based air forces were quite inadequate to protect Ceylon from the Japanese fleet.[59] The British fleet was more impressive on paper than in reality. The individual units had never operated together and the crews were inexperienced due to a lack of training. The air group consisted of only 57 strike aircraft and 37 fighters. The R-class battleships, despite recent refits, were in a poor state and unsuited for combat.[60] The battleships were, in fact, all veterans of the First World War with a squadron speed of only 18 knots.[61] The RAF—consisting of a few Grumman Wildcats, two-seater Fulmars and Hurricane fighters—was far too weak to seriously oppose the main Japanese naval aviation.[62] Admiral Somerville realized that his Fleet could not resist a concerted Japanese attack.

In contrast to the British fleet, the Japanese fleet consisted of modern, fast ships manned by well-trained crews; its aircraft carriers had a large number of aircraft flown by highly seasoned pilots who had fought in major battles in the Pacific, such as Pearl Harbor. Between Nagumo's five carriers, he had 318 aircraft compared to the 90 available aboard the three carriers of the Eastern Fleet.[63] The Japanese naval force comprised five aircraft carriers and four battleships, vastly outnumbering the small Royal Navy presence in the area.[64]

Orders Are Dispatched

Following the unconditional surrender of the Dutch East Indies on 9 March, Combined Fleet commander-in-chief Admiral Yamamoto issued 'The Combined Fleet Telegraphic Operation Classified Order No. 86'. It stated that the Southern Task Force commander Vice-Admiral Nagumo shall execute a surprise attack on the enemy fleet in the Ceylon area between mid-March and early-April.[65]

On the same evening, Vice Admiral Nagumo issued the following orders by means of the 'Southern Task Force Telegraphic Order No. 145': 'The 3rd carrier operation of the Southern Task Force shall be called Operation C, the scheduled date of attack shall be called Day C, and Day C shall be scheduled for 5 April 1942.'[66]

Operation C began on 26 March at 0800 Japan Standard Time, when KdB left Staring Bay on the east coast of Celebes (now Sulawesi). After departing Staring Bay, Kidō Butai (KdB) steered southward and the next day passed through the Ombai Strait, which separates Timor from the islands to its north. Now consisting of 20 warships, KdB continued toward Ceylon.[67]

Five fleet carriers the *Akagi*, the *Hiryu*, the *Soryu*, the *Shokaku* and the *Zuikaka*, along with four battleships the *Haruna*, the *Hiei*, the *Kirisbima* and the *Kongo*, accompanied by two heavy cruisers and ten destroyers, headed for Ceylon. In support were the 3rd Battleship Squadron, containing all four members of the Kongo-class, and the 8th Cruiser Squadron comprising the heavy cruisers *Tone* and *Chikuma*. Escort duties were undertaken by Rear Admiral Omori Sentaro, who commanded two divisions of destroyers (nine in total) from his flagship, the light cruiser *Abukuma*. The total aircraft complement of the fleet consisting of torpedo bombers, dive-bombers and fighters was 280. In striking power this fleet was virtually the same as the one used against Pearl Harbor.[68]

Having destroyed much of the American fleet at Pearl Harbor, Japan wanted to eliminate the British threat in the Indian Ocean. So they steamed westward to Ceylon, unopposed, to attack the Eastern Fleet in accordance with their master plan.[69]

Attacks on India's East Coast

Admiral Yamamoto's order included a raid in the Bay of Bengal to destroy all British merchant shipping and bring to a standstill the seaborne commerce between ports on India's east coast and strike Calcutta which was the logistical support base for British operations in Burma.[70] Working in cooperation with Nagumo on the Ceylon raids was Vice Admiral Jisaburō Ozawa. Ozawa's role was to destroy any merchant shipping and attack India's east coast installations, whilst Nagumo had the more vital role of finding and destroying the British fleet.[71]

Vice Admiral Ozawa commanded one light carrier, six cruisers and four destroyers.[72] The IJN attacked Allied shipping between Calcutta and Madras, sinking 21 ships—totalling 93,247 tons—and damaging four more. Japanese submarines sank five ships worth 32,404 tons. Conversely, the Japanese only lost 17 aircraft, and none of their ships were damaged.[73]

Five B5N aircraft launched from Ryujo to strike against various towns along the eastern Indian coastline, including

Visakhapatnam and Cocanada, caused considerable panic amongst the civilian population, who fully expected the Japanese to land troops and occupy India. Both towns were evacuated. The attack also caused chaos amidst Allied convoy commands with the port of Calcutta practically shutting down.[74]

The civil authorities in Madras, under Governor Sir Arthur Hope, were informed by the local military command that a Japanese 'invasion in force' was expected south of Masulipatnam on the Coromandel Coast. Sir Arthur's government issued a communiqué asking people whose presence was not essential to leave the city. About 200,000 people fled the city. They also ordered government offices and their staff to evacuate Madras and move inland. The high court shifted to Coimbatore, the inspector general of police to Vellore, the board of revenue to Salem, and other departments to various inland districts' headquarters. The bulk of the secretariat moved to the hill station of Ooty in the Nilgiris. Only the governor, along with the chief secretary and other senior officials, stayed on in Fort St George.[75] The balance of power had been totally overturned; the Bay of Bengal had been a 'British Lake' for over a century.[76] The whole scenario pointed to an invasion of Ceylon and India in conjunction with the drive through Burma followed by Imphal and Kohima.[77]

Operation C: The Attack on Ceylon

Whilst Ozawa was sweeping the Bay of Bengal, Nagumo was advancing towards Ceylon.[78] Nagumo's objective was to replicate the Pearl Harbor victory by catching an unprepared Eastern Fleet in Ceylon's harbour.[79] By midnight, 2 April 1942, Vice Admiral Nagumo was well into the Indian Ocean with the coast of Sumatra some 500 miles away. He was proceeding on a course that would take him directly to Ceylon. He was in no hurry and steamed slowly ahead. He had already decided to delay his attack from 4 to 5 April, Easter Sunday, because he thought it was more likely that the Eastern Fleet would be in port and Ceylon's defences less alert. It was much the same tactic that he had adopted at Pearl Harbor.

Squadron Leader Leonard Joseph Birchall of the Royal Canadian Air Force had arrived at Ceylon from Karachi in his Catalina with his eight-member crew.[80] At 0600 hours on 4 April, with a maximum fuel load that could carry a long-range operation until daylight the next day, Birchall took off with orders to patrol an area some 250 miles southeast of the island in strict radio silence.

Having been in the air for 10 hours, Birchall and his crew were beginning to work out a course back to base when they noticed a small speck on the southern horizon against the dim grey evening skies. With plenty of fuel still aboard, they went to investigate. It was to be a chance observation that changed the course of history. It was surprising to find any ship in this position and at first it was thought likely to be a Royal Navy ship. But as they got closer, flying at a height of 2,000 feet, they found it was part of a large naval fleet. At about 1600 hours on 4 April, Birchall had sighted the Japanese fleet southeast of Ceylon.[81]

Birchall flung his Catalina northwards at full boost but he was spotted. The Japanese had deployed a combat air patrol of Zeros that were circling high above the fleet. Unbeknownst to him, they were called down to intercept Birchall's plane and shoot it down.[82]

The slow, heavy flying boat was no match for these aircraft. Regulations required that radio messages be repeated three times but radio operator Sergeant Phillips had hardly started his second repeat when the Zeros struck. A cannon shell hit the radio set, completely destroying it, whilst another shattered the leg of Sergeant Calorossi, one of the gunners. The Japanese knew they must destroy the flying boat as quickly as possible before their fleet's presence was reported. The attack was intense and with a couple of fires breaking out on board and several of the crew badly injured, the Catalina started to break up in mid-air. Birchall fought on, taking evasive action as best as he could. [83]

They were still 350 miles from land when the aircraft crashed in the sea. The crew bailed out in the sea with their life jackets. The Japanese fighters kept strafing at the crew. They dived in the sea and disappeared as soon as an aircraft came in to strafe the crew. The bullets killed the two wounded survivors floating in their life jackets.[84] Fifteen minutes later, Birchall and five other survivors were picked up by the destroyer *Isokaze* and later transferred to Japan aboard the aircraft carrier *Akagi*.[85] The Japanese interrogators wanted to know if a sighting message was dispatched by Birchall. The crew said that they could not pass on the message as the plane crashed before they could do so. But then the Japanese intercepted a message from Colombo asking the Catalina to repeat its report. The message from Birchall's aircraft had been garbled, but its meaning was clear: a Japanese attack was incoming. The element of surprise had been lost. Birchall's message galvanized the British commanders.

As soon as the message was received, Admiral Sir Geoffrey Layton, c-in-c Ceylon, ordered all defences at Colombo to be at general quarters by 1500 hours on 5 April.[86] When Somerville received this news, he ordered Colombo's large harbour cleared of warships and merchant vessels. The garrison and the RAF units on the island were ordered to stand-to from 0300 hours the next morning. About 60 vessels had been sent out of harm's way following the 28 March SIGINT warning and another 25 were dispatched now, including *Cornwall* and *Dorsetshire*.[87] The Ceylonese people, like many around the world, had heard rumours of the atrocities carried out against civilians by the Japanese troops in China and did not want to become the next victim. The ferry from Talaimannar to India was packed night after night.[88]

At 0600 hours on 5 April, Nagumo's fleet was steaming

towards Ceylon from 200 miles south of the island.[89] Commander Mitsuo Fuchida, the general commander, had given the 'all go' at 1045. It was 0800 hours on Easter Sunday and an air of calm and tranquillity hung over Ceylon. Unbeknown to the general population, the radar stations at Colombo had picked up an early warning of the first wave of incoming Japanese aircraft. The message was not delivered until 0740 hours, 20 minutes before the attack began with a force of 53 Type-97 carrier-based attack planes and 38 Type-99 carrier-based bombers entering the air over Colombo, escorted by 36 Type-0 fighter planes.

This force of 180 aircraft was led by Commander Mitsuo Fuchida of the Akagi who had led the attack on Pearl Harbor. He was one of Japan's most experienced flyers who had already served for 25 years in the Imperial Navy. He was by far the oldest man to be flying on either side that day. However, the rest of the pilots were also significantly experienced, having participated in the Pearl Harbor attack.

The Japanese pilots took off in quick succession from the five carriers as they steamed into the wind and headed for Colombo.[90] For the first time, they faced stiff opposition as the incoming aircraft were met by a concentrated barrage of anti-aircraft gunfire and 28 British fighters who engaged them in a short and sharp dogfight.[91]

At first light on Easter Sunday, 5 April, two routine patrols flew out—one consisting of two Hurricanes from No. 30 Squadron, and the other of six Fulmars of No. 803 Squadron. The enormous battle formation of the expectant enemy—with dozens of Spitfire and Hurricane fighter planes—was spotted by the Fulmars.[92] In the 30-minute-long engagement, the Japanese Type-0 fighters brought down 19 Spitfires, 21 Hurricanes, 10 Swordfish and one Defiant, a total of 51 aircraft, while they only lost one fighter plane that had crashed itself.[93]

Air Combat over Ceylon

At Ratmalana, the early morning sun had risen high in the sky and there was no indication of an impending attack. Some felt it was another false alarm and at 0730 hours some of the men were sent to have their breakfast. Twenty minutes later the first Japanese formations roared overhead, taking everyone by surprise. Enemy fighters and light bombers—60- to 80-strong—approached Colombo en masse, flying in V-shaped formations of about six planes each. The majority of the planes were Mitsubishi Type-96s, Zero fighters, Seversky naval escort fighters and Kawasaki Army 97 light bombers. The attack opened with dive-bombing of the harbour and Ratmalana Aerodrome.[94]

Despite their long vigil, No. 30 Squadron—under leader G.F. Chater DFC—was caught out on the ground by the Japanese. But at this time the pilots of the squadron were faced with the simple fact that any aircraft, no matter how superior or inferior to an enemy aircraft, was at its most vulnerable just after take-off.[95]

From Ratmalana and the nearby temporary airfield at the Colombo Racecourse, RAF Hurricanes and Fleet Air Arm Fulmars were hurriedly taking off. The Zeros were already over Colombo and spotted the British fighters taking off—four Fulmars were immediately shot down. 258 Squadron's Hurricanes attacked a group of D3A attacking ships in Colombo harbour, shooting at least one of them down before the escorting Zeros took the matter in their hand.

Of the 14 Hurricanes that had taken off from the racecourse's airstrip, nine had not returned. Five pilots had been killed and multiple others injured whilst bailing out of their stricken aircraft. 258 Squadron could muster only nine aircraft. Together with the Fleet Air Arm, Britain had lost 27 aircraft over Colombo with 17 airmen killed and 11 injured. Only three Japanese aircraft were shot down over Ceylon.[96]

The Japanese strike force made its landfall at 0715 hours in the Galle area over Colombo's Marine Parade. The pilots headed for the naval harbour installations and oil depots at Kolonnawa to the east of the city. One formation attacked the ships in and around the harbour whilst the second—Fuchida's Type-97 attack bombers—came in low, strafing the rail yards at Ratmalana, the shopping areas, and the racecourse airfield, and bombed them. This initial attack was followed by high-altitude bombing aimed at the few ships that remained in the harbour—being repaired—sinking the destroyer *Tenedos* and an armed merchant cruiser named the *Hector* as well as severely damaging the *Lucia*, a submarine tender, and a freighter. One of those killed on the *Tenedos* was ordinary seaman Sir Robert Peel, Bt, son of the music hall comedienne Beatrice Lillie.[97]

As the Japanese turned to start their bombing run, they spotted six Swordfish biplanes armed with torpedoes approaching the city from the north. Their orders had been to refuel and proceed to attack the enemy fleet. At first the six Fleet Air Arm pilots were not perturbed as the fighters approached them; they were used to RAF Hurricanes coming up to take a look at them. Fuchida called up Lieutenant Commander Shigeru Itaya who was leading the fighter wing and ordered him to deal with the Swordfish. Interestingly, Itaya was one of the engineers who had designed the Zero back in 1938 when he was second in command of the Yokasuka Experimental Air Corps.[98]

The Zeros opened fire from a distance of about 600 yards with deadly accuracy. Most of the biplanes were hit in the first attack and their crews injured. A second attack swiftly followed and all six Swordfish were sent crashing to the ground. Not satisfied with downing the aircraft, the Zeros then swept in for a third time to strafe any survivors. Of the 14 men involved in this attack, five were killed and five badly wounded.[99] By 0835 hours, the action was over. The Japanese aircraft streamed out to sea, returning to their home ships.

A counter attack was launched by the British after the air

raid on Ceylon. The Blenheims of 11 Squadron had escaped the Japanese attack. Just a week earlier, they had been redeployed to the Racecourse airfield. 10 Blenheims were on alert status, fuelled and loaded up with 500 lb semi-armour piercing bombs. But they were forced to wait until all of 258 Squadron Hurricanes had flitted out of the way. At 1025 hours, nine unescorted Bristol Blenheim aircraft from 11 Squadron scrambled to locate and attack the Japanese carrier force. Zero fighters intercepted them and pouncing with a murderous rate of fire. Undeterred, the Blenheims went into a formation bombing run at a height of 11,000 feet targeting the *Akagi*. It was damaged by a near-miss. Another string of bombs fell near the cruiser *Tone* but did no damage. Five Blenheims were lost whilst the remaining four were badly damaged. It was the first time Nagumo's carrier strike force had been attacked either by surface or air forces since Pearl Harbor.[100]

After the air war, the ocean was empty and nothing disturbed the glassy, blue surface—not even the occasional flying fish which were found aplenty in the region. A pall of black smoke hung over the harbour at Colombo.[101] Admiral Layton was particularly scathing about the performance of his Fulmars and Swordfishes: 'Fleet Air Arm aircraft(s) are proving more of an embarrassment than a help, when landed. They cannot operate by day in the presence of Japanese fighters and only tend to congest aerodromes.'[102]

The Battle at Sea

It was a calm day with little or no clouds. A slight haze hung over the sun and visibility was good. Both Captain Augustus Agar on the *Dorsetshire* and Captain Percival Manwaring on the *Cornwall* had detected a second, shadowing seaplane on their radar. The first Japanese reconnaissance aircraft had been spotted by *Cornwall*'s lookouts passing 20 miles behind the British ships. The second was later detected loitering near the horizon. The *Dorsetshire*'s captain saw the Japanese spotter plane and concluded that it was a single-engine aircraft which signified the Japanese fleet being positioned close to the two British ships.

On the day of the attack, the ship's company had been at action stations since 0800 hours. The battle ensign was fluttering aloft and all gun crews were closed-up. Everyone on deck kept glancing skywards, ready for the attack they knew was coming.[103]

At 1455, a Type-0 reconnaissance seaplane of the Japanese cruiser *Toné* informed the captain about two warships who sent a wireless message to the aircraft: 'Confirm the enemy vessels. They can be destroyers, can't they?' At 1556, the reply of the aircraft of the *Toné* came in: '1545: Enemy cruisers are HMS *Cornwall* and *Dorsetshire*.'[104]

When the Japanese were attacking Colombo, *Cornwall* and *Dorsetshire* were 100 miles south of Ceylon. In 1941 *Dorsetshire* had been involved in the hunt for the German battleship *Bismarck*. It had fired three torpedoes at Bismarck. Two of them had found their target.

Having received this message, Carrier Task Force commander Vice Admiral Nagumo ordered at 1610: 'The 5th Carrier Division shall attack them with about one half of its carrier based attack planes and bombers.' At 1625, the 5th Carrier Division Commander Rear Admiral Hara ordered: 'The Attack Unit shall take off at 1700. Target: the Kent-class cruisers. Attack course 200°, distance to target 150 nautical miles.'

Nagumo directed Lieutenant Commander Takashige Egusa, Air Group commander of the *Soryu*, to lead the attack on the two cruisers. Egusa's pilots had been handpicked as an elite force and trained to destroy America's aircraft carriers but were thwarted when they arrived at Pearl Harbor to find none there.[105] Lieutenant Commander Takashige Egusa took off at 1130 hours with 80 Type-99 dive-bombers (Vals) from the Soryu, Hiryu and Akagi, and headed in the direction of the British cruisers. As soon as they spotted the two British cruisers they divided into two groups.[106] At 1300 hours, a large number of echoes indicated a force of aircraft was nearby. They approached the two warships directly from the front. Being of 1920s design, neither cruiser had anti-aircraft guns that could fire directly forward.[107]

At 1340, Dorsetshire's lookouts saw the first Japanese bombers directly overhead and opened fire. The Walrus seaplane and its catapult were hit. There was a blinding flash as the Fleet Air Arm's workshop—containing high-octane aviation fuel—exploded into an inferno.[108] The bombs fell in quick succession, accurately striking the ship's aircraft catapult, the wireless telegraph installation near the bridge, and the engine and boiler rooms. Her guns blazed away in defiance but were put out of action one by one. With her steering jammed hard to starboard, the ship swung in a wide circle and shuddered to a halt. There was a sudden explosion as a bomb hit one of the magazines.[109] At 1348, eight minutes after the first bomb struck, *Dorsetshire*'s bow lifted as her stern began to slip beneath the waves.[110]

Around two minutes later, Captain Agar, realizing that the ship was sinking, ordered all hands on deck. It was incredible how quickly the ship sank. To quote Captain Agar, '…she just took one plunge by the stern, and as we were thrown into the water, the bows towered up almost vertically alongside us.'[111]

First Lieutenant Geoffrey Grove later described his recollections of the attack:

> We watched the planes like hawks, and as the bombs showered down, we flung ourselves down on our faces. If the hit was close by, you were bounced like a ball. We had three hits almost directly under us and for one of them I was standing up and was enveloped in a great sheet of flame. I thought it was the end of me but my clothing saved me and I was unhurt.[112]

The *Cornwall*, though still afloat, had not fared much better. In less than five minutes after the attack started, all power had failed, and the boiler and engine rooms were flooding rapidly. Attempting to evade with a swing to starboard, several of her anti-aircraft gun mounts were obliterated as more bombs rained down. Thick black smoke was emanating from the foremost funnel uptake casings on both sides of the upper deck. It soon became evident that the ship was sinking and Captain Manwaring—who continued to direct operations while being wounded in the right shoulder—gave orders to prepare to abandon ship. Then—with the remaining bridge personnel—he left the bridge and made his way aft to oversee the launching of all available floats. At 1355, the final order to abandon ship was given.[113] The attack was swift and devastating. Cornwall managed to survive a few more minutes but ultimately sank quickly after suffering 15 total bomb hits. The attack had lasted less than 20 minutes. Over 400 men were killed. Not a single Japanese aircraft was lost or even suffered significant damage.

The Survivors

A large number of survivors from both cruisers found themselves adrift in the shark-infested ocean, 300 miles from land. The injured were transferred into two whalers and a skiff while the remainder swam around collecting wreckage to be improvised as rafts.

More wreckage surfaced as the ship continued to break up thousands of feet beneath the waves. A section of the ship's main mast floated up and proved to be a significant life-saver. Another useful item that surfaced was a 20 lb tin of dripping and some oranges. The survivors rubbed the dripping on their bodies to keep out the cold at night and protect against the hot sun by day.[114]

Throughout the night, the two groups of survivors occasionally heard each other enjoying singing duets out of sight and often joined in as chorus. Soon after sunrise on 6 April, the heat became intense and head coverings were fashioned from pieces cut from the battle dress. Sharks were numerous but they seemed content to wait for the corpses from the sunk battleships and made no attempt to devour anyone alive. The men quietly talked to each other, formed small groups and called out for news of their shipmates.[115]

Three of the four surgeons from the *Dorsetshire* perished in the battle, leaving Surgeon Lieutenant A.H.F. Wood to attend to the wounded. After establishing a sick bay of sorts in a whaler where he could attend to the wounded, Surgeon Lieutenant Wood worked tirelessly for 36 hours. Many of the survivors owed their lives to him.[116]

Early in the morning, the shrill sound of a bosun's pipe calling the *Dorsetshire*'s company to breakfast reverberated across the calm sea, causing much laughter amidst the crew. Breakfast? It consisted of salvaged oranges and canteen dripping. The men of the *Cornwall* fared a little better. They had tiny pieces of corned beef, tinned apricots, the ship's biscuits and some cans of juice.

Throughout the day the survivors continually scanned the horizon for signs of rescue ships until finally, at about 1700 hours, after spending 26 hours in the water, an aircraft flew overhead signalling, 'Hold on. Help coming.' With darkness fast approaching, at around 1800 hours the cruiser *Enterprise* and the destroyers *Paladin* and *Panther* arrived to pick up the exhausted survivors. 1,122 men—many of them wounded—were brought on-board.[117]

The Attack on Trincomalee

After the 5 April Ceylon raids, the Kido Butai had manoeuvred south of Ceylon with the intention of arriving in position to launch further attacks on the British base at Trincomalee.

Nagumo's force was sighted at 1517 hours on 8 April by an RAF Catalina. The island's defences were put on full alert and all seaworthy vessels in Trincomalee Harbour, including the aircraft carrier HMS *Hermes,* were ordered to sail. No further contact with the Japanese was made until 0706 hours the next day when the radar station at Trincomalee detected aircraft approaching at a range of 91 miles. The ships were also spotted by another Squadron 413 Catalina. This was shot down but not before it transmitted a partial sighting report.[118]

Admiral Nagumo started the attack on Trincomalee on 9 April 1942. The Japanese 91 B5N bombers, escorted by 38 Zeros, began the attack at 0706 hours The defending fighters were scrambled but there were only 23 of them—17 Hurricanes and 6 Fulmars—against 132 Japanese aircraft. A trio of Hurricanes on dawn patrol—from 261 Squadron—were vectored out to sea to intercept the Japanese. They managed to work themselves into a position behind the escorting Zero fighters and made a dash towards them through the clouds. Three Japanese fighters were quickly shot down, but one Hurricane was lost and another had to crash land. More Hurricanes from 261 Squadron arrived as the Japanese began their bombing runs against the China Bay airfield and attacked the B5Ns. However, the Zeros shot down half of the RAF aircraft.[119]

At 1030 on 9 April, the full force of the carrier-based attack planes and 37 fighter planes attacked Trincomalee, sank two large and one small merchant ships, caused serious damage to one HMS Leander-class light cruiser, blew up, set ablaze and mostly destroyed the naval facilities near the piers, anti-aircraft batteries, the residence of the commander-in-chief of Ceylon, and three barracks and oil tanks. The freighter *Sagaing* was set on fire, forcing the crew to beach the ship to prevent her sinking. The Japanese also blew up two large hangars on the airfield, hit merchant ship that caught fire and damaged HMS *Erebus.* Returning fire with anti-aircraft guns, the British forces managed to shoot down only four of the attackers while the RAF lost eight Hurricanes and one Fulmar.[120]

The China Bay Aerodrome was attacked by a force of about 54 bombers.[121] The 40 fighters escorting them dropped low to carry out their usual strafing runs and added to the destruction. The hangar housing 273 Squadron's old Vildebeests was hit and all the aircraft stationed inside were damaged beyond repair.

HMS *Hermes* Sunk by Dive Bombers

The most important of the ships anchored at Trincomalee Harbour was the aircraft carrier *Hermes* under the command of Captain Richard Onslow. It had arrived four days earlier, having patrolled between Simonstown, Mombasa, Mauritius, the Persian Gulf and the Maldives for the past few months. It had initially been scheduled to sail to Australia to help in her defence in case the Japanese moved southwards. A change of plans now included her in the Madagascar operations due to start the following month.[122]

On the evening of 8 April, the recall signal aboard the *Hermes* was hoisted for the benefit of those ashore and every measure was taken to get the message to them quickly. But it was 1900 hours before she weighed anchor and darkness was already falling when she left for the open sea. *Hermes* had to put to sea so quickly that she did not have the time to take the 12 Fairey Swordfish Mark I aircraft of the 814 Naval Air Squadron aboard.[123]

Japanese reconnaissance aircraft were scouring the coastal waters of Ceylon for Royal Navy warships. At 1055 a floatplane from the battleship *Haruna* reported the presence of HMS *Hermes* and three destroyers just south of Trincomalee, off the town of Batticaloa. Aboard the *Hermes* Captain Onslow realized he had been spotted and expected to be attacked at any moment. With little to retaliate with, he turned back towards Trincomalee, moving obliquely shoreward, hoping to come within range of fighter aircraft protection.[124] He repeatedly radioed for air cover but no one at the China Bay airstrip was in a position to help or even listen to his request. Only the Japanese picked up the signals.[125]

Nagumo had kept his dive bombers as a reserve for precisely such a situation.[126] At 1100 hours, the Carrier Task Force commander ordered: 'Bomber units and fighter planes, get ready for a sortie to attack the carrier.' The attack unit of 85 D3As, escorted by nine Zeros and led by Lieutenant Commander Takahashi Kakuichi, spotted HMS *Hermes* at 1330. The Japanese pilots were surprised to find the *Hermes* had absolutely no air cover. The dive bombing started at 1335.[127]

The dive bombers went into their tried-and-tested formation of line astern and plunged headlong into the attack. With little opposition, the pilots achieved an incredible percentage of direct hits with their bombs. Flames and smoke billowed upwards instead of the slender plumes of water from near-misses. Such accuracy was unparalleled even in future operations.[128] Lieutenant Brimble, second gunnery officer on the *Hermes*, recalled how the ship twisted and turned, desperately trying to deflect the pilots' aim. But—unlike a destroyer—an aircraft carrier is not entirely suitable for this sort of manoeuvre.

Suddenly the attack was called off and the aircraft took off towards the distant shore. Hermes herself continued in the same direction for a good half an hour. As the crew desperately tried to repair the damage, an estimated 70 aircraft were spotted flying at a great height overhead. The second rain of bombs fell thick and fast, and the ship was soon ablaze from stem to stern, sinking slowly. But the attack continued.[129]

Soon both boiler rooms were out of action. By 1350 she was listing heavily to port, the flight deck being awash; smoke was pouring out of the hangar and the starboard side. Captain Onslow gave the order to abandon ship. The end came very quickly, and at 1355, 9 April— 20 minutes after first sighting the enemy—the *Hermes* took her final plunge. 'So quickly did she, in fact, go,' records the navigating officer, 'that when I came to leave the ship I merely stepped off from the chart house level…into the water. Even at this list No. 1 4-in. gun was still firing.'[130]

Five miles out, the *Hermes* finally plunged beneath the waves into 30 fathoms of water, still fiercely blazing. Captain Onslow's calls were eventually picked up at Ratmalana and eight Fulmars of the 803 and 806 Squadrons took off at about 1000 hours to try to help. They headed out eastward across the island but arrived in time to see the final stages of the attack. Sub-Lieutenant Metcalfe later recalled that he saw 'the carrier and the destroyer lying stopped, like a couple of beetles being attacked by a swarm of ants.'[131]

The carrier sank beneath the waves within 20 minutes[132] and the enemy aircraft began dispersing. A jubilant Lieutenant Commander Takashige Egusa led his formations back to the carriers after 1100 hours, leaving many survivors floundering in the sea beneath the lingering smoke from the burning *Hermes*.[133] This was the first time in history that an aircraft carrier had been sunk by air attack.[134]

While the attack on the *Hermes* was still in progress, the tanker *British Sergeant* was attacked by six dive-bombers. She received four direct hits and two near misses in about 90 seconds, and was left to sink. Five of the aircraft also attacked the auxiliary tanker *Athelstane* at 1205, scoring several hits; she turned sharply to port and sank almost immediately. The remaining four aircraft then attacked her escort *Hollyhock* in pairs.[135] As the *Athelstane* sank, eight Fulmars engaged the enemy aircraft, shooting down at least three, and losing two of their own. The freighter *Norviken* was also sunk.

As soon as the *Hermes* had disappeared, the enemy turned their attention to the HMAS *Vampire* and attacked it with 15 or 20 bombers. *Vampire* was an Australian destroyer that was present in Trincomalee that day. When the enemy planes approached Trincomalee, HMAS *Vampire* was on patrol outside the harbour. She was immediately ordered to return to the harbour to help defend against the incoming attack. As the Japanese planes began dropping bombs, HMAS *Vampire* manoeuvred aggressively to avoid being hit. It engaged the planes with its anti-aircraft guns, shooting down several of them.

Ten minutes sufficed to finish her. A bomb struck the foremost end of the torpedo tubes; the warheads did not explode, but the ship broke in half, the fore end sinking immediately. The enemy ceased bombing and were making off when the ammunition storage depot exploded and the stem sank at 1105. Two minutes later there was a heavy under-water explosion, presumably the depth-charges.[136] 307 men from HMS *Hermes* and eight from HMAS *Vampire* were lost.[137]

The attack was witnessed by the hospital ship *Vita*, on passage from Trincomalee to Colombo. She closed the scene of action and picked up over 600 survivors. Others were rescued by local crafts or swam to the shore. The survivors from the *Hermes* thought she was a Japanese vessel and swam away from her. It was almost dusk when they reached a navigational buoy just outside the harbour at Batticaloa. Exhausted by the long swim, they secured themselves to the buoy for the night and stayed there until a local fishing boat came out to take them ashore.[138]

The navy sustained a total of 756 casualties in the two 'battles' over Colombo and Trincomalee. Twenty-one officers and 287 ratings lost their lives on the *Hermes*; 10 officers and 180 ratings were lost aboard the *Cornwall*; and 19 officers and 215 ratings on the *Dorsetshire*.[139] This led the British to suspend all shipping operations between Burma and India.

Admiral Nagumo set sail for action in the Pacific with his carrier strike force which had steamed more than 50,000 miles since attacking Pearl Harbor and won many battles, all with the loss of only a dozen aircraft.[140] The attack on Ceylon took place

119 days after the Pearl Harbor attack in Hawaii. In that relatively short time, the Japanese military had advanced westwards in the Indian Ocean with astonishing speed and success.[141]

Conclusion

Back in London, on 10 April, the British military was now concerned with trying to save India from a Japanese invasion. In Bombay, General Wavell—commander-in-chief of India—demanded more aircraft and protested that present naval forces were insufficient to protect either India or Ceylon from possible invasion.[142] As he put it: 'Our Eastern fleet was powerless to protect Ceylon or Eastern India; our air strength was negligible.'[143] Sir Winston Churchill diplomatically described it as 'our having narrowly avoided a major disaster. It is true to say we survived a severe trial but it was one in which we got no glory.'[144] The price was high. Churchill acknowledged that Squadron Leader L.J. Birchall had made one of the single most important contributions to their victory and called Birchall the 'Saviour of Ceylon.'[145] He would later write: 'Nothing like this had been seen in the Mediterranean in all our conflicts with the German and Italian Air Forces.'

At a press conference in London, Sir Winston Churchill was asked what he thought had been the most dangerous moment of the war. Some thought he would suggest the German invasion of Britain; others thought it might be when Rommel was heading at full speed for Alexandria and Cairo; and some thought it might be the fall of Singapore. After a moment's pause he declared, without any shadow of a doubt, the most dangerous moment of the war, the one that caused him the greatest concern, was when he received the news that the Japanese fleet was heading for Ceylon.[146]

THREE

Neutral Territory, Hidden Wars and Espionage beneath Goan Skies

Somewhere off the Indian coast in the evening swell of waves rolling and sweeping for miles in the Arabian Sea—with fish flying and skimming from one foam-capped crest to another—a U-boat periscope the size of a shark's fin sliced through the surface of the sea. Water gushed over the lens as the lieutenant commander of the submarine crouched and stared through the rubber eye pieces.

The lens was clouded by the grey and cloudy waters interspersed with bubbles of salty froth. When the obstruction weaned off, the officer saw the blue evening sky above the Indian Ocean stretched between Ceylon and East Africa. He slowly manoeuvred the periscope across the surface of the sea. At about two miles to the south, he saw the tossing outline of a cargo ship, her decrepit grey hull splashed with rust. He called the commander of U-181, Lieutenant Wolfgang Luth. 'In position, sir,' he reported as he perused through the Vessel Recognition Book and closely checked the ship's outline with the printed silhouette. A short paragraph gave details of speed, power, owners and tonnage. The vessel in question was now clearly visible through the periscope.[1]

As is customary, the U-181 had surfaced at an agreed-upon

time just before daybreak to intercept a radio signal from an unknown station somewhere on the Indian shoreline. The transmission directed the captain to intercept a Greek cargo ship at around 0730 hours and a British freighter at approximately 2030 hours, and had provided him with the bearings and courses. At precisely 0737 hours, Luth had sunk the 6,481-ton Greek ship *Mount Helmos*. Now, he was surfacing to sink the British *Dorington Court*, bound from Calcutta to Louren Marques and Durban.[2] They were safe from any attack from enemy aircraft or warships as the sea stretched wide and empty as the cloudless sky. Luth gave orders to fire two torpedoes. A grey wall of water rose as the torpedoes struck *Dorington Court* and an orange burst of flame engulfed her stern. Luth, peering through the submarine's periscope, watched the explosion. Immediately after the impact, he ordered his crew to bring the U-boat to the surface. On the deck of the stricken ship, the crew desperately scrambled to lower the lifeboats into the roiling sea. Amid the chaos, the helmsman of *Dorington Court* swung the ship hard over to port, aiming to present a smaller target to any follow-up salvos. Just as it shifted, the U-boat's gun roared to life, its first shell thundering toward the helpless vessel.[3]

Luth admired the accuracy of the radio transmission. He did not know who sent it or where the transmitter was located. The most he could fathom from the direction and strength of the signal was that it must be situated along the west coast of India, probably somewhere south of Bombay (now Mumbai). Every night, at a different time specified in a previous message, he would surface his U-boat, and while the generators charged batteries and hatches were opened for fresh air, the radio operator would listen for his next instructions. These came in a regularly-changed code which provided the details of the cargo ships. These messages had predicted for him the whereabouts of three American ships, *Alcoa Pathfinder*, *Excello* and *East Indian*, two Norwegian freighters *Gunda* and *K.G. Meldahl*, and the Greek

Mount Helmos. He had sunk them all.[4]

In five weeks, U-boats had sunk 46 Allied ships in the Indian Ocean. No matter where they were sailing or when, a German U-boat would rise from the depths of the ocean and destroy them. The U-boat commanders had complete and accurate information of the cargo ships' courses.[5] Shipping losses from German submarines in the Indian Ocean were threatening to cut off essential British war supplies for the defence of India against Japan.

Germany had rebuilt her merchant fleet after WWI and by 1939 had a substantial number of ships at sea. Inevitably, many of these were in foreign waters, some on the high seas. But many were in port when war was declared on 3 September 1939.[6] All German ships' masters carried secret orders to be opened on receipt of the code word '*Essberger*', which was issued on 25 August 1939. The orders directed them to leave hostile ports as soon as possible, or if at sea, to leave the usual shipping lanes. Shortly after, a second code word was transmitted ordering the ships to head for Germany or a neutral port. Those stationed in British or French ports were interned. Some were able to reach Germany, but most headed for the nearest neutral port in order to avoid capture or sinking.[7] *Ehrenfels* was one such ship. She was a newer, faster and more capable ship with twin diesel engines driving a single propeller, giving her long endurance on one engine and high speed on two. Such power also required the hull to be of significantly stronger construction than in a conventional merchant ship.[8]

Ehrenfels first came to the notice of the authorities in British India in 1939. The ship had visited Batavia in the Dutch East Indies where the Dutch Intelligence Service identified one of the passengers as a known Abwehr (German military intelligence) agent named Robert Koch (code-named Trompeta). The Dutch alerted the MI5 office in India so that when *Ehrenfels* arrived in Calcutta the latter were ready. The ship anchored in the

Hooghly River and was subjected to a 24-hour watch, with arrangements in place to detain Koch as soon as he ventured ashore, although, wisely in the circumstances, he did not do so. Plain-clothes policemen were sent aboard on a clandestine reconnaissance and the movement of all crew and passengers who went ashore was carefully monitored. After only two days in port, *Ehrenfels*'s captain—under cover of darkness and against port regulations—raised anchor and sailed down the Hooghly towards Sagar Island and disappeared into the Bay of Bengal.

British MI6 received intelligence that the *Ehrenfels* had entered the Mormugao Harbour in the neutral enclave of Portuguese Goa on the west coast of India. It became clear that the ship's captain had been alerted to the imminent declaration of war from the German consulate in Calcutta.[9] The following day, another German ship, *Drachenfels*, which had just left Goa for Rotterdam, returned to Mormugao. Three days later *Braunfels*, originally headed for Calcutta, also returned to Goa. One year later, in June 1940, the Italian ship *Anfora* also arrived in Goa.[10]

Mormugao was one of India's most ideal natural ports, based at the mouth of the river Zuari meeting the Arabian Sea. It was one of the busiest ports, and probably the richest, known in ancient times and frequented by traders from Africa, the Gulf, Europe, Southeast Asia and China.[11]

Legally, these ships were taking shelter while their crews were visitors. This meant that for as long as the ships lay at anchor, paid the appropriate harbour charges and chandlers' bills, and their crews acted with reasonable discretion, they were left to their own plans.[12] In Mormugao, the crew of the ship was allowed ashore and could roam anywhere within Portuguese territory without obstruction or interference. They prowled around the town, sailed in the harbour, canoed up rivers and took the train to the last station before the border with British India.[13]

The British Admiralty in London was concerned by the shipping losses from the German U-boats in the Indian Ocean.

A rear admiral from the Royal Navy sent a request to the Intelligence Bureau of the Government of India, asking them to discover the leakage of British shipping information as a matter of the highest priority. They reported some loose talk about ships docked at the Taj bar in Bombay Harbour and the Galle Face in Colombo. But there were no instances of people saying much more than generalities. The Germans were unable to discern the specifics of the cargo loaded onto ships at the Bombay Harbour or track alternative shipping routes through mere eavesdropping. Instead, they relied on a sophisticated intelligence network operating in both Bombay and Goa to gather these critical details.[14]

Based on a piece of information, the Intelligence Bureau apprehended a Bengali named Ramdas Gupta who was sympathetic to Germany and was operating from one of the shipping companies in Mazagaon, Bombay. After interrogation, the spy divulged that he obtained the sailing details such as course, speed and destination of British cargo ships from the Bombay port authorities. He then passed on the information to Robert Koch, staying at Altinho, Panaji, Goa. He was the head of the German intelligence operation in Goa. During further investigations, the spy revealed that Koch sent the information to MS *Ehrenfels* which was docked at Mormugao, Goa. The *Ehrenfels* transmitted this information through bursts of high frequency radio at predetermined times to the U-boats operating in the Indian Ocean.[15] The information was so precise that few ships using the port of Bombay could escape them. The Intelligence Bureau passed this information to MI6. The MI6 collaborated with the India Mission of the Special Operations Executive (SOE) at Meerut and intercepted coded messages to German Navy U-boats, relaying detailed information on the positions of Allied ships leaving Bombay Harbour and entering the Indian Ocean. From then onwards all activities of the *Ehrenfels*'s crew were closely monitored by the British consul-general,

Lieutenant Colonel Bremner, sending regular reports to the government in New Delhi.[16]

The Cabinet Defence Committee, naval and civilian officers gathered at the London MI6 office at the Broadway Buildings near Pall Mall in a cellar 150 feet underground. The cellar walls were distempered green. Red steel girders reinforced the roof. Metal ventilating ducts under the ceiling and a grey steel door with screw bolts like a warship's watertight door contributed to the sensation of being below deck in an old, iron-clad warship. The men gathered at the meeting were members of a secret Admiralty committee. They called for an investigation of the increasing shipping losses in the Indian Ocean.[17]

One of the rear admirals said 'German information is so good that when a U-boat confronts two or three of our cargo ships, and her captain doubts he has time to sink them all, he will invariably select the one carrying the most urgent cargo… That must mean he has details of all their cargoes—and their priority to us.'[18]

The C-in-C of India General Wavell was also present at the secret meeting. With permission from British PM Winston Churchill, he announced that they had to launch a military operation to destroy the enemy ship. This was the only possible way keeping British SOE team intact and avoiding a clash with the Portuguese.[19]

A civilian officer was the next to speak. He had grey hair and thick, bushy eyebrows, and had been a Cambridge don before the war. Now he worked for one of several intelligence agencies nominally under the control of the Ministry of Economic Warfare. 'I propose, sir, that we formalize Wavell's plan and send a copy of the plan to SOE in India. They have just set up an office out there.'

'Special Operations Executive,' said one of the captains present in the meeting, 'think they can do anything? Sound rather a mixed bag to me, from what I hear. Business men, schoolmasters, merchants.'

'You know something about them, then?' asked the commander.

'Should do,' replied the captain. 'Got a relative named Lewis Pugh in that lot.'[20]

The Special Operations Executive (SOE) office was in Meerut, 40 miles north of Delhi and 1,800 miles from the west coast. 'Maybe they'd like a breath of sea air,' replied the rear admiral drily. He turned to the professor. 'I'll inform the SOE, as you propose.[21]'

The SOE headquarters was housed in a Victorian bungalow on the Cavalry Lines Road, Meerut. In peacetime, this bungalow had been used by the brigadier commanding the British Cavalry Brigade on garrison duty in Meerut. On the gate post was bolted a small, black, wooden board painted in white letters: Ministry of Economic Warfare. Since SOE was under the control of this ministry, the notice provided a good cover for their activities.[22]

In India, the SOE did everything it could to stop the Germans from advancing into India from the Caucasus through Iran and Afghanistan, and the Japanese from Southeast Asia.[23] The mission was set up in India by a former businessman, Colin Mackenzie of J & P Coats, a clothing manufacturer. Colin Mackenzie reported directly to the viceroy of India—Lord Linlithgow at first and Lord Louis Mountbatten later. Its location was governed by the fear that the Germans might overrun the Middle East and Caucasus, in which case resistance movements would be established in Afghanistan, Persia and Iraq. When this threat was removed late in 1942 after the battles of Stalingrad and El Alamein, the focus was switched to Southeast Asia.

The India Mission had established training centres, including the guerrilla training unit at Kharakvasla, some 50 miles west of Poona, with water training, such as canoeing, being carried out on the nearby Lake Fife. The Mission had its own large communications organization, with radio transmitters and receiver sites, signal schools and various outstations. There were four main radio stations, two in Calcutta and one each in Colombo and Chungking. SOE (India)'s geographical area was vast, covering all of British India, Afghanistan, Burma, eastern Persia and Tibet.[24]

Lieutenant Colonel Lewis Pugh, Royal Artillery, was the director of Country Sections in SOE. He was also an honorary member of the Calcutta Light Horse (CLH) Regiment. He specialized in placing agents and trained saboteurs deep behind enemy lines in Burma and Malaya.[25] He recommended those countries to Mackenzie which he deemed ripe for setting up clandestine operations.

Pugh was a career soldier who had spent most of his service in India, which included being seconded to the Indian Police Special Branch in Bengal. During this period he was based in Howrah, the industrial centre located on the west bank of the Hooghly River, opposite Calcutta. Thus, he knew Calcutta and the British community well, and had many friends in the business community.[26] He was tasked with the secret Goa operation which was to be implemented without anyone being aware of any breach of Portuguese neutrality.[27]

The SOE had a plan and needed the men to accomplish it. Almost all the manpower needed for Operation Longshanks was found in Calcutta auxiliary units. Most came from the CLH, raised in 1872. Their purported role was to defend their area in the event of a foreign invasion. These units were essentially mounted infantry—using their horses for rapid movement but fighting dismounted. All personnel were Europeans, an unusual feature being that the officers were elected by the men, their commission then being confirmed by the viceroy, but promotions thereafter following the usual army practice.[28]

Pugh decided to approach the retired officers of the CLH for the operation. It was a reserve unit of the Indian Army and had been inactive since the Boer War (1899–1902). Its membership was voluntary and largely made up of former soldiers, civilian bankers, merchants, solicitors, businessmen and planters who received some training, but also hunted, played polo and provided an honour guard to the viceroy.[29] Admiral of the Fleets, the Earl Mountbatten of Burma, by long tradition was the honorary colonel of the CLH.[30]

Pugh called for an urgent meeting at the SOE bungalow to discuss the most immediate instructions they had received from London to deal with shipping losses in the Indian Ocean.[31] Colin Hercules Mackenzie sat at the head of the table. He was a director of one of Scotland's largest cotton thread firms but had the gentle, sensitive face of a scholar. Before the war, one of Mackenzie's fellow directors in the company had been a firm friend, Lord Linlithgow. Now, in 1942, Linlithgow was the viceroy and governor-general of India. He was short of qualified men to run this operation and suggested Mackenzie as an ideal candidate.[32]

Next to Pugh sat Alex Peterson. He had travelled around the country with Gavin Stewart, setting up an underground organization to continue resistance if the Japanese invaded India. Gavin owned an engineering business in UK with a branch in India. In this connection, Peterson had worked closely with Indian communists and other subversives, on many of whom Pugh had ironically collected detailed police dossiers before the war. One of Peterson's tasks in Meerut was to write items of propaganda camouflaged as news, and place them with newspapers and radio programmes in India.[33]

Walter Fletcher—who was in his early fifties—was also present. For many years he had been chairman and managing director of a large firm that supplied all grades of raw rubber. Fletcher was known for his organizational abilities and had planned some of SOE's more outlandish propositions into feasible projects, including kidnappings and political assassinations.[34] The other members of the group were Lumsdaine, Hilliard and Harrison.

At the meeting, Stewart said that Trompeta had provided

details of the various ships at the Bombay Harbour, their destinations, and where they would be at certain times, to the German ships anchored in the Mormugao Harbour.[35] Other officers in the room knew quite a lot about the German ships. All of them were owned by the German Hansa Line. Their cargoes included such unlikely items as cooked ham, sacks of flour, bags of explosives for mining purposes, marble slabs, locomotive spares, automobile batteries and even a Mercedes sports car originally intended for an Indian princeling. There were stocks of chianti in the holds of Anfora and several hundred crates of the best Bavarian beer in the others.[36] The *Ehrenfels* was more valuable as a floating radio station. She carried a powerful Deutz generator, for her transmitter and receiver had worldwide range.

Everyone sat in silence until Stewart spoke. 'Let's go in and deal with all those ships.'[37] Portugal's neutrality was of such incalculable importance to the Allies that the British Foreign Office had given the Government of India the strictest and most specific categorical instructions that no action was to be taken which Portugal could conceivably consider an infringement.[38] Fletcher made his proposal: 'Send an Indian SOE agent to Goa… We'll give him authority to offer Captain Röfer a bribe in any currency and hand over the ship to the SOE.' 'A good idea,' agreed Peterson. 'How much do you suggest?' The amount agreed upon was 10,000 pounds, and the discussion turned to other topics.

It was decided that attempts should be made to bribe the master of *Ehrenfels*, Captain Röfer, and carefully selected members of his crew. In a signal, London told SOE India that '…the Foreign Office will raise no objection if this operation is carried out without violence or overt action within Portuguese territorial waters, provided that the words "trickery" and "chicanery" in your letter mean "bribery" pure and simple, and nothing else.'[39]

Given the neutral status of the enclave, there seemed no way for the British to deal with the matter by force; any open violation of neutrality could lead to either retaliation, a general worsening of relations with other neutral countries, or, in the extreme, the entry of Portugal into the war on the Axis side. But one thing was clear: the radio transmissions to the waiting U-boats had to be stopped. SOE was tasked with the job, commanded by Colonel Lewis Pugh.[40] Operation Creek was launched on 9 March 1943.[41]

The Kidnapping

Robert Koch lived in Panjim with his wife Grethe, having arrived aboard the *Ehrenfels* in 1939.[42] SOE operatives Pugh and Major Gavin Burton Stewart journeyed to Panjim in the guise of businessmen with the objective of kidnapping Trompeta. They met at the Taj Mahal hotel, Bombay, bought a second-hand Ford V8 station wagon that same afternoon and immediately had it resprayed beige. It was a neutral colour used by civilian Indian army contractors and was unlikely to attract attention.[43]

Early in the morning, they got hard-boiled eggs packed from the Taj to eat on the way, settled their bill, and by 1500 hours were 100 miles closer to Goa. At the border, they showed the fake letter from the Midnapore Zamindary Company to a yawning immigration officer who ordered the guard to lift the barrier without even leaving his hut.[44] A few miles inside Goa, they stopped for a wash in a clearing in a palm forest before entering Panjim, the capital.[45]

Pugh proceeded to meet the British consul general who resided in Mormugao. 'What can I do for you, gentlemen?' he asked in a quiet voice. Pugh mentioned Trompeta's real name. 'We would like to know where he lives.' The consul looked at Pugh sharply, who carefully replied, 'Our business with him is of a more…ah…personal nature.' The consul nodded. 'I see.'

He did not ask any more questions in case one of his clerks, who often eavesdropped on his visitors, heard what he said. He put a finger to his lips and inclined his head towards the door.

Pugh understood the gesture—one widely used in India when dealing with confidential matters that could interest others not officially concerned. The consul wrote down an address and directions on a sheet of paper which Pugh put in his pocket.[46]

He also received information from his local contacts that Trompeta would be visiting the port of Mormugao. He and Stewart went out into the heat of the day to visit the port. A strong smell of oil and dried fish lay heavy in the air. Both arrived at the port-side boulevard and found a Goan restaurant while strolling along. One could see the cook at work through the window, which increased the appetite of people ambulating on the boulevard. The restaurant was a *tasca*, a type of restaurant which preserves the Portuguese furniture and serves authentic cuisine. A charismatic bunch of workers were serving rustic Portuguese food to colourful sailors from across the world.

The two men entered the restaurant. Stewart ordered a Portuguese soup called *caldo verde* topped with a smoked and spicy Portuguese sausage. Pugh ordered the tasca's specialties: a *bifana* (a traditional Portuguese sandwich with marinated pork meat), a *bife à la Gare* steak, a *bacalhau* (dried and salted fish), a *pasteis de camarão* (a shrimp-filled pastry) and *cabidela* rice. The restaurant owner approached their table and offered them *Polvo* à *Lagareiro* (roasted octopus with garlic potatoes), a rare Portuguese specialty requiring a lot of olive oil. After lunch Stewart ordered an *abatanado* coffee, while Pug settled for *cafe bombon* (a Portuguese espresso shot with condensed milk).

Just as the information had stated, Trompeta disembarked from a car in front of the restaurant. Pugh and Stewart discreetly followed him along the waterfront and noticed the four ships anchored in the harbour. Trompeta embarked on a small, four-seater boat and proceeded towards the *Ehrenfels*.[47] Pugh watched the boat sail across the harbour waters through his binoculars. The captain of *Ehrenfels* raised his glass in a silent salute as it went past.[48]

Trompeta was a tough, broad-shouldered, stocky man in his early forties. He was one of Germany's two most important and successful spy-masters in the East. The other was Richard Sorge in Tokyo, where he was ostensibly a correspondent for the influential German newspaper *Frankfurter Zeitung*. Both men were initially stationed there until Trompeta was ordered to leave for Batavia, then Calcutta, and finally Goa. When the war was declared, several other German citizens also raced across India to Goa, eager to escape internment.[49]

Trompeta climbed into the upper deck of the *Ehrenfels*, proceeded through the engine room, with its peculiar smell of warm oil and polished metal, and tapped on a grey steel door. Red skull and crossbones were painted on it with the warning: 'Danger of death. High Voltage.' Inside the room—beneath the radio controls—was a shelf full of code books with heavy lead covers, so they would sink instantly if thrown overboard in an emergency. Two decoded signals were handed to Trompeta. They reported four successful sinkings. Two were on 28 November and two more on 30 November. Trompeta checked the signals he had sent regarding the movements of certain ships and ascertained the casualties to be the British *Nova Scotia* and *Llandaff Castle* of 6,796 tons and 10,799 tons, and two small Greek freighters, *Evanthia* and *Cleanthis*.[50]

Pugh and Stewart returned to their hotel in Panjim by dusk. After dinner, they sat on the verandah watching small boats go busily up and down the river. A gramophone was playing in the next bedroom. Stewart's favourite song came through their wall clearly: 'South of the border, down Mexico way.' Pugh and Stewart raised their glasses of Portuguese brandy in a silent toast. Each hoped that by the same time next evening they would be safely north of the border with their prisoner.[51]

The plan to kidnap Trompeta was in motion. Pugh settled the bill in the hotel's reception, under a portrait of Vasco da Gama—the first European voyager to reach India in the fifteenth century.

Stewart was waiting in the car with their luggage. Trompeta rarely received visitors before 0900 hours, so they decided to call on him at 0800. Panjim would not be very busy and it was likely that Trompeta would still be on his own. Pugh turned the car and coasted downhill, and reached Trompeta's front yard soon. The two of them climbed the red brick steps to his bungalow and crossed the narrow verandah to the front door. The door opened a cautious three inches and Trompeta looked out enquiringly. He was wearing a short-sleeved check shirt and cotton trousers. It seemed unlikely he was carrying a gun. 'Who are you?' he asked in German. 'What do you want?' 'We have an urgent message for you,' Pugh replied in German. 'Let us in quickly.'[52]

Just as Trompeta opened the door, Pugh took out his Colt .32 automatic and prodded the muzzle into Trompeta's ribs. 'Don't shout or try anything, and you'll be all right. But do exactly as we tell you.' Stewart went into the front room. The table was laid for breakfast. He saw a glass coffee percolator, cups and saucers, and a loaf of bread. An ant sluggishly explored the sugar kept in a blue china bowl. Footsteps creaked on the wooden floor of the hall. Stewart drew his automatic. A woman entered the room. She had fair hair drawn back in a bun and wore a loose cotton dress. 'Who are you?' Pugh asked her. 'My wife,' answered Trompeta. 'Get into the back of the car, both of you, and sit quietly.' Trompeta and his wife walked slowly across the verandah and down the steps. As they reached the street, Trompeta suddenly shouted in English to the Indians going up the hill: 'Help! We're being kidnapped! Help us!' The Indians looked at each other in surprise. This was a matter for the sahibs, no concern of theirs.[53]

Pugh pulled the woman away and threw her in beside Trompeta. Stewart jumped in and jabbed his revolver into Trompeta's side. 'If you don't shut up, I'll shoot you.' Pugh quickly started the car and accelerated out of the town towards the border. He pulled up in the clearing where they had stopped on the way from Belgaum. Stewart opened the glove compartment and took out the hypodermic. 'Are you going to kill us?' asked Trompeta. 'No. It's just to make you feel drowsy for a bit.' Stewart jabbed Trompeta and his wife in their arms with the Pentothal needle. Slowly, their eyelids drooped and they sagged back against the seat.[54] He did not stop the car until they had reached Green's Hotel in Belgaum. By early evening they were in Bombay.[55] In Bombay the Kochs revealed what the British had already suspected: the *Ehrenfels* had a secret radio transmitter used for disseminating the information on British ships to the Germans.[56]

The Special Operations Planning

Pugh frequently visited the CLH clubhouse and sat upstairs in the bar overlooking the garden. The bar would be crowded with businessmen, jute merchants, bankers, brokers, solicitors and accountants who formed the membership of the CLH.[57] In early 1943 Lieutenant Colonel Pugh of SOE India Mission approached his friend, Lieutenant Colonel Grice, commanding officer of the CLH, with a request for help in the operation. He joined Imperial Chemical Industries (ICI) in India in 1919, enrolled in the CLH as a trooper in 1920, and took command as lieutenant colonel in 1939.[58]

The next day Bill Grice stood on an improvised dais in the CLH Club House in Calcutta. It was just after 1830 hours in the evening. 'Gentlemen,' he began, 'I have asked you all here for a special purpose. As you know, the Light Horse has not been in action as a unit since the Boer War in 1900. Tonight, I am asking for volunteers: 18 men for a special and secret job against Germans. I can tell you nothing about it except that the operation should take about a fortnight and will involve a short sea voyage. There it is, gentlemen. I leave it to you. Is anyone willing to volunteer?' Every man immediately raised his right hand. 'What name do we take this time, sir?' asked Breene. 'The Light Sea Horse?'[59]

The team was led by Lieutenant Colonel Lewis Pugh, the numbers being made up by veteran volunteers from the CLH. Despite essentially being a military sporting and drinking club, the CLH took its military operations very seriously.[60] The attack force comprised 24 men: six from SOE, four from the Calcutta Scottish and 14 from the CLH. There was one soldier (Pugh), one who had been a soldier (Crossley), four wartime soldiers (Stewart, Hislop, McEwan and White); the remainder were part timers. The oldest was Grice at 45 and the youngest was White at 25.[61] Pugh was tasked with procuring the weaponry and conducting training. Each of the men took leave from their respective jobs—stating that they were to attend a training course near Goa—and started preparing for the mission. Grice announced that the men would not receive any official recognition for their work as the mission was strictly unofficial.[62]

In Calcutta the men started intensive live weapons training and unarmed combat on 19 February. Each were given a personal list which included items like a military field uniform, service revolver, 18 rounds of ammunition, steel helmet, bedding roll, knife, fork, spoon, plate, mug, washing items and first field dressing.[63]

One expedient was attempted before resorting to large-scale violence—bribing Kapitan Johann Röfer, commanding officer of *Ehrenfels*, to move the ship out of the harbour to where it could be captured. This failed: '… Röfer was totally unwilling to accept any bribe and would not even discuss the matter.'[64] In order to allow maximum 'plausible deniability' by the authorities, nothing was said to Viceroy Linlithgow; and as far as the War Ministry and Foreign Office in London were concerned, they were told that the German crew was being bribed to sail the ship into international waters where she could be 'captured'. Around 100,000 pounds had been wired to India for that purpose.[65]

Pugh set about finding a vessel that could transport them to Goa. He managed to obtain a hopper barge '*Little Phoebe*'—a ramshackle tug which had been commissioned in 1912. One evening, 18 men crowded into the CLH bar to hear what Grice had to tell them. 'Gentlemen,' he began, 'you have all received your instructions, and I can answer no questions about them. Just make sure they are all carried out and you have all the items required. Once we leave here, it will be impossible to make up any deficiencies.

Grice said, 'We are going initially to Madras, by train.[66] Then in a smoky barge, the team will proceed to Goa after going to Cochin by train, with plans to split into three groups and board the *Ehrenfels*: one to take control of the bridge, another to destroy the anchor and the third to destroy the radio.' Stewart said, 'Our destination is Cochin.' This revelation caused much astonishment as Cochin was just 'a sleepy little hollow'.

'First aboard will be Colonel Pugh and his group. They will take control of the bridge and destroy radio equipment there and collect code books. The second group, under Corporal Manners, will go straight to the anchor chains and blow them apart with plastic explosives. I'll take the third group to destroy the other radio equipment. Then we'll report to the bridge to reinforce Colonel Pugh. Next, Mr Lumsdaine's group will stop the crew from interfering. If you take a prisoner, knock him out and tie him to the deck with handcuffs. The rest of you will stay and defend the *Phoebe* from other ships or from the shore, or from *Ehrenfels* herself.[67]

'Remember this cover story if you are caught by the Portuguese authorities: "You were in a party going to Bombay in a cargo ship. On the way, you persuaded your captain to cruise around Mormugao Harbour. He was reluctant to do so, but finally agreed. In the darkness, your ship bumped up against *Ehrenfels*. For a foolish drunken dare—a bet—you climbed aboard and their crew attacked you." But whatever you do, on no account involve the Light Horse or Calcutta Scottish, and do not expect any help from the Government of India, because they know nothing whatsoever about this. Our code word for this whole exercise is "Operation Creek". And if anything goes wrong, we'll all be up that creek without a paddle!'[68]

Before relieving the group, Grice reiterated that this was not an exercise; it was real. 'The other day I saw on an army notice board this information: "Good health - keep your bowels open. Good security - keep your mouth shut." Remember, careless talk costs lives. And on this operation, the lives it costs can be our own.'[69]

The team assembled for the operation on 26 February. The members made their way through the Calcutta traffic towards Howrah Station, a red brick reminder of the solidity of Victorian architecture. The Howrah–Madras Mail waited, engine steaming, on platform 12, all doors open. They walked straight to their reserved compartment where they would spend that night, the following day and night, and reach Madras on the morning of the third day. A guard locked their door and saluted. He blew his whistle and waved a green flag. The train jerked forward. The two volunteer groups from the Light Horse were on their way—one travelling by the train and the other by the *Phoebe*.[70]

Upon reaching Madras station, the team took a taxi to the Connemara Hotel, where another group—which had travelled ahead of them—was waiting in the main lounge. The air was thick with cigarette smoke, which the ceiling fan's blades paddled through dimly. Red Mac raised his glass. 'To our colonel, and all who ride or sail with him.'[71] They were ordered to be discreet, so most of the members remained in their rooms, playing craps or cards. Others found a private swimming pool while a few of the more athletic members hired bicycles and toured the surrounding countryside.[72] The members departed from Madras to Cochin.

Meanwhile, Jack Cartwright from CLH had been sent to Goa overland. His task was to distract as many sailors and crew of the *Ehrenfels* and other ships as possible. He bribed a brothel keeper in Goa to offer free services that night to those seamen. He also managed to bribe a Goanese *fidalgo* to throw a party and invite the many port officials and ships' officers and made sure that there would be no taxis available to take the Germans back to their ships when the party ended.

After the arrangements were made, Cartwright casually asked the manager at one of the hotels in Mormugao whether any fiestas or carnivals were due. He enthusiastically responded that some local cafe owners were organizing a carnival of their own that week. There would be *fado* singers singing the old sad songs of Portugal, and he was sure that the *senhor* would enjoy himself if he visited those cafes around midnight. Cartwright was relieved to know that his arrangements seemed to be working.[73]

Two Portuguese cruisers, *Gonzales Zarco* and *Alfonso D'Albuquerque*, had arrived with 1,600 African troops. They had left Mozambique for Timor and were now stationed there.

'But the Japs have been in Timor for months,' said Cartwright cautiously.

'That is why they are here, senhor, on their way home.'

'Their officers will be at your reception tonight?'

'They have received invitations. There will also be a celebration in the cafes. It might sound like the firing of guns, senhor, but it will only be local people setting off fireworks to show they are happy. We are a happy people, senhor. There is much happiness in our hearts.'

When the conversation drew to a close, the manager smiled and bowed out of his presence, sitting in a car to be driven home. Cartwright waited until its tail lights diminished in the darkness before walking back to his hotel.[74]

The Voyage of Hopper Barge Number 5

To carry out the raid on Mormugao Harbour, Pugh persuaded the Calcutta Port Commissioners to lend him an old but serviceable hopper barge.[75] He went to meet a businessman named Lomax who owned a shipping company in Calcutta. Pugh said he had to transport 20 men from Calcutta to do a special job somewhere in the Indian Ocean before sailing on to Bombay. Lomax looked at the pages in a record book. 'This is what we can do for you,' he announced. 'I can provide you the Hopper Barge No. 5. Affectionately known as *Phoebe*, the barge is 30 years old and owned by the Port Commissioners in Calcutta.'[76] It had a displacement of 1,200 tons, with a length of 61 metres. *Phoebe* was powered by two coal-fired steam engines driving two three-bladed propellers, which gave it a maximum speed of no more than eight to nine knots at best.

'Can she make the distance?' asked Stewart. Lomax shrugged. 'She's basically just a hull, a bloody great floating iron bath with an engine. Although built specifically for coastal and estuarine work, it is to her credit that in 1913 it safely made the 8,000 nautical miles delivery voyage from the Clyde to the Hooghly.[77] We use her up against a river dredger. You will be responsible for all wages, salaries, mooring fees, pilotage charges, fuel, rations and insurance against act of war, collision, storm, malpractice, mutiny, foundering, and so on.[78] She was never designed for open sea work, you know. Purely a river boat, and like the fellows you're taking, a bit old for rough stuff.'[79]

A retired British naval commander, Bernard Davies, who was employed by the Port Commissioners of Calcutta agreed to sail the old barge down the east coast of India via Trincomalee to Cochin.[80] Davies had recently commandeered a destroyer in action, making him an ideal man for this job.[81] The members loaded sufficient amount of coal for the entire voyage to Bombay alongside water and rations. She also carried military stores, including Bren and Sten guns, rifles, ammunitions, explosives and items needed for the attack, such as bamboos, timber, railway sleepers, rope, grappling irons, fire extinguishers and bags of cement.[82]

Two radio sets were installed for this operation. The main set was an SOE Wireless Set Type-B which was required to enable the vessel to communicate with the SOE at Meerut. Also, a Type-1154 transmitter and Type-1155 receiver were installed in order to report the approach of hostile ships, submarines or aircraft. Strict wireless silence was imposed throughout the voyage.[83]

Meanwhile, the CLH team arrived at Cochin from Madras and spent four uneasy days at Hotel Malabar and the Harbour House, waiting for Little *Phoebe*'s arrival. On the fourth day Grice asked his compatriots to 'come and see if there's any sign of it.' Melbourne, Breene and Squire walked gingerly past the fishermen drying their fish on poles towards the harbour. Several freighters were discharging cargo. About 300 yards out, a small, shabby craft with an absurdly long funnel was letting down her anchors. Immediately, Melbourne went through the corridors of the Malabar Hotel beating on the doors of his friends' rooms. Breene and Squire did the same thing in Harbour House, relaying the same message: 'Meeting of all visitors in the Harbour House lounge - now.'[84]

'Gentlemen, you are looking at the ship that's come to take us on to our assignment.'

The men crowded at the window, disbelief and disappointment drawn on their faces: 'That little tiddler?' 'We thought we were going to have a destroyer, or at least a proper landing craft.' 'Are you serious, sir?' 'Absolutely,' Grice assured them. It was 1630 hours when Harrison approached Davies on *Phoebe*'s bridge. 'First of our passengers coming aboard, sir,' he reported.[85]

The *Phoebe* picked up Pugh and the SOE troop of five officers and 14 men from Cochin and steamed on to Mormugao Harbour. Among the SOE troop was Lieutenant Colonel William Grice as well as Lieutenant Colin Sandys-Lumsdaine, Charles Tindall, Captain Robert Duguid, William Miller, Gilman Wylie and James Patterson, a Lloyd's Surveyor.[86]

Davies took her south for several miles until the coast fell away and they were surrounded by sea, no longer visible to any watcher on land. Dusk followed them at tropical speed but Davies deliberately lit no navigation lights. The risk of collision was far less than the risk of being spotted by an enemy submarine that had surfaced to charge her batteries.

In Calcutta, these men controlled companies essential to Britain's economy. They managed jute mills and vast tea estates the size of English counties. In air-conditioned offices they regularly handled sums of money larger than the budgets of many countries. But here they slept like schoolboys on a summer camp, in shorts or underpants, feet facing a pile of coal, heads barely a yard above the hissing, rushing sea.[87]

The men were briefed about the operation. They were also told that British agents would encourage some locals to organize parties which would be attended by at least some of the *Ehrenfels*'s crews. So there would be reduced manpower to deal with on the ship. The meeting closed with them being issued 30 rupees each and told that if anything went wrong, they were to get ashore and make their way to the Burmah-Shell Refinery whose manager had been informed of the possibility of 'visitors'.[88]

'In a couple of hours, there'll be supper and a mug of hot tea each, courtesy of P. Milliard and the cook.'

The Light Horsemen looked at each other gloomily in the deepening dusk. At this hour, in more civilized surroundings, they would be reaching out for the first drink of the evening, the glass misted by chunks of ice. Then there would be a leisurely bath and a change into clean clothes, laid out by their bearer, a car and driver waiting to take them out for dinner or to visit friends. Instead, they faced a night on a bare metal deck, only feet above the swiftly running sea.[89]

'Gentlemen,' Grice began. 'We are now on the final lap of our journey. We are heading for the neutral port of Mormugao, where a German ship *Ehrenfels* lies at anchor. Our task is to sink her at anchor.'[90]

The men trained throughout the voyage and were given the exact routes to follow. Rehearsals were carried out and passwords were issued. The morning of 8 March was devoted to preparing for action, with bamboo ladders and other stores placed ready, while a protected emplacement was constructed on the bridge wing for the Bren gun. At 2100 everyone blackened their faces and hands, donned helmets, checked weapons and then rested. The weather was fine with good visibility and high tide was at 0036.[91]

Phoebe was now barely holding her own against the tide, creeping in as close to shore as Davies could bring her. Through the bridge house windows they could see occasional flickers, like fireflies, from houses near the sea, and faint moving cones of light from car headlamps on the Goan coast. High on the hill, behind Portuguese fortifications that dated from the sixteenth century, the doors of the big house were wide open to the warm night. Lanterns had been lit above the red-tiled patio and fado singers were strumming guitars and singing.[92]

At 0100, 9 March, everyone took up their positions. On the forecastle were the assault groups with ladder and grappling irons ready, and a man whose task was to answer challenges in either Portuguese or German. Amidships were the carrying parties ready to launch their ladders and carry any stores requested. At 0145 *Phoebe* approached the buoy marking the entrance to the harbour and Davies ordered members of the ship's crew to suspend ropes and fenders over the starboard side.[93]

The Operation

'Five minutes to go,' whispered Grice. *Phoebe* moved slowly towards the *Ehrenfels*. Davies began to bring her alongside with inestimable care. The second hand crept around the dial of Grice's watch. 'Three minutes.' The bridge had four storeys and the rail around her deck stretched to infinity.[94] A gramophone played on the *Ehrenfels*'s deck and warm yellow bulbs still burnt. Grice could hear men talking. But no one hailed them; no one seemed to have noticed them.

'One minute.'

The men in the bows, holding the ladders, stretched their necks to see the top of *Ehrenfels*'s deck. All around *Phoebe*'s hold others lay silently on their stomachs in case the impact of the two hulls touching flung them off their feet.

'Who are you?' shouted a lookout from *Ehrenfels* in German. The men aboard *Phoebe* peered up into the darkness towards the sound of the enemy voice. 'Just a harbour barge,' Pugh called back in German.

'Why are you sailing without lights?'[95]

Pugh shot the sentry in response. Within minutes he was up and over the German ship's gunwales, the first to board her. Everyone in *Phoebe* could hear shouts in German from the deck of the cargo ship. '*Achtung*! *Achtung*!' someone was calling urgently. And then the whole night exploded in the blaze of a million candles. *Ehrenfels*'s searchlight focused on little *Phoebe*. The sight of the barge baffled the Germans and many stared at it in disbelief. They had expected a small water-boat or an oiler but found this instead. Red Mac raised his Sten gun, took careful aim and fired deliberately along the beam. His gun chattered like a chain and the searchlight exploded in a blue flash and great puff of white smoke. Darkness dropped around them.[96]

'Come on, up the ladders!' shouted Grice. The soldiers were still dazzled and blinked their blinded eyes in the sudden dark. Each one of them began to climb. Men who were in the habit of using a lift to reach even a first-floor office in Calcutta now heaved themselves up the swaying, creaking bamboo ladders. The noise of the gunfire awakened Captain Röfer, always a light sleeper. He was in a small sea-cabin above the tiered bridge. He switched on the light, swung down from his bunk and pulled on his trousers. The officer of the watch burst into the room. 'Enemy boarding party alongside, sir!' he reported breathlessly. 'How many men?' 'I counted about 20, sir. Must be the advance party.' 'Sound the alarm.' The officer pulled a rope handle that hung from the roof. The siren motor whirred for a second before bellowing like a thousand car horns. It was so loud and unexpected that soldiers still on the ladders, paused, bemused by the sheer thunder of its iron clamour. Then they continued upwards, grimly determined to complete their tasks.[97] Meanwhile, Kapitan Röfer had barely reached his ship's bridge when the first of the SOE party burst upon it, and when Röfer refused to stop advancing, he was immediately shot and killed.[98]

Up in the house on the hill behind wide windows edged by gilded frames, the singers were in full throat. Guitarists tore at the strings as they recalled the loves, glories and memories of old Portugal in their traditional songs. Several couples were dancing, and everywhere the buzz of conversation sounded like the drone of distant bees over the constant tinkle of empty glasses being exchanged for full ones on silver trays. Through this cacophony of enjoyment the first wild wail of *Ehrenfels*'s siren sliced like a sharpened knife. Officers dancing with Portuguese ladies stopped mid-step and released their partners.

'We must find out,' said an officer. 'We beg your permission to leave.' 'But how will you get back? There are no taxis or tongas at this hour. I have ordered cars to pick you up later on. It is a long way down to the harbour, senhors. You will have to walk.' 'We'll run,' retorted the German shortly.[99]

Corporal Turcan, one of the volunteers, and his CLS group followed the SOE up the boarding ladder to the bridge where they saw the captain lying dead. In accordance with the plan, the bridge was cordoned off while the other groups fanned out around the ship to capture any remaining crew.[100]

Meanwhile, *Ehrenfels*'s chief engineer reached the engine room to secure the steel doors behind him, lit the scuttling charges, ordered his men to open the seacocks and began the planned sabotage of the engines. When the raiders reached the engine room, Captain White, the SOE explosives man, used a magnetic charge to blow the door off its hinges. But it was immediately obvious that he was too late. The incendiary charges went off with a bang and the explosion led to intense fires which eventually engulfed the whole ship, following which the engineer jumped into the sea and swam ashore.[101]

Crossley had seen a wire from the main masthead aerial leading down to a glass insulator outside a deck cabin. 'This would be the cabin that had contained the ship's radio,' Grice said to Lumsdaine, Hilliard and Harrison. 'Let's have a look at that door,' suggested Lumsdaine, pointing to the metal door with the warning 'Danger of Death. High Voltage', with a skull and crossbones drawn upon it.[102] Lumsdaine quickly attached a charge to the door and burst it open. 'There should be a transmitter behind one of the bulkheads here.' He opened the heavy door and went inside the tiny cell from which so many messages had been sent. The shelves were empty of code books, but the radio was still bolted to the wall. The front of the set was of black, crackle-finished metal with tuning dials, plugs for earphones, a Morse key, and a list of wavelengths pasted on a piece of cardboard. Hilliard ripped this off the facia and pocketed it. Then they smashed the set with the butts of their Stens.[103]

A German officer crouched on the floor, surrounded by bundles of papers and thick books with shining lead covers. The officer threw one of the lead-covered code books at Breene's face who squeezed his trigger in response. The gun jammed. The officer jumped up, fumbling for a weapon. Crossley threw himself at him and the incendiary went off between them. A blazing jet of flame, thick as a man's wrist, roared out of the nozzle. Its intense heat scorched the ceiling and lit the papers. Breene kicked it out of the way, but nothing could stop the cascade of fire. The German officer grabbed a dub from beneath his bunk, and he and Breene fought hand to hand, stumbling over the blazing incendiary. It rolled to one side and the flames engulfed the papers and code books. The lead began to wilt and ran like liquid silver. Red Mac, running past the open door, saw the fighting and inferno within. He hit the German on the head with the butt of his Sten gun.[104]

Meanwhile, Manners and Squire had reached the starboard anchor chain. The plastic explosive felt clammy as they crammed it hurriedly between a link and the giant eyehole through which the chain ran down to the anchor. But it would not adhere to the rust on the metal, already damp with spray. They squeezed it in, wedged it somehow. 'Right,' said Manners. 'Now the detonator.' Squire handed him the detonator. Manners set the mechanical timing device and pushed the tiny metal cylinder into the plastic. Then they dashed across the deck. The explosion temporarily deafened them both, but the link broke. With a screech and roar of rusty metal, the heavy chain disappeared down into the sea.[105]

Inside the *Ehrenfels* three German sailors were trying to move the valve. They began to open slowly. Sea water bubbled and frothed at the mouth of a pipe in its fury to be free. The first wheel suddenly spun easily and the man gripping it slipped and fell against it before he realized it was fully open. Water roared like a whirlpool from the pipes and streamed against them. Its pressure knocked them off their feet and swept away the torch. Almost instantly, they were up to their thighs in swirling water. Pieces of wood bashed their bare chests as they groped, gasping, for the metal ladder bolted to the side of the hull. They hauled themselves up—out of the swiftly rising flood—into the space beneath the engine room.[106]

Below decks, as tens of thousands of tons of sea water streamed through the open Kingston valves, the floor heaved slowly like some great sea beast rolling over into a more comfortable position. More lights dimmed, flickered and went out. 'She's going over!' shouted Grice through the darkness. 'Up on deck.' They began to cross the oily floor of the engine room, feeling water rise as they moved through the darkness, hands outstretched.[107]

Blue sparks blazed across terminal gaps near fuses. Wires smoked with the heat of direct short circuits. One by one, hidden charges exploded below decks. Portholes splintered and glass showered over the sea like confetti as the crew leapt into the water. The men who stayed behind now leapt over the rails, grateful for the cool salt water dousing the flames that had already scorched their clothes.[108]

Shortly afterwards Grice shouted, 'Everyone aboard?' Crofter replied, 'So far as I can see, sir. I have counted them.' Grice ran up the steps to the bridge. Davies turned the telegraph to 'Full Speed Ahead'. Everyone looked for friends, shaking hands warmly, slapping each other on the back in a general euphoria of reaction and relief. Bottles of rum and brandy were passed around. They drank greedily. They were all alive! Relief poured through their blood as intoxicating as the alcohol. Lumsdaine and Pugh marshalled several men with Bren guns in the stern. If any boat put out after them, they were to fire below the water line, to try and sink them. But if either of the Portuguese crusiers made one hit on *Phoebe* with even their smallest gun, the barge would sink like a stone.[109]

On shore, the Germans and Italians, breathless from running down the hill, had reached the docks. Searchlights on both sides of the harbour played on the four ships. They could see *Ehrenfels* clearly, for flames soared above her funnel, almost reaching the top of her masts. Figures were running on her deck, and they heard shouts, and the crack of gunfire. Then came the deep sonorous boom of an explosion. The flames guttered with its force and then dimmed momentarily as the air filled with flying debris. Marble slabs blown into tiny pieces, logs, metal bars, bags of flour erupted like rocks from a blazing volcano.[110]

From Goa to Bombay

On the night of 9 March, *Ehrenfels*'s radio equipment was quickly destroyed while the ship's captain and four of his men were killed in the skirmish. The harbour was not deep enough to allow the ship to sink completely. By 0235 the *Ehrenfels* had settled on its sides at the bottom with the funnels, masts and structure visible out of the sea, still burning furiously.[111] Evacuation was completed by 0240 and as soon as all men were accounted for, the *Phoebe* cast off. By 0315, she passed the outer buoy and set course for Bombay.[112]

Davies moved the engine telegraph lever to 'Full Speed Astern', *Phoebe*'s propellers thrashed the sea like a mill race.[113] Above the barge, the long funnel poked out its busy puffs of black smoke. The whole harbour now erupted like a spectacular firework as drum after drum of kerosene caught fire. Reflecting the flames, the water glowed and glittered like a sea of gold.[114]

In *Phoebe*'s boiler room, the stokers laboured furiously, shovelling coal with relentless vigour, their bare torsos gleaming with sweat in the furnace's blistering heat. The tide had turned and the waves hammered the ship—a chaotic, relentless barrage. In synchronized effort, bankers, accountants, insurance agents and jute merchants—bodies caked in coal dust, streaked with sweat—hauled shovels full into the furnace's ravenous mouth. Davies steered *Phoebe* close to the shore, careful to keep the Portuguese army's searchlight from falling on them. All it illuminated for the sentries in the fort were the crashing waves of the harbour and the dark plume of smoke from *Phoebe*'s long funnel blending with the black trail rising from the burning ship.[115]

Pugh asked his permission to send a signal over *Phoebe*'s radio transmitter. Once well on the way, the success signal was transmitted, the only known occasion on which silence was broken. In both cases the message was the same: the single word 'Longshanks'. This had been chosen because it was inspired by Stewart's long legs. Both messages were received at the SOE signal stations and passed to Meerut.[116]

~

Walter Fletcher was reading *The Times of India* at the SOE office in Malabar Hill, Bombay, when a messenger arrived with a note. He read the single word typed on it and at once went into the next room. Alex Peterson was sitting at his desk. 'Longshanks,' said Fletcher. 'They've done it.'[117]

Dawn lit the sky and the flames, which had seemed so bright in the night, paled against the power of the rising sun. Explosions still rippled the morning air. Showers of sparks still cascaded occasionally over the sea as though from some marine display of fireworks, while the soldiers aboard *Phoebe* sailed farther and farther away.[118] When MI6 received word of the successful destruction of *Ehrenfels*, it sent an open message to announce that the British was about to invade Goa, which was a bluff. The crews of the other two German ships at Mormugao—as well as several Italian ships—scuttled away to prevent British capture.

The members of Creek Force shared the remains of their liquor ration. They tended to Crossley's burns and the cuts and nicks from bullets and knives which others had suffered in the fighting. Gradually they began to sing the songs they used to sing at pre-war concerts, around campfires, and after rugged matches. The words—defiant, rude and belligerent—drifted out on the evening wind. Mission accomplished, they thought. But none of them guessed at the real magnitude of their achievement.[119]

Fifteen miles to the west, and several hours later, Lieutenant Luth's U-boat No. U-181 shook off her weight of water, and soared like a giant seal from the sea. The conning tower hatch opened. Luth and another officer climbed down the slippery steps to the long narrow deck space. The last instruction Luth received had been to surface at 0115 hours on 10 March at a certain bearing. He was well on time. At 0130 he climbed back inside and approached the radio operator. The man removed his headphones. 'Nothing, sir.' 'Give it another half an hour then,' Luth told him. In fact, they gave it another one-and-a-half hours, but still there was no message. At 1500 hours, Luth, much puzzled and perplexed, gave the order to submerge.[120]

Peterson typed a press release claiming that morale was so low among the Axis crews in the ships in Mormugao Harbour that they had set fire to their own vessels. He would submit these reports to the Indian news agency Associated Press of India, which would transmit them to English language and vernacular newspapers throughout India. Other countries would also pick them up and print them. Over the next few days, other reports would appear. He had acquired several photographs of the ships at anchor before the fire, and had made arrangements for other photographs to be taken within the next few days.[121]

At 0600 hours on that same Wednesday morning, *Phoebe* arrived off Bombay. Davies anchored her well out in mid-stream, feeling disreputable and scruffy along naval ships in their camouflage and freighters being loaded. He hoped that a representative of the Port Commission or the Customs or the Police might wonder at the arrival of such an unlikely vessel and come out to enquire their business. But no one came near them.

Pugh and Grice disembarked and proceeded to the Army HQ on the Colaba Causeway. It was nearly 1100 and the British sentry, smart in whitened belt and gaiters, looked dubiously at these men in dirty uniforms who claimed to be officers and sought an urgent interview with Colonel Freddie Hutson. They were shown into the colonel's office by a sergeant major. He roared with laughter when he saw them. 'You've probably heard some rather extraordinary story about Goa?' asked Pugh. 'You're right,' said Hutson. 'I have indeed heard some extraordinary stories.' He pushed across a copy of *The Times of India* and another of *The Statesman*. Both had two news items which were released earlier by Peterson. 'Did you do it?' asked Hutson bluntly. 'As a matter of fact, we did,' replied Pugh. 'With a lot of help from the locals from Calcutta.'[122]

The Light Horse and Calcutta Scottish dumped their kits at the Army HQ and crowded into the Taj Mahal Hotel. Standing near the Gateway of India, it was Bombay's most elegant hotel with a magnificent view across the sea. Some stayed to the Bombay Yacht Club, so they took friends there for a wash and brush-up.

That night, the Calcutta Mail left on its long trans-India journey. In the harbour, Davies was already preparing to take *Phoebe* out to sea. Soon he began on his 2,500-mile trip back to the Hooghly as unobtrusively as he had arrived. As dusk deepened into darkness, *Phoebe*—navigation lights now lit—beat steadily south again, keeping well within sight of the coast. A new bearing was in her engine and her crew was happy about the bonuses they would collect upon arrival in Calcutta.[123] By the end of the week, the Light Horses were back in their homes and offices.[124]

Colin Mackenzie returned to Scotland. He later became chairman of the Scottish Council and then chairman of the Scottish Arts Council. Alex Peterson went back to teaching. He served in Malaya during the 1950s' emergency as the director general of Information Services. He was subsequently appointed director of the Department of Education at Oxford University. Walter Fletcher was elected the Conservative MP for Bury in 1945 and remained in the House for 10 years, latterly representing Bury and Radcliffe. He was knighted in 1953.

More importantly, not one word seems to have leaked out after their return—no rumours were reported from the Calcutta waterfront, no startling revelations printed in the local newspapers.[125] Most of the public and the press accepted that the Germans had mutinied and scuttled their own ships, and the SOE actions escaped detection. In fact, the Goan court found the Germans guilty of disturbing the tranquillity of the port and sentenced 111 seamen to jail, out of whom 34 were Italian and were detained. Twelve Italians and 21 Germans who were onshore, partaking in the festivities, managed to escape jail.

Shipping losses were reduced to single digits after the operation and life went on at the Calcutta Club as before. The Light Horse Bar, located at the Saturday Club in Wood Street Calcutta, did brisk business. The U-181 did not get any more messages from Indian spies and its commander Wolfgang Luth spent only a few more months captaining it. After sinking 27 ships, the U-boat was transferred to the Japanese navy as I501.

The last viceroy of India Earl Mountbatten recalled his own association with the regiment when he contributed the preface to their official history. 'One of my saddest duties in India in 1947 was to give the order for the disbandment of the Calcutta Light Horse, of which Regiment I was then Honorary Colonel,' he wrote. His words held a secret and special significance for the 14 members who travelled to Goa in March 1943.[126]

FOUR

Drama on the High Seas in 1975

Sometime in the early 1950s, on a cold November evening, Fleet Admiral Sergey Gorshkov and Colonel General Sergey Arsent'yevich Gulyayev, commander of Naval Aviation of the Baltic Fleet and hero of the Soviet Union for his exploits during the Second World War, met at the Soviet Fleet HQ in Moscow. Gorshkov realized that the primary naval threat to the Soviet Union was from the US aircraft carrier task forces. At a time when the Cold War was just taking shape, the WWII era Soviet Union's conventional naval fleet was insufficient to counter the new US threat of aircraft carriers. At the meeting, Gorshkov and his team decided to introduce the first change in the direction of the Soviet Navy since the Russian Revolution: the launching of the naval anti-carrier programme consisting of a new large fleet of anti-submarine warfare (ASW) destroyers armed with anti-ship missiles that would be able to destroy the aircraft carrier before it arrived in range of the Soviet mainland.[1]

In 1960, Colonel General Sergey Arsent'yevich Gulyayev and his team started work on Project 1135 which consisted of Burevestnik-class destroyers.[2]. The *Storozhevoy* was a part of the first fleet of the Krivak-class (Soviet designation Project 1135 Burevestnik-class) of large ASW ships launched in 1970.' The destroyer earned the class a nickname among the US Navy derived from their foreign ship silhouette identification training: 'Hot dog pack, smokestack, guns in back – KRIVAK.'[3] The

Storozhevoy was a sleek and low-slung warship whose poised silhouette, even while secured at the moorings, evoked the flexed anticipation of a greyhound at the starting line—primed to surge forward at a moment's notice.[4] The *Storozhevoy* was not only a lethal Soviet warship, but also beautiful, with graceful lines and a design that US Navy analysts would later call 'neat, workmanlike, and elegant'.[5]

The *Storozhevoy* was a handsome ship which was designed for both speed and manoeuvrability. Her assortment of comprehensive and impressive armaments made a ship of her class a significant force on the high seas.[6] She bristled with weapons systems, rocket launchers, torpedo tubes, guns, rotating radars, antennas and dozens of electronic warfare systems that many of the visitors can only guess and marvel at.[7] The *Storozhevoy* was loaded with ASW weapons. The RBU-6000 launchers on the stern could fire rocket-propelled depth charges. She was armed with an SS-N-14 torpedo launcher. The *Storozhevoy* had 76.2 mm guns mounted on the stern, 30 mm Gatling guns and two surface-to-air missile launchers for close-in air defence. The *Storozhevoy* was equipped with state-of-the-art electronics, including the Head Net C search radar, a pair of Eye Bowl radar systems to control the SS-N-14 missiles, Pop Group radars for the SA-N-4 missiles, plus Owl Screech radar for the guns, Don Kay, Palm Frond Surface Search radars and a complete suite of ESMs equipment to detect any sort of electronic noise from a submarine or any other ship. In 1973 the Soviet minister of defence, Marshal Grechko, sailed onboard and 'evaluated' highly the mastery of the anti-submariners in their firing of ASW missiles. He stated that the *Storozhevoy* 'had all the requirements necessary to win first place in the Soviet competition among outstanding ships.'

Riga in Latvia was a major port city on the NATO border. So the Soviet military presence was strong, with many army, air force and naval units based nearby. Many citizens from other parts of the Soviet Union, including officers with their families, gradually settled down in the city.[8] Riga provided Soviet warships with a new harbour. The port of Riga is on the banks of the Daugava river, which empties into the Gulf of Riga 10 miles to the north. The lighthouse on Rukhnu Island in the Gulf of Riga directs outgoing ships to turn west and incoming ships to turn south.[9]

On 7 November 1975, the *Storozhevoy* had come to Riga to take part in the celebration of the fifty-eighth anniversary of the Great October Socialist Bolshevik Revolution which was celebrated to commemorate the October Revolution of 1917.[10] *Storozhevoy* was assigned a buoy in the middle of the Daugava River. The ship had been open for tours by local citizens all day. The next morning it took part in the naval parade that sailed down the river, passing the Baltic Fleet flagship and rendering honours to it. Afterward, a detachment of sailors from *Storozhevoy* marched in a workers' parade down the wide riverside promenade past the distinguished Latvian artist Valdis Alberg's sculpted memorial to the Red Rifleman.[11]

Early in the evening, visitors were admiring Riga's beautiful architecture while some were strolling along the Eksporta lela Krastmala Street, which runs along Riga's waterfront. Some had arrived from as far as Vladivostok to watch the stellar display of advanced warships. Approximately half of *Storozhevoy*'s crew of 250 men had been given shore leave to join in the anniversary festivities.[12] But others, led by the ship's political officer, were planning to defect to Sweden.[13]

Valery Sablin was the *zampolit* or the political officer aboard the *Storozhevoy*. The zampolit was assigned to every unit of the Soviet armed forces to guard against subversion and educate servicemen in party doctrine. In a major combatant ship like *Storozhevoy*, the zampolit is the third in command. He has a completely separate chain-of-command within the military-political directorate (*Gla*vPuR).[14] The zampolit thus sits in the unique position of being the one person to whom all sailors are encouraged to take their welfare problems, like with an ombudsman. He is sensitive to their problems, the one officer who could establish some sort of rapport with the sailors.

Sablin had grown up as a privileged member of Soviet society. He was a descendant of the Decembrist[15] N.S. Bestuzhev, who took part in the 1825 revolt against Czar Nicholas the First.[16] When war came to Russia in 1941, Sablin's father Mikhail was attached to the Northern Fleet staff. Ships from this fleet dodged German bombers and submarines, escorting merchant vessels from the North Atlantic to the port of Murmansk in the Soviet Union. This was a vital lifeline to Soviet, supplying aid from the US and Britain.[17] Valery's maternal grandfather was a sailor, his paternal grandfather was a cavalry man, and his great-grandfather went down with the cruiser *Pallada* in World War I. All had seen combat in at least one war.[18]

Officer Nikolay Cherkashin, Sablin's colleague, recalled: 'He had always thought globally… He tried to deeply understand social phenomena. He was a natural politician.' In 1973 Sablin joined the Lenin Military Political Academy. He was offered the command of a destroyer, an extraordinary accolade for a 30-year-old officer. To the surprise and dismay of his family, Valery turned down the offer of a commission in favour of becoming a political officer.[19] Sablin was responsible to the KGB and one of his tasks was looking out for deviation from the Party line.

The winter frost rode heavily on the stiff ocean breezes in the harbour on the morning of 8 November 1975. Aboard the destroyer *Storozhevoy*, moored beside an Alpha-class nuclear-attack submarine, the sound of reveille echoed through the ship. On this chilly predawn, all of Riga was sleeping. It was time for the 200 men and officers to rise from their slumbers, dress in trousers and *telnyaschka*—the long-sleeved blue-and-white-striped undershirts that sailors wear no matter the time of year—and muster on deck for exercises. A strange undercurrent of anticipation permeated the ship, though only two men knew the reason.[20] After the exercises, the enlisted men were served *kasha*—a gruel made of hulled buckwheat—and a couple of thin pieces of bread with a little butter, while the officers were served a special *kasha* made of processed oatmeal, cheese and *kielbasa* sausages.[21]

During two years of service on the *Storozhevoy*, Valery Sablin talked to the crew and shared his thoughts with them, searching for allies for his plan. In November 1975, when the Soviet Union celebrated the fifty-eighth anniversary of the Revolution, Sablin decided that his time had come.[22] One such meeting was taking place with those remaining onboard the ship that afternoon in November 1975.[23]

The holiday was over and the people of Riga were doing their own thing—family gatherings, playing chess, watching television—the Bolshoi Ballet was doing a matinee performance of Giselle. The next day the *Storozhevoy* was to head to the shipyard for repairs. Hence, the missiles and torpedoes had been taken off the ship.[24]

The Mutiny

Unlike many other political officers, Sablin was popular with the sailors as he maintained good relations with the crew. He took advantage of this while planning the mutiny. Sablin had to find supporters for his plan as he wanted to defect *with* the *Storozhevoy* to the west, and for the ship to find a new home. He chose Seaman Alexander (Sasha) Shein, a young proletarian with the honest, frank face of a typical Russian *muzhik* (peasant) who, on his own admission, was a 'bit of a rebel'.[25] On 5 November 1975, immediately after leaving Baltiysk on the way to Riga, Sablin persuaded Shein to help him plan and execute the mutiny. Shein was a good mechanic and had a talent for art. Shein recruited a few more co-conspirators among friends within the crew.[26] Shein effectively became Sablin's second-in-command during the mutiny.[27]

The date chosen for the mutiny was Saturday, 8 November 1975. The evening was suitable for a defection, as a large part of the Soviet military was on leave or still celebrating the anniversary. But there was another reason, and that was a decisive factor. Sablin had had just over a year to get to know the crew and the ship. But immediately after the celebration in Riga, the *Storozhevoy* would go to Liepaja to get a new crew and be prepared for transfer to the Pacific Fleet to be deployed on operational duties.[28] If Sablin wanted to bring this warship—equipped with the latest armaments, electronics, communication devices, cipher systems and code books—along on his defection to Sweden, this was his last chance.[29]

The last entry in the *Storozhevoy*'s log on Saturday was entered at 1900 hours, when a new duty officer signed in—one of those who supported Sablin. That night, he chose to show Sergey Eisenstein's groundbreaking 1925 film *Battleship Potemkin*, which was about a mutiny on a Russian ship in connection with the revolution of 1905. In the film, the Tsarist fleet gathers to stop the bold mutineers on the Potemkin, but when it comes down to it, the honest sailors on the Tsarist ships refuse to open fire at the mutineers. The Potemkin continues right through the Tsarist fleet, towards freedom and revolution.[30]

At 1900 on 8 of November, while the film kept the rest of the crew occupied, Anatoly Potulniy, the captain of the *Storozhevoy*, was sitting in his cabin when Sablin burst in without knocking, pale and disturbed. 'Comrade Commander, we have a CP!' CP was the Russian acronym for *chrezvychainoe polozhenie*, an extraordinary situation—the call word for an emergency aboard ship. Potulniy jumped up out of his chair. 'What happened? Where?'[31]

Sablin told him that some of the sailors were drinking in the Second Radio Technical Centre (RTC) post, a forward sonar compartment below the main deck. A remarkably diligent commander, Potulniy decided to sort out the incident himself. So below decks they went, Potulniy leading the way and Sablin dutifully following him. They went to the lowest deck, 15 feet below the waterline, with Potulniy calling back to him, 'Here?' and Sablin answering, 'No, lower.' Finally, the captain entered the foremost compartment on the ship's lowest level, the second sonar post. Potulniy entered the cabin and saw that it was empty and turned back to speak to Sablin. In a moment's notice Sablin shut the hatch. Potulniy heard the loud noise and looked around the compartment, bewildered. In the corner he saw an envelope with 'Potulniy, A.V.' written on it, along with several books from the ship's library. His first thought was to call someone, but then he noticed that the phone had been ripped off the wall. The envelope contained a note from Sablin. It explained what Sablin was going to do with his ship.[32]

Subsequently, Sablin, in his capacity as the senior officer present on board, summoned the remaining officers to a meeting at 1930 hours. He lined up all 150 officers and sailors who had come over to the destroyer after enjoying Riga and its festivities. Sablin announced the mutiny against the Soviet system. While he wanted to defect to Sweden, Sablin lied to gain their loyalty. He told the crew that officers in the Northern and Pacific Fleets were waiting for a word from *Storozhevoy* and then they would join the revolt.[33]

Later at 2210 hours, Sablin assembled the officers in the dining room and gave a small speech on how the bureaucracy, censorship and corruption had taken over the Soviet Union. 'What are you saying, Comrade Zampolit?' one of the officers asked. No one talked about these things. No one was allowed, by law, to talk about these things. To be in the same room with a man talking this way was treason. Senior Lieutenant Nikolai Vinogradov rose to his feet. He, too, had had enough and was ready to walk out. 'Sit down!' Sablin shouted. 'Right now! That's an order!' Slowly, the other officers—starting with the ship's medical officer, Oleg Sadkov—reluctantly sank back into their seats, followed by Proshutinsky and Vinogradov, both initially involved in the mutiny. A strange, uneasy silence fell over the officers' mess.[34]

A counter-revolt was launched by some of the officers. A couple of them made an attempt to stop Sablin and free the captain. One of the sailors, Seaman Sakhnevich, came to Sablin and informed him that several of them were meeting in one of their cabins and plotting against him. Sablin and Sakhnevich went there to confront them. Three officers, Saitov, Stepanov and Kovalchenkov, had pistols, and they squared off against Sablin in their stateroom. They grabbed the zampolit and tried to disarm him, but Sakhnevich along with several sailors came to his defence. They overpowered the other officers and locked them inside the cabin.[35] Most of the crew chose not to oppose the mutiny, either because they supported Sablin or because they did not dare to overrule their superior officer.[36] Others, like Sadikov, refused point-blank.

Undeterred, Sablin swept all resistance aside and demanded a vote.[37] He asked them to vote their support or opposition to his scheme by choosing backgammon pieces from a board in front of them.[38] He pointed to several pieces on the table in front of them. Take a white piece if you support this mutiny, he told them, and a black piece if you do not. Far from any active opposition, the officers did as they were told, laughing and joking as they chose their pieces. One by one all the officers cast their votes. Besides Boris Gindin and Kuzmin, those voting against mutiny included Captain Lieutenant Nikolay Proshutinsky, Senior Lieutenant Vinogradov and warrant officers Gritsa, Khokhlov and Zhitenev. Conversely, Lieutenant Dudnik supported the mutiny and midshipmen Viktor Borodai, Gomenchuk and Kalinichev also each dropped a white backgammon piece into the basket. The vote was made. Eight officers supported Sablin and eight did not. Sablin assured that no harm would come to those who were against him. The mutineers led them towards the deck below and locked them up.[39]

The news that at least half of the officers had decided to back the mutineers had an immediate and electrifying effect: 'From that moment on there was great enthusiasm,' recalled Shein with a wry smile: 'Everybody's spirits were lifted. We thought we would be such heroes!'[40]

Senior Lieutenant Vladimir Firsov, in charge of a section of the ship's electronics as well as chairman of the party committee onboard the warship, decided to leave the ship to sound the alarm.[41] He had supported the mutiny in the officers' meeting, so he had not been detained. After the voting, one of the officers told Sablin that the mutiny was over because Senior Lieutenant Firsov had jumped ship.

After Sablin's meeting with the crew around 2230 hours, Senior Lieutenant Bulat Talipovich Saitov, another loyalist who had earlier voted for Sablin, assisted Firsov in climbing down from the deck of the ship to the buoy at which the *Storozhevoy* was moored. Ensconced in the frigid darkness of the massive anchor hawsehole, Firsov finally connected the dots. A couple of weeks ago, Sablin had enquired about how the electrical systems aboard the ship were supposed to work. During the conversation Sablin made not-so-subtle comments about what a mess the bureaucrats in Moscow had made of Lenin's fine ideas.

Firsov looked over the side of the fortifications. A dark and intimidating nuclear submarine, the S-263, was at the same mooring as the *Storozhevoy*. He could make out a dim red glow from the open hatch on top of its conning tower. The sub's captain would know what to do. Firsov looked over his shoulder to make sure there was no one to see him, then lowered himself through the hawsehole, the filthy mooring line getting his uniform dirty, and swam towards the sub.[42]

He managed to get the attention of a sentry on the quay next to the S-263. After some confusion, the submariners sent a small boat to retrieve Firsov from the buoy.

'Is your captain aboard the submarine?' Firsov asked.

'Yes, sir.'

'With compliments, tell him that Senior Lieutenant Vladimir Firsov from the *Storozhevoy* is on deck and would like to have a word with him. Tell him it's urgent.'

'Yes, sir,' the sailor replied, and he disappeared, presumably to use the submarine's interphone to call the captain. A hatch opened at the base of the sail and a warrant officer beckoned from inside.[43]

Upon arrival, he alerted the submarine's commanding officer, Captain L. Svetlovskiy, who in addition to being commanding officer was also serving as the temporary duty officer for the ships on the River Daugava. This made him responsible for any sudden emergency among the ships at the anchorage.[44]

When Firsov told his story to the sub's skipper, Captain Second Rank Svetlovskiy, he was met with stunned disbelief.

'A mutiny of the officers is impossible,' Svetlovskiy fumed. 'Such things no longer happen aboard Soviet warships. Where is your KGB officer?'

'He's been reassigned, sir. The mutiny was ordered by our zampolit. He's arrested Captain Potulniy and a few of the officers who tried to stop him.'[45]

Svetlovskiy immediately telephoned the chief of staff of the 78th Ship Security Brigade for the protection of the water area, Captain Second Rank V.S. Vlasov, and the head of the Brigade Special Detachment Captain Second Rank V.G. Yudin. They were in charge of the Ust'-Dvinsk neighbourhood in northwestern Riga on the left bank of the Daugava. Just as Svetlovskiy before them, Vlasov and Yudin found the story hard to credit.

Back on the destroyer, the fact that their plans had been betrayed to the authorities caused a momentary vacillation. The sun had set at 1730 hours. As the air cooled, mist rose from the water and spread throughout the city like a night watchman making his rounds.[46] When Sablin found out that Firsov had skipped out, he realized that they could not wait any longer. Faced with the possibility of overwhelming odds, Sablin hesitated, but decided to go ahead anyway. Significantly, what stiffened his resolve was the firm attitude of the ordinary sailors, most of them still teenagers, who insisted on continuing the revolt: 'We have started this; so we might as well see it through!' The attitude of the men settled the matter in favour of action.[47]

Sablin began preparing the *Storozhevoy* for departure at about 0100 hours.[48] It was now 2300. Sablin went to the bridge and ordered the crew to weigh anchor. 'This is an order! Start all four engines now! I need full power as quickly as possible! Call me on the bridge when everything is ready!'[49]

At midnight on Saturday, 8 November 1975, the rumble of a ship's engines broke the stillness of the Daugava. The destroyer unhooked from its mooring buoy.[50] Once she started her engines and lurched forward, they struck the stern of the submarine in front of her. The man at the helm was an accomplished seaman but because nobody expected one of the ships to break parade formation, they were closely moored together. However, this was the least of their worries. The 400-foot ship now had to turn around in a shallow river crammed with other ships and submarines. The helmsman did so, skilfully putting the bow downriver.[51] The bridge of *Storozhevoy* was dark. The only lights in use were subdued red or blue ones for marking a passageway or reading a chart. *Storozhevoy* was now sailing at a comfortable speed.[52] She left Riga at 0100 hours on 9 November.[53]

Around 0250 hours she moved out into the Gulf of Riga. Sablin set a course for the Baltic Sea, heading west with a speed of just over 15 knots in the direction of the Irben Sound, which led out into the Baltic Sea. He did not want to be noticed, so the *Storozhevoy* proceeded without turning on either her air/surface search radar or her navigation radar. For this reason she could not move very fast in the darkness.[54] The only instrument activated was the fathometer which kept track of water depth.[55]

Several attempts were made by the Soviet Navy to contact the *Storozhevoy* by radio, but as decided nobody onboard responded. It was too late by the time the news reached the Soviet Naval General Staff. By then, the *Storozhevoy* had already left the anchorage and was heading out towards the Bay of Riga.[56]

Once the master had successfully turned the ship around and pointed it downstream, it was all ahead full. Carried by the tide and travelling at top speed, *Storozhevoy* was now sailing north along the Daugava. The warship would continue on this course for another 10 miles until the freshwater river emptied into the saltwater Gulf of Riga.[57]

The destroyer disappeared into the night.[58] The ship was headed to the Swedish island of Gotland. At an average speed of 15 knots, the journey of 175 nautical miles—through the Irben Sound—to freedom could take no more than five and one-half hours. Sablin was counting on the fact that the Soviet holiday would give them a head start.[59]

On the way, the *Storozhevoy* nearly collided with a gasoline tanker.[60] 'I looked out and saw a ship coming out of the harbour,' said Maksimenko, one of the defectors reliving the experience. 'I thought it was going to block us. The *Storozhevoy* made a sharp turn to the right, I was nearly thrown overboard; I was just clinging on. It felt as though we were at 45 degrees. And this other ship kept on coming. Then it suddenly turned left.' The crew breathed easy again. The 'Sentry' had got out of Riga![61]

The feeling of uncertainty became overwhelming as the ship was gathering speed. There was a feeling of freedom. A kind of contentment as if one's heart was going to take flight. During the next six hours, all kinds of contradictory feelings of success and failure arose among the crew.

It took approximately four hours for news of the *Storozhevoy* mutiny to reach Moscow. KGB Headquarters got wind of it at

0400 hours on 9 November. Vlasov and Yudin finally contacted the command post of the Baltic Fleet.[62] They called Navy Headquarters, but the duty officer there had not yet heard about it. He had to call the Baltic Fleet HQ to find out the details.

It was only when the amazing message 'Mutiny onboard the *Storozhevoy*: we are heading for open sea' was received on an emergency frequency by the Naval High Command that chaos erupted at the Naval Headquarters. All this while, Soviet radio traffic was being intercepted and decoded by the Swedish Intelligence.[63]

In Kremlin

Fleet Admiral Gorshkov had stayed up until nearly 0300 hours, talking and laughing with his friends, before he finally went to bed after another long, exhausting day. Having learned of the mutiny, Vice Admiral Kosov immediately contacted Gorshkov in his villa outside Moscow. The admiral opened his eyes, instantly awake despite the fact that he'd only had one hour of sleep. At around 0415 hours, Gorshkov, in turn, informed the minister of defence, Marshal Grechko.[64] Gorshkov always imagined that the global thermonuclear war they had dreaded since 1945 would begin this way. The Americans and the Soviets were nuclear powers who led the NATO and the Warsaw Pact against each other.

'Da, what is it?' the admiral asked, softly so as not to disturb his wife sleeping next to him.

'No one is sure, Admiral,' Lieutenant Markin whispered. 'But it's possible that a mutiny may be in progress aboard one of our ships in the Baltic Fleet.'

Gorshkov sat up in bed. By the time he had tossed the covers aside and gotten to his feet, Markin was there with his robe and slippers.

'Would you like tea?'

'Yes,' the admiral said and marched out of his bedroom, down a long corridor, through a glassed-in unheated porch, to his office at the back of the house. During the day it looked down a wooded slope to a small stream from which he pulled some trout in happier times.

Mutiny! Not in his navy!

He switched on the desk light and telephoned Naval Headquarters. The duty officer, a young lieutenant, answered on the first ring.

'What's going on?' Gorshkov demanded. He didn't bother to identify himself. It was up to his people to recognize his voice. He was reporting directly to arguably the third most important man in the Soviet Union, behind party general secretary Leonid Brezhnev and minister of defence Andrei Grechko.

'Admiral, from what I have been able to piece together so far, a mutiny may be in progress aboard the *Storozhevoy*.'

Markin was there, unobtrusively, with a glass of tea in a filigreed silver holder, which he placed on the desk at the admiral's hand. He lit a cigarette from a box on the desk and perched it delicately on the edge of a large marble ashtray, a gift from the president of North Korea.

Markin left, softly closing the door.[65]

'First, I want a reconnaissance aircraft sent to locate the *Storozhevoy*. When the ship has been found, no action is to be taken against him, but I must be personally informed. Immediately. Not one hour later.'

'Yes, sir.'

'I want the captains of every ship and boat at anchor in Riga to be awakened and ordered to prepare to get underway within the hour on my orders.'

'Yes, sir.'

'You will personally see to it that nothing of this incident is broadcast to anyone else for any reason. No matter who that might be. Do you understand that order?'

'Yes, sir.'

'Now, move it, Lieutenant,' and Gorshkov slammed down the telephone.

Markin appeared at the door. 'Will we be dressing in full uniform or civilian attire with medals this morning, sir?'

'A civilian suit. No medals.'[66]

Premier Brezhnev was woken from his sleep. Gorshkov arrived at the Kremlin before dawn. The guards at the Spassky Gate let him through, having been alerted of his arrival beforehand. The armed, uniformed guards in front of the Council of Ministers Block came to attention and saluted the admiral as he got out of his car and entered the building which was all but deserted that morning. Only two long, black ZIL limousines were parked in front—one of them Grechko's, and the other Premier Brezhnev's.

'The Party General Secretary is waiting for you, Admiral.'

'Da,' Gorshkov brushed past the man and entered the conference room where Brezhnev and Grechko were seated at the small mahogany table.

He took his seat across from the two men dressed in dark suits, worn without a tie, drinking tea and smoking cigarettes. 'We have a mutiny on our hands,' Gorshkov said.[67] Brezhnev read the communiqué, his irritation turning to alarm and he burst out, 'A mutiny!' *He* ordered every ship and plane in the Baltic Fleet to hunt down *Storozhevoy*. 'Bomb that ship and sink it!' he shouted.[68] He authorized lethal force to prevent a humiliating defection.

Moscow could not allow the *Storozhevoy* and all her military technology to fall into enemy hands. The ship had to be sunk rather than allowed to escape. As the head of the navy, Gorshkov had to stop the *Storozhevoy* by any available means. So he was given command of the Border Troops' vessels in the area of operations in addition to those of the navy which he already controlled. As a result, at about 0745 hours, Admiral Gorshkov assumed personal command of the operation to intercept and regain control over the *Storozhevoy*.[69]

Gorshkov spoke to the commanding officer of the Baltic Fleet, Vice Admiral Anatoliy Mikhaylovich Kosov.[70] His orders, direct from Brezhnev, were to find the *Storozhevoy* and stop it or sink it. 'The mutineers have given up their right to our consideration, and Captain Potulniy should never have allowed his ship to be taken from him. Find the *Storozhevoy*, Admiral, and kill him. That order comes directly from Secretary Brezhnev.'

Kosov was momentarily taken aback. 'He knows?'

'Yes, and in the next few hours half of Moscow will probably know,' Gorshkov said. 'Carry out your orders, Admiral. Quickly.'

'Yes, sir,' Kosov replied.

An old hand who had commanded a nuclear submarine and until recently had been the chief of staff of the Baltic Fleet, Kosov reacted much faster than the overly cautious Svetlovskiy, Vlasov and Yudin. He ordered the Baltic Fleet's warships to immediately set out in pursuit of the *Storozhevoy*. The first warship soon left Riga to intercept the destroyer. [71]

On that chilly morning, Vice Admiral Kosov sat in his official car and reached the Baltic Fleet HQ at Kaliningrad. From the radio room he called Sablin. Chief of operations Captain Third Rank Viktor Badim looked up from the plotting table as Kosov walked in and shouted 'Admiral on deck!' The eight staffers on duty stiffened to attention. 'As you were,' Kosov grumbled.[72]

'*Storozhevoy*, this is Vice Admiral Kosov speaking. Let me talk to Captain Potulniy.'

'I'm sorry, Admiral, but Captain Potulniy is no longer in command,' Sablin responded.

'What are you talking about?' Kosov shouted. 'Put the captain on, immediately! That's an order!'

'I'm sorry, sir; I cannot do that.'

'Who is this?' Kosov demanded.

'Captain Third Rank Valery Sablin, sir. I am temporarily in command of the *Storozhevoy*.'

'Mutiny?'

'Sir, I have to announce that the *Storozhevoy* is no longer a part of the Baltic Fleet. This ship is now in a free and independent territory, no longer under the authority of the Soviet Union.'

Sablin hesitated again before he keyed the microphone. He'd never disobeyed a direct order. He had been a good Communist. 'Sir, I'm sorry, but I cannot comply with that order.'

'Report your situation, Sablin.'

'Respectfully, sir, I cannot do that either. Sir, since this ship is no longer a part of the Baltic Fleet, I am no longer under your command. I am no longer accountable to you.'

'Sablin!' Vice Admiral Kosov's voice rose to a shout again.

'*Storozhevoy*, out,' Sablin radioed. He replaced the microphone on its bracket and turned off the VHF radio.[73] He soon received a direct order from the commander-in-chief of the navy: 'Stop the ship and return to port immediately.' Sablin refused again. The *Storozhevoy* sailed on.

The Assault on *Storozhevhoy*

Kosov glanced at the large table displaying a detailed chart of the Baltic region, including all of its islands, inlets, rivers and bases, as well as those of Sweden and other bordering nations. Every warship that the Soviet Navy was tracking was represented as a tiny wooden model on the table, and talkers, connected by headsets, moved the pieces around as if they were chessmen in a deadly game. Kosov took his position at the command console at the head of the table. One of the ratings brought him a glass of sweet tea with one small piece of lemon, just as he liked it.

Badim came up. 'The fleet at Riga is underway.'

'Order as many units of our air wing as you think necessary to help with the hunt.'

Badim went off to order the air wing into action as Kosov sat back with his tea and watched the talkers push the fleet down the River Daugava toward the Baltic. The *Storozhevoy* had at least a five-hour head start, and the fleet was unlikely to catch up with him before the air wing did.[74]

A large interception force consisting of a number of warships sailed from the Liepaja Naval Base. It was commanded by Captain First Rank Leonid Semyonovich Rassukovannyy, who led the force aboard the patrol ship *Komsomolets Litv*.[75] Two naval Il-38 'Ilyushin' reconnaissance aircraft were ordered to take off immediately from the Skirotava airfield on the southeastern outskirts of Riga. Nine other Baltic Fleet ships were also dispatched in the chase including another of the Krivak-class and a patrol boat from Riga.[76] By 0800, the *Storozhevoy* was passing between Saaremaa Island and the Latvian coast. In less than an hour, it would be in international waters.

The first reconnaissance aircraft, under the command of Captain Anatoliy Grishkin, was in the air. An Il-38 commanded by Lieutenant Vasili Barsukhov was flying some 300 feet above sea level. His copilot Warrant Officer Yevgenni Levin, and flight engineer Warant Officer Ivan Zavorin, monitored the navigational and engine instruments. Flying this fast and this low was dangerous. The slightest mistake in the dense November fog could send them into the cold waters of the river or the gulf.[77]

The Swedish intelligence community did not know about the dramatic events which were unfolding in the Baltic Sea just east of Gotland Island. There was a secret National Defence Radio Establishment (Försvarets radioanstalt/FRA) SIGINT station on the island near the city of Ostergarn.[78] But Swedish intelligence personnel were not on duty on weekends. Although some employees worked shifts outside of office hours, there was no one who processed and analysed the intercepts.[79]

The first event that piqued the interest of a Swedish radar

operator on Gotland Island was the take-off of two planes detected on the air search radar screen. He wondered why two Il-38 May reconnaissance aircraft had left the airfield in Latvia early on a Sunday morning and were flying over the Irben Channel.[80]

Once Sablin turned on his surface search radar in the Irben Channel, the Il-38s picked it up and sent the ship's location to ground control at Skirotava Airfield.[81] There were several fast torpedo vessels of Soviet designation Project 205P Tarantul ('tarantula') from the Border Troops pursuing the *Storozhevoy*. The Border Troops was an operational arm of the KGB which was responsible for preventing Soviet citizens from fleeing the country. They had a chain of command separate from the navy. The *Smirnov* was one of the KGB boats fast approaching the *Storozhevoy*.

Doris Sampsonn, a radar intercept and evaluation officer at the FRA station, suddenly sat up at her console in the small, dimly lit room. Half a dozen other electronic intelligence (ELINT) officers were monitoring the consoles. Sampsonn was receiving a strong shipborne radar signal from the southern edge of the Irben Channel. They'd been warned of some unusual activity in the Gulf of Riga—on the surface and in the air—earlier in the morning. The Soviets were filling the airwaves with all sorts of wild, frantic messages.

Something big was in the works, and all of Sweden's military and civilian ELINT capabilities had been placed on high alert. It was possible, no matter how unlikely, that the Soviet Union was launching an attack on NATO. But they had to be sure before they sounded the alarm. Sampsonn consulted a manual containing a list of Soviet warships. Each ship's radar suite broadcast a signal different from others. She was an experienced intercept operator, but it took her the better part of a half hour to finally come up with an identification and exact location.[82]

A hotline phone connected her directly with the ELINT duty operator at the FRA Headquarters at Lovon.

'Sir, this is Doris Sampsonn, intercept officer at Ostergarn Station.'

'Go ahead,' the duty operator replied crisply. It had been a busy morning.

'I've identified the lead Soviet ship that just came out of the Irben Channel. She's an ASW destroyer, the *Storozhevoy*. She is on a course of three-two-zero degrees, making thirty knots.[83] She is heading into directly towards Sweden.'[84]

At 0730, twenty new radar blips showed up on the screen.[85]

'*Storozhevoy*, *Storozhevoy*, this is the coastal patrol vessel *Smirnov* off your port quarter,' the VHF radio on the overhead blared. 'Immediately shut down your engines and prepare to be boarded.' The *Smirnov* was a Pchela-class fast-attack hydrofoil boat capable of much higher speeds than the *Storozhevoy*. It was armed with four 23 mm cannons with which the gunners could take out the *Storozhevoy*'s bridge. The boat was also equipped with depth charges that could be laid out ahead of the destroyer. By now every military unit in the Soviet Union knew exactly where the *Storozhevoy* was headed: to Sweden, where Sablin and his mutineers meant to defect.[86]

The above order was rescinded before he could carry it out, as Moscow suddenly altered the chain of command to deal with the extraordinary situation. The coastal patrol was withdrawn from the chase and the Soviet Navy and Air Force took over. This was now a serious National Security matter to be handled by the higher authorities. The *Storozhevoy* accordingly continued on her way through the Irben Sound, henceforth accompanied by the KGB flotilla.[87]

Following wartime protocol, Gvozdikov ordered the entire Soviet Naval Aviation Yak-28 regiment to take off immediately. Pilots only received a description of their target when the first planes were in the air. At 1000 hours, there were about 20 Yak-28s in the air. At about 1020 hours, the Yak-28s carried out attacks with bombs from a height of 1,000 to 1,500 feet towards what they thought was the *Storozhevoy*. However, it was soon obvious to the airmen that they had attacked the wrong target, because the targeted ship's crew immediately radioed for help. The attack was aborted before anybody was killed or wounded. The target was not a warship at all but the Soviet cargo ship Volgo-Balt 38, en route from the Latvian port Ventspils to Finland.[88]

The cloud base was still at an altitude of about 2,000 feet, so it was difficult to get a visual overview of the situation. After the mistake with the cargo ship, the pilots received repeated orders to attack only when the *Storozhevoy* had been positively identified. They finally got their target, a proper warship of the right appearance, in their sights at around 1028 hours. The pilots were ordered to attack 'straight at him'.[89]

Zhernov was lined up for his run on the *Storozhevoy* and his squadron was fanned out behind him. They were to make their attack in five waves of four aircraft each.

'Control, we are commencing our attack,' Zhernov radioed. 'Have they surrendered yet?'

'Does it look like it?' Guliayev shouts. 'Follow your orders!'

'On my lead,' Zhernov radioed his squadron and pushed the stick forward.

His aircraft was equipped with the Initiativa radar bombing system and 30 mm cannons. It was carrying conventional bombs large enough to take out the *Storozhevoy*.

'I have the target,' his weapons officer reported.

'Roger,' Zhernov responded. 'Report weapons lock.'

'Roger,' the weapons officer reported and returned after a momentary pause. 'I have a weapons lock. Do I have permission to fire?'

His controller in the Ilyushin above was shouting in his headphones, as were at least two others, one of them probably Guliayev. Zhernov ignored them.

Two of his wingmen dropped their bombs but they aimed wide of the mark. Zhernov wondered if it was purposefully done.

The *Storozhevoy* loomed large outside his canopy and he could even imagine picking out individual faces through the bridge windows while firing his cannon, the shells tearing up the foredeck and along the hull as he screamed past, leaving the ship in his wake.

Off to port, Zhernov spotted a flash and sudden plume of smoke. One of the bombs dropped by his wingmen had found a target. But the wrong ship!

It's the fog. It's the lousy orders.

'Break off! Break off!' he ordered his squadron.[90]

Now the *Storozhevoy* would be hit, not just warned. Four minutes later, a Yak-28 dropped bombs which fell 150 feet in front of—*not* the *Storozhevoy* but the slightly smaller *Komsomolets Litvy*, the lead warship of the pursuit force from which Captain First Rank Rassukovannyy was commanding the chase of the *Storozhevoy*! Being inexperienced in naval matters, the Frontal Aviation airmen had failed to spot the difference between the two warships. The bomb fragments spread far and wide, and a fire broke out on the *Komsomolets Litvy*. Rassukovannyy's ships were about 10 miles behind the *Storozhevoy*. His ship fired signal rockets to make the Yak-28 pilots understand that they were attacking the wrong target.[91]

Later the Yaks found the *Storozhevoy*. One silvery jet pocked the port side of the destroyer with 23 mm cannon shells. Despite boasting two rapid-fire three-inch dual-purpose guns on the stern and SA-N-4 Osa anti-aircraft missiles, it did not return fire, either lacking loaded ammunition or under orders from Sablin.

Something hit the starboard side of the ship with a tremendous bang, nearly knocking Sablin and the others off their feet. Almost immediately, more sledgehammer blows hit the ship, this time on both port and starboard sides. Sablin looked up in time to see at least six jet aircraft bracketing either side of the *Storozhevoy*, bright pinpoints of light coming from beneath them as they fired their cannons. As the jets roared past just a few metres above the level of the bridge, the banshee scream of the jet engines all but blotted out the noise of the incoming shells impacting the ship's hull.

'They're attacking!' Soloviev shouted needlessly.

Sablin wanted to get on the radio to tell the pilots that they were making a dreadful mistake. But he could not move.

The jets had been so low and close that he was certain he could see the faces of the crew. Two men in each cockpit.

But they were gone now, and the shooting has ceased.

'Is it over—' Makismenko had barely started to ask when a tremendous explosion slammed into the ship somewhere aft. This blow was so massive that Sablin was actually knocked off his feet.

'It was a bomb!' Maksimenko cried. 'Captain, they're bombing us!'

More jets appeared out of the fog, shooting their cannons at the *Storozhevoy*'s hull, the ship shuddering like a mortally wounded animal with each hit.

It suddenly began to turn to the left. Soloviev tried fighting the wheel, but it had no effect.

Sablin scrambled to his feet. 'Come back on course!'

'I can't,' Soloviev responded. 'I think the rudder has jammed.'

'Captain, we need to stop and surrender before it is too late!' Maksimenko shouted. 'We're going to die here!'

'Nobody's going to die!' Sablin retorted, reaching for the radio as a second laser-guided 250-kilogram bomb hit the stern, shoving the ship about 65 feet off-track.[92]

From their headquarters in Moscow, Grechko and Gorshkov ordered the commander of Naval Aviation of the Baltic Fleet, Sergey Gulyayev, colonel general of the air force, hero of the Soviet Union, and Second World War veteran, to commence preparations for sinking the *Storozhevoy*. The KGB boats were ordered to move at least six miles away from the *Storozhevoy* as a group of Tu-16K bombers, belonging to Soviet Naval Aviation, approached from Skirotava.[93] They were outfitted with AS-2

Kipper and AS-5 Kelt anti-ship missiles that could be used against aircraft carriers at long range but were unsuitable for attacking a runaway destroyer in heavy merchant traffic.[94]

Nine Tu-16K bombers under Colonel Savinkov had taken off from Bykhov in the morning. From about 0910 hours, the groups gradually converged in the area where the *Storozhevoy* had been found. Captain Grishkin's Il-38 from Riga henceforth followed and reported the *Storozhevoy*'s movements to Colonel Savinkov's bombers. The naval aviation pilots thus had a good idea of what was happening down at sea level. This was necessary because visibility was poor and the cloud base was only 300 to 400 feet above sea level. Above the clouds there was no opportunity to see what was happening below.[95]

The Swedes detected the Tu-16 Badger bombers flying at different altitudes, at one point as low as 50 feet above the sea. What were they doing? Everyone was watching the blips on the radar scope. All the signals and voices were being taped and saved for subsequent analysis.

Colonel Savinkov and his men went below the clouds to read the bow number of the ship. They descended until they could fire warning shots with the rearward-facing cannon.[96] He then made a low-level pass across the destroyer. Consequently, in a standard evasive manoeuvre, the destroyer turned towards Sweden. Sablin was not on his way to Leningrad after all, despite what he claimed in his speech to the crew. It was certainly a more prudent move for a determined revolutionary to seek safety in Swedish waters, from where he could make his appeal to the United Nations, than to sail straight into a Soviet naval base. Moreover, during the heat of the action, the Soviets could easily interpret the *Storozhevoy*'s movements as her aiming directly for Sweden.

The Tu-16K pilots rehearsed the attack procedures. Each bomber carried only one anti-ship missile, the nearly 30-foot-long Kometa K-10S Luga-S. In order for the missile to carry out the final dive towards the target vessel, the radar needed to be locked on. To that end, a Tu-16K bomber kept its radar locked on target even after launch. In addition, the missile had to be launched at least 65 miles from the target, or the onboard steering mechanism would not have time to aim correctly.[97]

Colonel General Gulyayev took the task seriously. He had ordered Savinkov to launch an anti-ship missile only on his direct order. Colonel Savinkov and his unit were now asked to prepare for weapons launch against the *Storozhevoy* from an altitude of about 2.5 miles at a range of, as far as could be ascertained, 100 miles. Gulyayev immediately gave the order to 'use the weapon'. In addition, he executed the special protocol for the launch of nuclear missiles. This protocol necessitated a mutual confirmation so as to avoid any chance of error. On his side, Gulyayev confirmed the launch order in a communication in part transited by radioman Kargin on Captain Grishkin's Il-38.[98]

Still, Savinkov did not launch his anti-ship missile. He explained to the others in the group of three that his radar had malfunctioned. The magnetron had failed. Without an operational magnetron—a high-power vacuum tube used in radar systems, notorious for the time it took to start up—Savinkov's missile was blind. Since it needed to be guided by the radar, Savinkov couldn't fire despite being in position. Instead, he ordered the other two bombers to attack the *Storozhevoy* independently. The Tu-16K bombers were on course for the target, and the three men were well aware that the nuclear launch protocol had been confirmed.[99]

At this very moment, in the command post of the headquarters of the Baltic Fleet, Vice Admiral Kosov sat with one telephone receiver in each hand. In one, he received instructions from Defence Minister Grechko. In the other telephone receiver, Kosov forwarded Grechko's orders to Colonel General Gulyayev. Then, suddenly, the head of the Operations Directorate, Rear Admiral Yakovlev, ran into the room and shouted: 'The *Storozhevoy* has halted, Comrade Commander. We must abort the attack on her!' The men at the command post quickly began to issue orders down the various chains of command to abort the attack. At 1044 hours, moments before Savinkov was to launch his anti-ship missile, frantic radio messages from the *Komsomolets Litvy* and her sister ship, the *SKR-14* which had set out from Riga 45 minutes after the *Storozhevoy*, ordered 'everyone in the air' to 'suspend the use of weapons'. At 1046, Savinkov ordered his men to abort the attack. No missile was launched.[100]

Swedish military surveillance posts were watching these developments with growing alarm. Blips filled Sweden's radar screens, showing what appeared to be every ship and plane in the Soviet Baltic Fleet heading straight at their position.[101]

Grechko realized that the Tu-16K bombers had the wrong kind of weapon load for the mission. Automatic cannon fire from the Yak-28 aircraft hardly impressed the fugitive ship and the Tu-16K bomber pilots' anti-ship missiles were lethal weapons whose use could only have one outcome. The weapon load was carefully selected for the aircraft's regular task and not dimensioned for anything else.[102] The bomber was more suited to long-range nuclear bombing missions, could be used effectively as a strike platform for anti-aircraft carrier operations or attacks against ships much larger than the *Storozhevoy*. The Yak-28 bombers were the first to open fire on *Storozhevoy* but they were completely ineffective in their attack runs; many had simply ignored their orders to fire on their own ship. Gorshkov decided that naval aviators could not be trusted and turned to the air force. He jumped several levels in the chain of command and personally ordered an aviation regiment based at Tukums Air Base, Pribaltiysk Military Region, 30 miles west of Riga, to send its new Su-24 Fencer fighter-bombers to stop the renegade vessel.[103]

Two dozen crewmen had already assembled, and before Makarov could take his seat, Air Regiment commander

Colonel Nikolai Teplov walked in and charged to the podium at the head of the room.

Everyone jumped to attention, but Teplov—normally a stickler for military etiquette—waved them down.

'Your aircraft have been fuelled, and ordnance is being loaded at this moment. In addition to ammunition for your cannons you will be carrying laser-guided bombs. You are to take off as soon as you can get to your aircraft. Captain Makarov will be in overall command once you're in the air.' Teplov gave them a hard stare. 'Dismissed.'

Makarov jumped to his feet as he stepped away from the podium, striding towards the door. 'Colonel, where are we going?'

'The Baltic!' Teplov shouted. 'Once you're in the air and assembled you'll be given the coordinates of your target.'

'Yes, sir. What target?'

'A ship, which your squadron will stop,' Teplov said. 'This is not war, I assure you. Your mission is to prevent a war, and the orders come from Minister of Defence Grechko himself.'[104]

Several Su-24 Fencer fighter-bombers took off from the airfield at Tukums, loaded with live ammunition and 500-pound bombs.[105]

'Do you mean to sink him?' Ryzhkov asked.

Makarov looked over at his co-pilot/weapons officer and nodded. 'We have our orders.'

They were flying low and slow, about 300 feet above the waves, at around 400 knots. They couldn't miss. The *Storozhevoy* was on fire and circling to port a couple of miles to the west. Perhaps the ship was slowing down, but at this speed and angle it was hard for Makarov to be sure.

He keyed his helmet mike. 'Unit Three, on my lead, let's finish this.'

They were the next wave of attack jets that had not dropped their laser-guided bombs.

This time the *Storozhevoy* had no chance whatsoever of surviving. Within a few minutes he and his crew would be at the bottom of the Baltic.

The Swedish intelligence community had begun to get a picture of what was happening. On 10 November, the collected intercepts from the weekend were compiled at the FRA Headquarters on Lovön Island, near Stockholm. The results were then reported to the intelligence and security departments of the navy, air force and the military intelligence service of the defence staff.[106]

Mutiny Over

Meanwhile, some sailors aboard the *Storozhevoy* realized where things were headed and, at 1020 hours, a group headed by Seaman Lykov joined captain lieutenants Kuzmin and Proshutinski, and Senior Lieutenant Vinogradov, in freeing Captain Potulniy, who got a pistol from one of the armouries and insisted upon going to the bridge himself. As *Storozhevoy*'s captain, he felt that he should be the one to regain control of the ship. He ordered one armed group to cover him from the fantail and another from the bow.[107] Potulniy ran onto the bridge, where Sablin was still broadcasting at the radio. After a moment's hesitation, he raised his pistol at the man who had once been his trusted advisor and pulled the trigger. Sablin fell into the corner, grasping his leg in pain. Potulniy disarmed him and sent him to his stateroom under guard. He had time to study the images on the radar screen. It looked as if the entire Russian Navy had them surrounded.[108] He quickly got on the radio and shouted in a hoarse voice, 'Ceasefire, I have regained command of the ship!'[109]

'Fighter squadrons attacking the *Storozhevoy*, this is Captain Anatoly Potulniy.'

Makarov slammed his stick hard right and full forward, ignoring the urgent voice in his headset. His jet peeled off to starboard in a steep dive toward the ship he meant to kill.

In 30 seconds the mission would be accomplished.[110]

Potulniy keyed the VHF radio again. 'Baltic Fleet Headquarters, this is Captain Anatoly Potulniy. The mutiny has been put down. Ceasefire; ceasefire! I am in command of the ship!'

'Who is this?' the radio blared.

Potulniy recognized the voice of the chief of staff. 'Admiral Kosov, it's me: Potulniy. Can you recognize my voice?'

The radio remained silent for several ominous seconds. Potulniy stared out the windows, the jets looming ever larger.

'Report your situation,' the admiral demanded.

'The mutiny has been put down, and I have regained command.'

Potulniy spoke in a breath. 'My engines have been shut down and we are slowing to a stop. Call off the attack!'

The radio went ominously silent again.

The jets were less than 200 feet out.[111]

'Break off the attack! Break off the attack!' a voice shouted in Makarov's headset.

'Ready for weapons release,' Ryzhkov reported.

Seconds.

'Break off the attack!' the same voice screamed in Makarov's headset.

He keyed his mike. 'This is Sukhoi-24 Squadron Leader Captain Makarov. Identify yourself.'

'This is Vice Admiral Kosov. Break off the attack now!'

'Unit Three, Unit Three, break off. I repeat, break off.' Makarov barked into the radio as he hauled the heavy jet hard to starboard and pulled back on the stick, sending it climbing into the sky. They had accomplished their mission. Time to go home.[112] The Su-24 dropped 500-pound bombs on the fantail, disabling the rudder, then raked the ship with cannon fire.[113] She lay dead in the water only 30 nautical miles from Gotland. The mutiny was over.

At 1100 hours, Soviet Naval Paratroopers came on board with automatic rifles. When the ship was boarded there were plain-clothes men among the new arrivals. The KGB was already taking charge. The boarding parties met no resistance; on the contrary they were met with appropriate salutes and normal military courtesies as if nothing had happened.[114] When they got back to the city, the mutineers were taken to KGB Headquarters at the corner of Lenin and Engels streets, while the enlisted men were taken to the Voroshilov Barracks near the train station.[115] The entire crew was interrogated—first by the KGB and then by senior naval officers, including Gorshkov himself.

The Soviet leadership did its best to sweep the mutiny under the rug. A story was disseminated that the activity on 9 November had, in fact, been a naval exercise during which a specially prepared target barge was attacked. The barge then drifted away until Soviet units rediscovered it on 11 November off Gotland, where it was recovered by Soviet ships.[116] Shortly after the drama, a Krivak-class destroyer in perfect condition bearing the *Storozhevoy*'s number made a conspicuous cruise along the Soviet Baltic Coast participating in a number of official celebrations in order to quell the rumours and accounts that had begun to emanate from that area.[117] Having returned to base, Colonel Savinkov and his men were ordered to destroy all documentation of the incident and not tell anybody about it.[118]

The *Storozhevoy* was towed to Liyepaya, a Latvian city on the Baltic, for repairs.[119] Among the dockyard workers was one who had a special interest in the ship as he worked for the Swedish intelligence service. He had a secure communication channel to a man in Sweden named Alex Milits who worked for the GBU, the Swedish human intelligence (HUMINT) service. He informed his contact that a warship with combat damage had been brought into port.[120] Milits asked for the name of the ship on which the mutiny had taken place. The worker reportedly answered '*Storozhevoy*' and then hung up without waiting for more questions.[121] It was not until 3 February 1976 that the CIA knew enough about it to inform President Gerald R. Ford. The news went on page 3 of the CIA's 'President's Daily Brief'.[122] *Storozhevoy* sat, ignored and rusting, at a pier in Vladivostok in the Russian Far East for decades. In 2004, it was sold to India for scrap metal.

On the morning of 10 November, Sablin, Shein and 12 others were taken to Skirotava Airfield outside Riga for a direct flight to Moscow. Two An-24 transport planes were waiting for them. They were accompanied by KGB troops. Sablin, Shein and 14 others were sent to Moscow's notorious Lefortovo Prison for interrogation. The *Storozhevoy*'s crew was detained for months, but in the end, only a handful of officers were tried. Lieutenant Shein received eight years in prison. Captain Third Rank V.M. Sablin was given the death penalty and the sentence was carried out by a firing squad in the basement of Lefortovo prison soon after a three-day trial.[123]

FIVE

The Frozen Frontier over the Ussuri

Many places in the northern hemisphere were starting to emerge from winter, but Zhenbao Island was not one of them. Icebound for half of the year, the tiny island is situated near the west bank of the Ussuri River, on the boundary between Russia and China. Just a mile long and half as wide, it seems an unlikely catalyst for a nuclear war. Yet, it nearly was just that in the spring of 1969.[1]

The Ussuri had been designated as a boundary between Russia and China in 1860 when the Treaty of Peking transferred the vast area east of Manchuria from the Qing Empire to Russia. Consequently, Russia gained a long Pacific coastline, including the port of Vladivostok. The arcane question of whether Zhenbao Island was an island in the river or a feature of the Chinese bank became tense as relations between the USSR and China floundered in the 1960s due to a mix of ideological, strategic and political disagreements. Clashes, with occasional casualties, had become frequent at several spots along the border, though none were as serious as the Zhenbao Island skirmish.[2]

There were several border-related issues that led to the build-up of Sino-Soviet tensions: differences over the exact location and ownership of Zhenbao Island; validation and differences over border treaty implementation; and problems of administering the border area, including river navigation. The number of Chinese 'systematic provocations' began to increase in mid-1962. By 1967, border relations were leading towards a conflict.[3]

Mao Zedong and other Chinese leaders continued to pledge eternal friendship with the Soviet people, but undertook no measures to support these claims in practice. In the mid-1950s, Chinese newspapers began to publish articles on the border question with the USSR. The People's Republic of China's (PRC) government publishers were already publishing maps identifying Soviet territories as having at one time been lost by China. Starting in 1960, hostility in relations with the USSR became open, and it was at this time that a long-term practice (lasting up to 1969) of organizing all kinds of provocations at the border began.

In 1959, after the festive celebrations in honour of the tenth anniversary of the Chinese Communist Party (CCP), Mao invited Soviet Premier Nikita Khrushchev to his residence near Peking. He met him in the swimming pool and suggested that Khrushchev join him. The problem, however, was that Khrushchev could not swim. He could only go into the water up to his waist and sit down to immerse himself, as he had done on a vacation in Pitsunda, Abkhazia. His predicament was unimaginably awkward when compared with his host, who could swim across the almost mile-wide Yangtze!

Khrushchev was furious! That very evening he announced that he was postponing the week-long trip across China and returning to the Motherland. The reasons for the fall-out between Peking and Moscow, which sustained a 30-year confrontation and fighting on Damansky Island, were not only ideological disagreements, but also the personal enmity between the two leaders. Recollections of his helplessness while floundering in the swimming pool next to 'the great helmsman' strengthened Khrushchev's rage.[4]

In 1964 Mao pronounced at the Communist Party Plenary

session: 'Approximately 100 years ago the region east of Baikal became Russian territories, and since then Vladivostok, Khabarovsk, Kamchatka, and other points have been territory of the Soviet Union. We still have not submitted a bill for this list.' There was no delay in submitting the bill: soon the Chinese leadership announced a list of claims: one million square miles of Soviet territory, including the cities of Khabarovsk, Vladivostok, Blagoveshchensk and others, which rose to about two million square miles in unofficial talks.[5]

Sun Yatsen, the first president of the Republic of China, also viewed the expansive lands of neighbouring countries as Chinese. Chiang Kaishek even compiled a special list of territories that had been 'torn away' from the Chinese: Burma, the Amur River basin, Annam. It also included territories from which Chinese overlords had extracted tribute: Thailand, Nepal, Bhutan, Borneo, Java and Ceylon. Mao moved this problem to a practical plane.[6]

As Sino-Soviet tensions heightened in the 1960s, ownership of the tiny, uninhabited islands along the Ussuri became bones of contention. The Soviet Union argued that China had no legal claim to them. According to Moscow, the Treaty of Peking clearly identified the boundary line between China and the Soviet Union in this area as running along the Chinese riverbank.[7] Both countries recognized the Amur and Ussuri rivers as their boundary. But they could not agree on the exact demarcation line along the rivers which had legal implications concerning the ownership of hundreds of small islands in the rivers.[8]

In January 1966, the Soviets signed a mutual defence treaty with Mongolia which allowed Soviet troops and military equipment to be stationed there. The Chinese threat was a key reason for the new alliance. According to the treaty, the Soviet and Mongolian forces would 'jointly' defend their respective territories. In 1967, the Soviets deployed the Scaleboard (SS-12) tactical nuclear system, a single-stage, liquid-fuelled, road-mobile missile with a 500-mile range and a 500-kiloton warhead to the border.[9]

Mao read Sun Tzu but he also read books on warfare written by Western writers. He particularly favoured Charles Tilly's famous dictum, 'War makes the state.'[10] He saw the need to create an international conflict to divert public attention from domestic problems. Politically, the Sino-Soviet military clashes were primarily the result of Mao Zedong's domestic mobilization strategies connected to his concerns about the impasse of the Cultural Revolution. The Chinese were in the midst of the 1965 military strategy debate; the power struggle preceding the Cultural Revolution had led to the purge of the army chief of staff, Lo Jui-ch'ing, and the army had lost capability due to Lin Piao's efforts to use 'Mao Zedong Thought' to enhance military prowess. Additionally, the Vietnam War directed Chinese military attention primarily to its southern flank. Thus, they were unable to counter the Soviet build-up.[11]

The Cultural Revolution and factional party politics constituted a dramatic decline in China's ability to project power over territory disputed with the Soviet Union. As the instability of the Cultural Revolution deepened, the PLA became the bulwark of maintaining law and order.[12] In 1967 and 1968, PLA units assumed administrative control of the provincial governments and deployed troops around the country to maintain domestic stability.[13] China's leaders viewed the growing Soviet military pressure during the chaos of the Cultural Revolution as being designed to profit from China's weakness and compel a change in its domestic and foreign policies. Mao was facing political rebellion, instability and social disorder. He apparently believed that the Soviets might intervene in China to support the 'revisionist' faction in the Cultural Revolution.[14]

Another key moment in escalating Sino-Soviet tensions was the Soviet invasion of Czechoslovakia in August 1968 and the proclamation of the 'Brezhnev Doctrine' that the Soviets had the right to overthrow any communist government that was diverging from what was defined by the Kremlin. Mao saw the

Brezhnev Doctrine as the ideological justification for a Soviet invasion of China to overthrow him and launched a massive domestic propaganda campaign attacking the invasion of Czechoslovakia.[15]

In remarks to an Albanian delegation on China's national day, Zhou Enlai linked Soviet actions in Eastern Europe with further 'provocations' against China, including 'deploying large numbers of troops on the Chinese-Soviet and Chinese-Mongolian border.' Zhou gave a speech that tied Soviet revisionism with a possible invasion, while chief of the People's Liberation Army (PLA) General Staff Huang Yongsheng stressed concerns about Soviet troops on the border.[16] Chinese fears of war intensified when Beijing learned that Moscow was asking Warsaw Pact nations on how they would respond to nuclear attacks on the PRC.[17] The Sino-Soviet rivalry was centred on leadership of the communist bloc and it was one that China was losing in the late 1960s, especially after the start of the Cultural Revolution.[18]

Approximately 70 per cent of the USSR's troops in the Far East were based along the border with Manchuria. Although this was dictated by the need to defend the Trans-Siberian Railway which ran along the Chinese-Soviet border, it was nevertheless threatening to the Chinese.[19] By 1969, the total number of Soviet Army divisions facing China had increased from 14 in 1965 to as many as 34. These deployments represented a dramatic increase in the number of Soviet troops facing China since the late 1950s.[20] The Soviets had about 600 tactical aircraft in the region, while China had only 294.[21]

By contrast, China deployed only nine divisions near the border, placing the rest in reserve 300 or more miles away.[22] Marshal Chen Yi, a prominent Chinese military leader, politician and diplomat, suggested in an interview published in a Brazilian paper that the Soviet Union was planning to attack China in alliance with the United States.[23] For China's leaders, it was likely not a coincidence that Soviet military deployments increased during the Cultural Revolution.[24] China was worried about a second front apart from the Vietnam War.

The Chinese historian Li Danhui wrote, 'Already in 1968, China began preparations to create a small war on the border.' She noted that prior to March 1969, the Chinese troops had twice attempted to provoke a clash along the border, 'but the Soviets, feeling weak, did not accept the Chinese challenge and retreated.'[25] As China's position in the dispute declined during a period of internal political instability, China's leaders chose to respond with force.[26] Historian Niu Jun noted that 'it cannot be denied that the limited attack against the Soviets and China's internal political situation were closely linked.'[27] Zhou told Mao that the Soviet Union might use nuclear weapons. Mao replied that nuclear weapons simply were not a relevant factor in the conflict as it was a limited, one-time effort designed to signal resolve and deter future aggression.

CCP leaders were concerned that Soviet leader Leonid Brezhnev might act more aggressively than he had in Czechoslovakia, and not just send Soviet tanks steamrolling into China to reaffirm Soviet leadership over international socialism but make good on Moscow's threat of a nuclear strike.[28] Mao had devised a pre-emptive scheme to deter Moscow from launching a large-scale invasion.[29] The secret Third Front Project[30] was an enormously costly endeavour, relocating Chinese heavy and military industries from coastal cities to a remote inland base. The project was well underway by the time of the border clash, but the fighting only confirmed PRC fears of the Soviet Union and caused redoubled efforts to pour money into a project that dramatically altered the economic trajectory of the nation.[31]

Majority of China's industrial clusters were situated in the 14 big coastal cities. These industries were prone to air raids or a nuclear strike and so the General Staff suggested researching measures to guard against a sudden attack.[32] Afraid that the Soviet Union could demolish Chinese industry with a few air raids or nuclear strikes, nearly 400 state-owned enterprises were moved from coastal cities to clandestine mountain locations.[33] Third Front construction picked back up in 1969 in response to Sino-Soviet border clashes at Zhenbao Island.

The Planning

Mao held a meeting with the CCP National Congress and the Central Committee at the Communist Party HQ in Peking. It was decided to launch an attack on Soviet border forces on Zhenbao Island. The armed clash was to be used to incite nationalist feelings in the PRC and use it to strike against the internal enemies of the CCP. This would be a step along the road to ensuring Maoist supremacy and as a means of mobilizing support for the upcoming 9th Party Congress.[34] At the meeting Mao said: 'We should let the Soviets in, which will help us in our mobilization.'[35] A common external enemy that might provide cohesion was valuable for the survival of China's leaders.[36] Mao also presented another goal of the armed clash—to start rapprochement talks with the Americans.

The ambush on Zhenbao Island was part of a larger endeavour to deter future Soviet provocations and force Moscow to recognize that the current Sino-Soviet border was to be re-negotiated. Moscow knew well that such an admission would raise into question large tracts of its territory and rejected Beijing's assertions.[37]

China's Central Military Commission (CMC)—the highest national defence organization in the People's Republic of China—ordered the Beijing and Shenyang military districts to prepare for a plan for the ambush. The MDs were instructed to select a politically advantageous time, place and situation, make preparations in advance, create an action plan that accounted for multiple possibilities, and conduct a focused and planned attack against the Soviets. The CMC emphasized that border patrols were to strictly follow the principle of proportionality in engagements with Soviet forces. Mao instructed commanders to limit the scale of conflict to a local border skirmish.[38] He authorized Premier Zhou Enlai to oversee the operation and the CMC took direct control of the attack.[39]

Xiao Quanfu—deputy commander-in-chief of the Shenyang Military Command (responsible for China's northern borders)—visited the PLA chief of staff in Beijing to discuss the plan. Prior to Xiao's visit, the Shenyang Military Command had submitted a report to the top PLA leadership, Mao and Zhou.[40] In accordance with these instructions, the Shenyang MR dispatched a small group of select troops to Qiliqin to begin preparations for an attack.[41] The General Staff instructed the military districts to 'strive for suddenness of action', 'fight quickly' and 'avoid entanglement'. The forces were ordered to retreat to a safe location after achieving victory, and to obtain 'reliable proof', such as confiscating Soviet weapons and equipment or taking pictures.[42]

At the end of January 1969, China's Heilongjiang MR, with agreement from the Shenyang MR, proposed the 'Zhenbao Island Counter Interference Struggle Plan', which was essentially a continuation of the 1968 preparations for an attack at Qiliqin. On 19 February the Central Committee of the Chinese Communist Party, the PLA and the Ministry of Foreign Affairs approved the plan. Zhenbao was the ideal place for an attack because it was on the Chinese side of the river. An attack at Zhenbao had important tactical advantages for China: the area along the Chinese bank was elevated, thereby giving troops, artillery and commanders stationed there superior line-of-sight; the Chinese bank was approximately 300 feet from the island, whereas the Soviet bank was around 1,300 feet away; and the nearest Chinese border post was much closer than the nearest Soviet post.[43] Zhenbao was the only such island in the Ussuri River that was situated near a hilltop on the Chinese side, which created a substantial tactical advantage for the ambush, as the Soviets lacked any high ground on their side of the river.[44]

Kang Sheng—the Chinese intelligence chief in the Ministry of State Security—provided crucial details for the operation. He recommended 2 March for the attack for two reasons. Firstly, considerable Soviet border guard forces were involved in joint exercises with the troops of the Far Eastern Military District and therefore could not immediately take part in the battle. Secondly, around this time Russia celebrated Shrovetide, that is, bid farewell to winter. The organizers of the provocation were relying on the hospitality of the local Soviet authorities, for whom an invitation to dinner for the chief of the border guards seemed to be a completely natural matter. Thus, the advance of the Chinese was well thought out and organized in absolute secrecy.[45]

Afterward, the Shenyang Military District transferred around 600 elite troops to the Zhenbao area to begin preparations for the ambush. Senior commanders from the CMC and Shenyang MR supervised the preparations.[46] The Shenyang and Beijing MRs increased their alert status and strengthened border defence preparations. The Heilongjiang Military District (MD) proposed a plan for attacking Soviet patrols using three companies, with one of them hidden from view to surprise the Soviets.[47]

The Skirmish

The 2 March Ambush

A PLA regiment arrived at Damansky. The Soviet border guards attentively followed what was happening on Chinese territory. It was established that mass rallies, with the participation of Chinese military personnel, had taken place in populated border areas, at which 'Repel the Soviet revisionists' could be heard.[48] On 2 March, after preparations were complete, the PLA local command post ordered two groups to patrol the island, one in plain view and the other hidden from the Soviets.[49]

On the night of 1–2 March 1969, around 300 PLA infantrymen crossed over to Damansky Island and lay among the bushes and trees on the higher western bank of the island. The Soviet soldiers were in their tents in the snow, warming up with rice vodka and snacking on biscuits. The vodka was rationed at 100 grams per man, with the condition that it be used in small swallows over a long period of time on the advice of military doctors. The temperature had dropped to minus 27 degrees Celsius. To support the subunits landing on Damansky Island, recoilless rifles, medium machine guns, and mortar positions were outfitted on the Chinese riverbank. Hundreds of PLA infantrymen lay biding their time.[50]

Soviet border guards Private Aleksandr Shevtsov and Private Vladimir Koyakhov were stationed at the Mount Kafyla Observation Post, but they neither saw nor heard anything—no fire, no sounds. The distance of the post from the island was more than two miles, and visibility was obscured by snowfall.[51]

At around 2240 hours Soviet local time, they noticed the advance of a group of around 30 armed men from the Hunzy Border Post on the Chinese side in the direction of Damansky. Meanwhile, at first the Chinese had held a small rally, accompanied by the waving of Mao's quotation books; then they set off for the island. Private Shevtsov, who was the senior man of the border detail, immediately reported this by telephone to the Nizhne-Mikhaylovka Outpost, which was located about four miles southeast of the island. Senior Lieutenant Ivan Strelnikov, chief of the outpost, called his subordinates 'to arms' after which he called the border detachment's duty officer and his neighbour, Vitaly Bubenin.[52]

Commander Strelnikov and his subordinates set off for the island in two armoured personnel carriers—a truck and a command car. After arriving, Strelnikov and several others dismounted and moved out to warn the oncoming Chinese that they were trespassing on sovereign Soviet territory, as they had done several times before. Up to this point, these confrontations had typically involved little more than shouting, fistfights and the occasional use of clubs, sticks and fire hoses.

The Soviets strapped their automatic rifles to their chests and linked arms to prevent the Chinese from passing. A verbal altercation took place at this point. The Chinese arrayed themselves in rows and appeared to be unarmed. Then suddenly the front row of the Chinese stepped aside to reveal a second line of soldiers. At that point, the 300 Chinese troops who had secretly dug foxholes on the island the night before emerged from their hiding places and pulled submachine guns from under their coats, opening fire on the Soviets.[53] Strelnikov and six others were killed outright. Mortar, machine-gun, and anti-tank fire also commenced from the Chinese bank.[54] After two hours of fighting, there were 31 dead Soviet border guards and 14 wounded.[55] Reinforcements from a nearby Soviet border outpost arrived and forced the Chinese to retreat to their side of the riverbank.[56]

The 15 March Skirmish

An operations group of officers from the Pacific Ocean Border District Headquarters was created for the purpose of directing the combat operations against China. Located at the Nizhne-Mikhaylovka Outpost, the group was headed by Colonel G.P. Sechkin. After the ambush on 2 March, the 135th MRD—consisting of infantry, tanks and artillery—commanded by General Major V.K. Nesov was deployed in the rear several miles from Damansky. Another army operations group headed by Colonel N.A. Yegerev was organized to coordinate operations with the border guards. Soviet border guard details continuously arrived on Damansky Island.[57] The troops were supported by large numbers of tanks, armoured vehicles, heavy-calibre guns, one motorized infantry battalion, one tank battalion, four heavy-artillery battalions, 50 tanks, and approximately 10,000 artillery rounds.[58]

The Soviet Air Force conducted an air reconnaissance over the area. The aircraft detected a large number of campfires on the Chinese side, around six miles from Damansky. The Soviet Air Commander assumed that this was a concentration of infantry about the size of a battalion. At the same time, technical equipment for listening to any sounds on the island showed that there were no Chinese on Damansky. At 0330 hours on 15 March, a new order arrived from General Lobanov: occupy the island. Lieutenant Colonel Yanshin—the commander of a motorized manoeuvre group of the Iman Border Detachment—was assigned the task. At 0530 hours, Nikolay Ivanovich Popov gave the command to disperse along the swamp ice interspersed with grass and dry branches. The other two groups (Klyga's and Senior Lieutenant Solovyev's) set up behind a bend in the swamp. The Soviets lay in the trenches, listening to the terrain. They were thirsty but had no water; therefore, they resorted to 'Duchess' hard candies.

After dawn fully broke, the Chinese turned on their loudspeaker and began their propaganda against the Soviets. The first: 'Officers and soldiers of the Soviet Army, you have violated the border of the PRC, this is an armed provocation against the Chinese people. You must leave Chinese territory, otherwise you will be held responsible for what happens.' The second was a long speech, which said that Damansky Island and other islands were Chinese. It ended with: 'Down with the new tsars. Down with Brezhnev!'[59]

At 0940 hours, the PLA launched their attack with the support of covering fire. Troops started advancing to the island from behind their support rampart located on the Chinese riverbank (apparently left behind by the Japanese). Immediately after automatic fire from small arms, the Chinese opened heavy mortar and artillery fire from the hills along the island. Two Soviet groups (Solovyev's and Klyga's) fell under this fire. A furious battle began. Soviet APCs began to fire from the turret machine guns, simultaneously manoeuvring so as not to fall into the field of fire.

Colonel Sechkin reported the situation to the Far East Military District Headquarters, saying the observers from 135th MRD's artillery regiment had detected the location of Chinese mortar batteries and artillery which were firing on the Soviet troops. The one thing needed was permission, but there was none. Despite strong shelling, Soviet border guard casualties were minimal—five wounded, none killed. Communications were lost between Yanshin and the riverbank; it was explained later that antennas on the APCs were cut by their own machine-gun fire from the rotating turrets. The Soviets fought for an hour and a half. By 1100 hours, the defenders' ammunition had begun to run out and three APCs had been damaged. Under these conditions, Yanshin decided to leave the island for a while to carry off the wounded, replace the APCs and replenish ammunition. The Chinese, seeing the withdrawal of the border guards from Damansky, quickly occupied positions along the bank in the southern and western parts of the island.[60]

The fighting on the island took on a sporadic character: disparate groups of border guards continued to attack and repel the Chinese, who were significantly superior numerically. Several tanks involved in the battle substantially helped the border guards. Despite all the reinforcements, however, the numerical superiority of the Chinese was very sizeable—approximately 10:1. After 1400 hours, around 200 Chinese ran across to Damansky. They continued to come in large groups, and the firing almost stopped.

A Soviet mortar battery from the 135th Motor Rifle Division opened fire along the channel between Damansky and the Chinese riverbank, but all this was not enough to repel the expected enemy attack. Thus, the real threat of losing Damansky arose. It became obvious that a command decision had to be made quickly. However, none of those invested with power wanted to take the responsibility—neither the division command, nor the district command, nor the generals from the Ministry of Defence and General Staff. Everyone understood that in case of complications one could lose not only one's position and rank but also something more serious. As for the top officials of the state, general secretary of the Soviet Union Brezhnev was on his way to Budapest to participate in a meeting of the Warsaw Pact's Political Advisory Committee.[61]

The news of the second Chinese attack soon reached General Secretary Brezhnev. He called the generals and ordered them in no uncertain terms to use all resources on hand to liberate the island. The Soviets deployed the top-secret T-62 tanks, and after a Politburo debate and Brezhnev's approval, used the top-secret BM-21 Grad System—a truck-mounted system with a 40-tube rocket launcher—for the first time.[62]

The Russians, adopting American Korean War tactics, allowed the Chinese to advance and then counter-attacked with a large number of tanks, armoured cars and infantry in armoured personnel carriers. Soviet artillery launched a fierce barrage at 1400 hours, raking Chinese positions as far as four miles inland. Three such attacks were mounted, each breaking through Chinese positions.[63]

At 1700 hours, two artillery battalions, a rocket battalion and a 120 mm mortar battery from the 199th Motorized Rifle Regiment opened fire against areas of concentration of Chinese troops and their fire positions.[64] The Soviets fired 10,000 artillery rounds in a nine-hour engagement with the Chinese. A ground attack was carried out by 36 sorties conducted by Soviet MiG fighter aircraft.[65] After the shelling and suppression of the gunners, the Chinese ran off the island. The Soviets didn't have any spare barrels, so it was necessary to detach and cool it down in the snow (a barrel had to be changed after 500 shots). Otherwise it overheated and firing would be ineffective.[66]

The raid was exceptionally precise: artillery and mortar

shells destroyed the Chinese weapons systems and soldiers. Information from radio interception attested to the hundreds of dead PLA soldiers and commanders. Approximately 120 soldiers from the 199th Regiment's 2nd Motorized Rifle Battalion on 12 APCs (commanded by Lieutenant Colonel Aleksandr Ivanovich Smirnov) and 80 border guards on 6 APCs (commanded by chief of the Political Department of the Iman Border Detachment Lieutenant Colonel Aleksandr Dmitriyevich Konstantinov) took part in the attack. At around 1830 hours, Damansky was completely liberated.[67]

Soviet soldiers withdrew to their riverbank while the Chinese made no more attempts to capture the island. PLA understood that further continuation would lead to a wider conflict which would be detrimental to China.[68] The battle was over at 1900 hours, having lasted more than nine hours. By 2000 hours on 15 March, after the Chinese had been completely driven off the island, the Soviet sapper units mined the southern part of the island.[69] The Russians lost about 60 men while the Chinese lost 800.[70]

In the aftermath of the conflict, Moscow alerted the Strategic Rocket Forces in the Far East. Mao told the Central Cultural Revolution group, 'We are now confronted with a formidable enemy… Our nuclear bases should be prepared for the enemy's air bombardment.'[71]

A cold Antarctic breeze, scattered with ice-cold drops of rain, was sweeping over Washington, DC. Fog had settled on the empty streets which were slippery with the sleet that had formed the previous evening. CIA director Richard Helms was working late in his Langley office. He was being briefed by the CIA, director of analysis, chief of European Bureau and the Soviet Bureau on the Sino-Soviet crisis. At 0530 hours, Helms rushed to the White House to meet President Richard Nixon. After a quick security check at the main gate, Helms stepped out of his car and hurried along one of the narrow, carpeted hallways in the West Wing of the White House. Nixon was already sitting in the Oval Office flanked by Henry Kissinger, who had taken over as the president's national security advisor in January 1969. Helms described the conflict as having explosive potential which could have wider ramifications in the Far East and Europe. He stated that 'the potential for a war between them clearly exists,' including a Soviet attack on Chinese nuclear facilities. China appeared to view the USSR as its most immediate enemy. Nixon was concerned about the crisis unfolding parallel to the Vietnam War, but Kissinger sat quietly on a cushioned chair beside Helms. In his typical husky voice, he said, 'We should shake hands with China.'

How It All Ended

Though Beijing never prepared for—or wanted—a war, the ambush was the most serious instance of violence between China and the USSR and was perceived as an act of treachery by Soviet leaders, requiring a firm response. This raised the dangerous prospect of a larger war along the vast border extending from Central Asia to the Sea of Japan.[72] Moscow interpreted China's actions as aggressive and emblematic of an increasingly revisionist and antagonistic regime in Beijing.[73]

A meeting was arranged by Brezhnev's political secretary at Kremlin. In it, Brezhnev directed the top military generals to recommend the future course of action. The Soviet Union decided to implement diplomacy backed by force. The Politburo members unanimously arrived at the conclusion that the force would be nuclear. Brezhnev implemented an effective strategy of superior but measured demonstrations of force and consistent communications across numerous channels, including through foreign interlocutors. The military strategy was to be led by marshal of the Soviet Union Matvei Zakharov and the coercive diplomacy was led by Soviet Premier Alexei Kosygin. The final objective was to send a message to the Chinese leadership that the escalatory ladder will lead to decapitation strike on its top leadership.[74]

Moscow immediately sought high-level diplomatic talks within a week of the 15 March clash. China's shrill propaganda warnings had disappeared after 15 March, likely signalling that the leadership had soberly reassessed the discrepancy in military power in less ideological terms.[75] Six days after the 15 March clash began—and one day after Moscow took its Strategic Rocket Forces off high-alert status—Soviet Premier Alexei Kosygin called the Chinese leadership on a direct hotline set up during the days of socialist solidarity. His call was rejected by the operator, who called him a 'revisionist element'. Brushing this off, Kosygin had the Soviet Embassy in Beijing contact the Chinese Foreign Ministry to arrange a top leadership call. This too was rejected, with the ministry telling the Soviet government that traditional diplomatic channels should be used instead of a direct phone call.[76]

On 29 March 1969, in light of the unsuccessful attempts to reach out to Chinese leaders, the Soviet government dispatched a formal diplomatic note proposing consultations.[77] When Moscow followed up on 11 April to propose border consultations on 15 April, Beijing mentioned, 'We will give you a reply, please calm down a little and do not get excited.'[78]

Exercising forbearance and understanding China's chaotic political climate, Moscow sought to use other channels. First, Moscow proposed—and Beijing accepted—lower-level talks on the topic of river navigation beginning in mid-June. The talks went nowhere but they got the diplomatic ball rolling.[79] Second, Moscow took its message directly to the Chinese people early on through Chinese language radio broadcasts that described in great detail the Soviet Union's missile superiority, exclaiming that 'the destructive range of these rockets is practically unlimited.'[80]

On 1 August 1969, US president Richard Nixon visited

Pakistan, a close ally of China, and requested General Yahya Khan to pass a message to Mao that he wanted to normalize relations with China, especially due to the Ussuri crisis with the Soviet Union. China responded with unprecedented speed to the proposal, and in early 1969—in a highly unusual manner—Mao Zedong ordered the publication of the newly-elected President Richard M. Nixon's inaugural address in all major Chinese newspapers. Henry Kissinger secretly visited China for a meeting with Zhou in 1971. Three years later, Nixon would visit China and personally meet Mao in Beijing.[81]

Most importantly, Soviet diplomats and agents around the world planted the seeds of nuclear threat, understanding that Beijing would eventually get wind of these messages.[82] The Soviets increased the pressure on the military side. The minister of defence Marshal A.A. Grechko planned to deliver a preventive strike against Chinese nuclear facilities. In the 1960s the United States was probing the level of Soviet interest in joint action against Chinese nuclear weapons facilities; now the Soviets probed what the US reaction would be if the Soviets attacked the facilities.[83]

Thus, on 18 August 1969, a very unusual conversation between B.N. Davydov, second secretary of the Soviet Embassy in Washington, DC, and William Stearman, a mid-level State Department official in the Bureau of Intelligence and Research, took place during lunch in the Americana Hotel. Davydov began the conversation with some secondary questions about Vietnam but quickly switched to the Ussuri crisis. The Soviet diplomat asked what the reaction of the American leadership would be to a preventive strike by the USSR against Chinese nuclear facilities. Struck by this news, the American made it clear how serious this conversation was. Davydov confirmed the seriousness of the conversation and then explained the goals that the USSR was pursuing in planning such an operation. First, the Chinese nuclear threat would be eliminated for decades. Second, such a strike would weaken and discredit Mao and his group to such an extent that the army commanders and party cadre who did not agree with him would be able to topple him in a coup.

Stearman, surprised by the question and cautious in his answer, replied that while he was 'in no position to predict exactly what the US would do,' he believed the nation would view a major Sino-Soviet conflict 'with considerable concern' and would 'most certainly want to keep out of any such conflict.'[84] Given the drawbacks of overt support for either side, the US concluded that a policy of neutrality would 'provide maximum flexibility'.[85]

Thus, Moscow threatened a nuclear response. In June, Soviet bomber units were moved from Western Europe to Mongolia and Siberia, where they engaged in military exercises that included practice strikes on Chinese nuclear facilities.[86] Moscow also announced that Colonel General Vladimir F. Tolubko, the former deputy commander of the Strategic Rocket Forces, had been appointed as the new head of the Far Eastern Military District. Beijing did not miss the significance—or, in its view, the apparent signal—of the appointment of a commander with significant experience in nuclear weapons to oversee Soviet forces in the Sino-Soviet border region.[87]

In Washington, DC, Richard Helms told the press that the Soviets had been approaching the Warsaw Pact nations about an attack on China's nuclear programme. Several newspaper articles discussing the CIA and State Department's views on the Soviet probes appeared over the next few days, thereby ensuring that Beijing was informed of Moscow's activities.[88]

The Chinese leadership became increasingly concerned about the possibility of a Soviet nuclear strike, particularly an attack on China's nuclear facilities in Xinjiang. Upon learning of Helms's announcement, China immediately issued orders for war preparations. On 27 August, the Central Committee and the CMC issued an order establishing a 'Leading Group for People's

Air Defence', headed by Zhou. The group issued orders for the preparation of large-scale evacuations of the population and dispersing critical industries out of large cities. Beijing instructed citizens in major cities to dig air-raid shelters and stockpile basic necessities.

The next day, the Central Committee issued an order for 'General Mobilization in Border Provinces and Regions', which instructed both citizens and the military along the border to be fully prepared to fight a war against aggression. Military personnel were ordered to stay at their posts and protect key military positions and transportation routes. Mass revolutionary organizations were to be 'dissolved immediately', factional struggles had to be 'stopped immediately', all weapons 'handed back', and all labourers were to return to work 'so that extensive support can be given to the front-line'. By 30 August, the US press was reporting troop movements, military training and other war preparations in China.[89] In response to the Soviet threat, local authorities in China started the construction of multi-level underground bomb shelters (repurposed in the 1980s as seedy shopping malls).[90]

The reliance on conventional forces for deterrence reflected a prevailing view in Beijing that China's nascent nuclear arsenal could not effectively deter a Soviet nuclear attack. China had been a nuclear power for less than five years and its forces were small in number and highly vulnerable to a first strike. The CIA estimated that China had less than 10 single-stage, liquid-fuelled DF-2 medium-range ballistic missiles and a handful of strategic bombers—a strategic arsenal that a capable opponent could destroy in a pre-emptive or preventive strike. Moreover, China had paid scant attention to nuclear strategy and doctrine beyond a commitment to a minimalist force posture and a 'No First Use' policy. In November 1968, Mao told E.F. Hill, a leader in the Australian Communist Party, 'Our country, in a sense, is still a non-nuclear power. With this little nuclear weaponry, we cannot be counted as a nuclear country. If we are to fight a war, we must use conventional weapons.'[91]

On 5 May 1969, after the eruption of the Ussuri River crisis, Kosygin travelled to India to discuss the possibility of a Soviet-Indian alliance against China with Prime Minister Indira Gandhi. China was India's enemy and the two countries had fought a war in 1962. PM Indira Gandhi was hesitant to sign the proposed Indo-Soviet Treaty considering US and domestic political opposition. But US secretary of state Henry Kissinger's secret visit to China with Pakistan's assistance and his subsequent conversation with the Indian ambassador to the US, L.K. Jha, changed the military dynamics of South Asia. Kissinger told Jha that the US would not get involved if China intervened in a war between India and Pakistan. Jha immediately briefed Indira Gandhi about the US position which compelled her to authorize the Indian Ministry of External Affairs to proceed with the treaty. China was a common enemy of Soviet Union and India.

The Soviets proposed an article that would plan for a mutual defence in case of an outbreak of conflict with a third party. Article IX of the treaty stated, 'In the event of either Party being subjected to and attach or a threat thereof, the High Contracting Parties shall immediately enter into mutual consultations in order to remover (sic) such threat and to take appropriate effective measures to ensure peace and the security of their countries.'

Both countries signed the 'Treaty of Peace, Friendship and Cooperation' in 1971. During the Ussuri crisis, the Soviet Union had deployed 18 army divisions on its border with China in Siberia. The Soviet force structure was maintained in accordance with Article IX of the treaty to deter China from launching an attack on India in support of Pakistan during the Indo-Pak war of 1971.[92]

Soviet threats to launch missiles against China's nuclear programme in Xinjiang finally brought the PRC to the negotiating table. The first meeting was held on 11 September

1969 in Beijing.[93] The Chinese agreed for the meeting on one condition: that the meeting was to be informal and take place outside of the Chinese capital. Peking Airport was deemed to be the best place. On the early morning of 11 September 1969, the staff of Beijing Airport observed an unlikely scene: Chinese premier Zhou Enlai and his Soviet counterpart, Aleksei Kosygin, were having a polite conversation over breakfast. Other Soviets in attendance were secretary of the Soviet Union K.F. Katushev and deputy chairman of the Supreme Soviet M.A. Yasnov; other Chinese in attendance were deputy premiers of the PRC State Council Li Xiangnian and Xie Fuzhi.[94]

Kosygin particularly stressed the need for the quickest resolution of all differences that had accumulated between the two countries. Zhou Enlai did not object but his main priority was the resolution of the border issues. He declared that 'China has no territorial claims with regard to the Soviet Union' and acknowledged the current border.[95] At the outset, Zhou brought up the rumours of a possible Soviet attack on China's nuclear facilities and asked Kosygin to clarify the Soviet intentions. He sought to convince Kosygin that nuclear aggression against China was unnecessary and candidly commented that the Soviets 'must be well aware of China's nuclear weapons capability'. He reminded the Soviets that China's nuclear capability was small and rudimentary, and not a serious threat requiring pre-emptive action. Zhou also reminded the Soviet premier that China 'had its hands full' with domestic issues, especially the Cultural Revolution, and had no desire for war.[96] The discussion continued for about three hours. The Soviets had successfully coerced—or, more precisely, *compelled*—China to come to the negotiating table.[97]

But on the evening of the meeting, Chinese officials became concerned that the session was a trick—a Trojan Horse—designed to get a Soviet airplane into Beijing airspace carrying Soviet special forces apart from the premier and his delegation. The Soviet Union had used a similar tactic the year before in Czechoslovakia. As a result, Mao ordered Zhou to put military forces in the area on alert and move several units to the airport. Army officers and civilians alike were told to expect an inevitable attack.[98] Lin and Mao came to the conclusion that Kosygin's visit was actually a 'smokescreen' for a future strike, just like the Japanese special envoy's meeting with President Roosevelt before the attack on Pearl Harbor.[99]

To make matters worse, just as Beijing was beginning to pore over the details of the airport meeting, a 16 September article in the *London Evening News* further stoked Chinese concerns, as it contained some of the most specific Soviet nuclear threats of the Sino-Soviet conflict. The author of the article was Victor Louis, a Soviet citizen with close KGB connections. His article said there was not 'a shadow of a doubt that Russian nuclear installations stand aimed at the Chinese nuclear facilities.' The Soviet Union, he wrote, clearly 'prefers using rockets to manpower' and had 'a variety of rockets to choose from'. As if hinting at the possibility of a surprise attack, Louis wrote, 'Whether or not the Soviet Union will dare to attack Lop Nor…is a question of strategy, and so the world would only learn about it afterwards.'[100]

The Louis article and the re-examination of the airport meeting prompted more extensive emergency war preparations in China. Mao ordered the CMC to transfer elite military units from the south to the north; the air force began moving surface-to-air missile battalions to the northern city of Zhangjiakou; and new tank divisions were formed. At a PLA conference on 22 September, Zhou remarked that the situation was 'extremely tense', and that China 'must be fully prepared'. According to the Indian Foreign Ministry, China had even stepped up efforts to move some of its nuclear facilities to Tibet.[101]

On 23 September, China conducted its first underground nuclear test, and just six days later, it tested a thermonuclear device. In conducting these tests, Beijing was uncharacteristically quiet and circumspect. While China had widely publicized its previous nuclear tests, Beijing delayed the public announcement of the September tests until early October. Even then, the tests were 'virtually ignored' by the Chinese press. The Chinese leaders were acutely sensitive to the political and military dangers of nuclear saber-rattling and consequently sought to underplay the tests in order to avoid overtly antagonizing Moscow.[102]

On 26 September, Kosygin responded to Zhou's 18 September letter and proposed that formal negotiations begin in Beijing in early October. Zhou responded favourably to Kosygin's offer, suggesting in his reply that negotiations commence in Beijing on 20 October.[103] The Chinese leadership—especially Lin—became even more concerned about a nuclear sneak attack. Chinese National Day, an annual celebration commemorating the founding of the PRC, was scheduled for 1 October, and Lin was worried that the Soviets might 'take advantage of the holiday to launch a surprise attack'. In order to be prepared for such an attack, Lin ordered the military to enter 'first-degree combat readiness'. Airplanes stationed at airports around Beijing were dispersed to other locations; obstacles were placed on runways to prevent Soviet planes from landing; and airport workers were given weapons and told to be prepared 'to shoot at enemy paratroopers'.[104] China was preparing for a nuclear attack by the Soviet Union. Lin, second to Mao, ordered 940,000 soldiers, 4,000 planes and 600 vessels to scatter from their bases, and the transfer of major archives from Beijing to the southwest. Lin's concern was so great that he even proposed emptying the water at the Miyun Reservoir to prevent the Soviets from blowing up the dam. Zhou quickly opposed this plan since it would flood dozens of communities downstream.[105]

China set the new date for a Soviet assault as the eve of the negotiations in Beijing. Apparently based on incoming intelligence, Mao and Lin worried that the airplane transporting Kosygin and the Soviet delegation to Beijing might actually be armed with nuclear weapons.[106] Mao said, 'The concentration of all of the members of the central leadership in Beijing is not good; one atom bomb would kill many. We should disperse a bit. Some old comrades can be evacuated to other places.'[107] The Central Party Committee advised all party, military and civilian leaders to leave Beijing before 20 October. Mao fled to Wuhan in central China; Lin flew to Suzhou in the east; key military officials went to a hardened wartime command centre under the Hundred Hope Mountain in western Beijing; and the State Council and the party's Central General Office took refuge in hardened posts in Elephant Nose Valley, also in western Beijing.

In anticipation of an attack, and without Mao's prior approval, Lin sent a message to General Huang Yongsheng entitled 'Urgent Directive Regarding Strengthening Combat Readiness to Prevent an Enemy's Surprise Attack'. The orders directed the regional commands, especially the three in the north, to 'disperse and protect their heavy weapons, such as tanks, aircraft, and artillery' and to 'rapidly accelerate the production of anti-tank weapons…and anti-tank guns.' Intelligence units were told to maintain constant surveillance.[108]

Most importantly, the second directive of order instructed China's strategic forces, the Second Artillery, to conduct 'launching preparations'. For the first—and only—time in history, China's nuclear weapons were put on combat alert. Given the sensitivity of the order, and the secrecy with which China conducted its nuclear activities, the directive was transmitted only to the Second Artillery Headquarters. Lin was also emphatic that Mao must personally approve any missile launch. One of his aides warned, 'The Second Artillery fires by pressing a button; if they fail to be cautious, even a single shot could start a world war.' Despite the obvious caution in dealing with issues related to China's nuclear forces, at least one mistake was made. Specifically, Lin included the DF-3 intermediate-range ballistic missile in his directive to the Second Artillery, but none of the missiles were yet operational.[109] Lin's order also raised the possibility that Moscow would detect and misinterpret these preparations as signs of an impending launch and decide to pre-empt.

As the Soviet airplane approached Beijing, Lin asked for minute-by-minute intelligence updates and situation reports, and refused to sleep until the plane had landed. Not until the plane touched down in Beijing without incident did he relax and go to bed. After eight months of violence, threats and scathing political rhetoric, China and the Soviet Union finally sat down at the negotiating table. Negotiations were protracted and complex, lasting several decades, before a final agreement was reached. Beijing claimed on more than one occasion that its bargaining position was disadvantaged because 'above the negotiating table hangs the Soviet atomic bomb'.[110] But for Mao, Lin, and the rest of the Chinese leadership, the immediate threat of a Soviet nuclear strike had at last subsided.

The Soviet success wasn't easy; it took seven months of coercive diplomatic overtures backed by demonstrations of military force. Even more effective was Moscow's carefully crafted hints of a looming missile attack, which led the CCP leadership to finally fear for its own survival.[111]

SIX

Operation Able Archer: The Military Exercise That Almost Started World War III

The year 1983 was the stellar interplay of heightened geopolitical tensions, superpower crisis situations, near misses of nuclear war, arrival of the pop culture revolution and the release of a blockbuster Hollywood movie. Many acclaimed musical works—some bonafide classics—were launched, changing history. Prince took over once and for all; Michael Jackson's blockbuster album *Thriller* topped the charts; Madonna stepped into the spotlight; and Lionel Richie learned to dance. Amid the entertainment explosion, artists also responded to the apprehensions of nuclear annihilation. The second track on U2's album *Seconds* was the most direct in this regard. 'It takes a second to say goodbye,' sang Bono about the brief moment between nuclear detonation and annihilation. U2 soon grew into one of the world's most popular bands. The song 'Two Suns in the Sunset' was part of the Pink Floyd album *The Final Cut*, 1983. It wasn't played until Waters added it to his solo shows in 2018. The first sun is the actual sun. The second sun is an atom bomb. Little did anyone know that the world would actually be on the brink of a nuclear war in 1983.

At the geopolitical and military levels, there were several events and incidents which led to a crisis situation in

November 1983. Back in 1981, the Soviets interpreted President Carter's 1980 'Presidential Directive 59: Nuclear Weapon Employment Policy' as preparation for a nuclear first strike.

PD-59 sought to destroy all military, industrial and economic targets in the Soviet Union and Eastern Europe. Secretary of Defense Harold Brown was doing exactly that in a military exercise where he was 'chasing enemy general purpose forces in East Europe and Korea with strategic weapons.'[1]

The Soviets had deployed the new Hen House over-the-horizon radars and launched ICBM-detection satellites capable of providing 15 to 30 minutes warning in the event of a US nuclear attack. However, the impending deployment of US intermediate-range Pershing II missiles to Europe created a new vulnerability for the Soviets because they had the ability to strike targets in the USSR in as little as 10 minutes—too little time for the leadership to react. On 22 June 1981, Defence Minister Dmitri Ustinov publicly condemned the Pershing IIs as an attempt by the US to safeguard North America by shifting the focus of World War III to Europe.[2] Just weeks before the Able Archer 83 military exercises by NATO, Ustinov characterized the NATO missiles 'as means for a first strike, the "decapitation strike"', in a meeting with fellow Warsaw Pact officials.[3]

In the early 1980s, new leadership in the US and Soviet Union ended the period of détente. Rising tensions and an accelerating arms race led to increased mistrust. This culminated in NATO's 1983 military exercise, Operation Able Archer, which the USSR mistook for a possible nuclear attack, bringing the world dangerously close to war. The election of President Ronald Reagan in 1980 saw the return of heightened Cold War tensions after a period of détente during the previous decade.[4] Soviet leader Yuri Andropov, who assumed power the following year, came to the job after heading the KGB. From the first days of his presidency, Reagan accelerated the largest peacetime military build-up that had begun in the last year of the Carter administration.[5] A new version of the B1-B aircraft was given the go-ahead. A new generation of ground-launched Cruise and Pershing II missiles were planned, all of which could carry nuclear warheads.[6] The M-1 Abrams Main Battle Tank, powered by a gas turbine engine, was inducted by the US Army. Thermal imaging and laser range finding systems made US weapons accurate and deadly. Production lines for the F/A-18 Hornet and the F-117 Nighthawk jets went into full action mode.[7] The US Navy also saw huge growth during the Reagan presidency, with an increase from 479 to 610 vessels that were organized around 15 aircraft carrier task groups.[8]

Reagan appointed William 'Bill' Casey—a lawyer, long-term friend, and his successful campaign manager—as head of the CIA. 'Bill Casey came to the CIA primarily to wage war against the Soviet Union,' and victory was the only acceptable outcome.[9] Physicist and hydrogen bomb designer Edward Teller spoke to Reagan about a weapon consisting of a laser beam that would destroy a volley of missiles. This was the 'Star Wars' programme, named after the futuristic George Lucas movie. The top-rated motion picture of the year 1983 was *Star Wars: The Return of the Jedi*. Many moviegoers saw Darth Vader's galactic 'Empire' as a stand-in for the Soviet Union. In fact, President Ronald Reagan gave a speech in March 1983 in which he labelled the Soviet Union an 'evil empire'.[10]

Later on 23 March 1983, Reagan announced plans for the Strategic Defense Initiative (popularly dubbed 'Star Wars'), which aimed to intercept incoming Soviet nuclear missiles from space. Reagan viewed it purely as a defensive measure, but the Soviet Union saw a defensive shield that would protect the US against the Soviet missiles and enable them to take offensive action.[11]

US Naval Exercises

In March 1981, Reagan authorized the US Navy to conduct

operations in waters near the Soviet Union where it had not treaded before. These provocative manoeuvres, known as 'freedom of navigation' operations, were designed to test Soviet defences. The US Air Force (USAF) also increased reconnaissance flights just outside Soviet airspace to monitor military activity and detect gaps in Soviet radar and air defence coverage.

In August 1981 a carrier battle group of 83 US and Allied ships, led by the carrier USS Dwight Eisenhower, managed to transit the Greenland-Iceland-United Kingdom (GIUK) Gap undetected through carefully crafted and previously rehearsed concealment and deception measures. The battle group evaded Soviet reconnaissance satellites and came close to Soviet naval bases. A combination of passive measures (maintaining radio silence and operating under emissions control conditions) and active measures (radar-jamming and transmission of false radar signals) turned the Allied force into something resembling a stealth fleet, even eluding Soviet low-orbit, active-radar satellites.[12] Meanwhile, US Navy fighters conducted an unprecedented simulated attack on the Soviet planes as they refuelled in-flight, flying at low levels to avoid detection by Soviet shore-based radar sites.[13]

In the second phase of the exercise, a cruiser and three other ships left the carrier battle group and sailed near the militarily important Kola Peninsula—bordering the Barents Sea and the White Sea—the site of an extensive complex of Soviet military bases. They remained there for nine days before rejoining the main group. Aircraft carriers with submarine escorts were also anchored in Norwegian *fjord*s close to the Soviet border. US attack submarines practised assaults on Soviet SSBNs stationed beneath the polar ice cap.[14]

Fleet EX

On 3 April 1983, V.K. Bondarenko, the captain of the Soviet Victor II attack submarine, K-305, was celebrating his thirty-eighth birthday somewhere below the surface of the Okhotsk Sea in the western Pacific. He suddenly received orders from the commander of the Soviet Pacific Fleet to track the aircraft carrier USS *Enterprise* as it crossed the western Pacific on its way to San Francisco.

Bondarenko sailed through a narrow passage called Bussol Strait near Kurile Islands, and in open waters, decided to navigate to a position where he could monitor the aircraft carrier. The K-305s sophisticated electronic surveillance sensors picked up alarming sounds. The crew opened up their guides of the US Navy ships and signals and compared the *pings* and *bleeps* to the emitter characteristics on file. They matched those of a Spruance-class destroyer—a type of ship not supposed to be in the area. The electronic warfare officers informed Bondarenko that the destroyer was headed toward the Kurile Islands.[15]

At 0300 hours Moscow time, the submarine's sonar detected a large fleet of US ships. Fusing sonar, radio and radar returns, he searched for a place to hide so he could track them without being detected. He found a blind spot about 3.5 miles behind the USS *Enterprise* itself. It ran silently from then on out. No radio messages came in or went out. When the K-305 ascended to periscope depth, Bondarenko saw that the *Enterprise* was being restocked with supplies by a ship to its starboard, cruising next to the USS *Bainbridge*. This electronic dance continued for hours. The K-305 would peek up to see what was happening and then dive down and take evasive action.[16]

The K-305 remained at periscope depth for two hours, monitoring communications between the nearby ships. When it surfaced, a Sea King anti-submarine helicopter was hovering directly overhead, circling tightly. The Soviet submarine was right at the centre—caught in the open. But Commander Bondarenko stayed calm. These were 'peaceful times' and there was no need for evasive action. The Americans had found him—just as he had found them.

The submarine went back underwater. For the next few days, Bondarenko monitored radio traffic indicating the imminent arrival of a third carrier, the USS *Coral Sea*, which was steaming toward them from the West Coast. He could see other ships of all types rendezvousing at a staging point. Three aircraft carriers and two dozen other ships had assembled. They were headed toward the Kamchatka Peninsula. Bondarenko sent a flash message to the Soviet Fleet Commander.[17] He had stumbled into the biggest US Navy fleet exercise of the year, Fleet Ex 83. The *Midway*, the *Enterprise*, and the *Coral Sea* were the anchors of a 40-odd conglomeration of naval ships conducting a massive show of force involving 23,000 crew members and 300 aircraft.[18]

The US carrier battle groups sailed within 450 miles of the Kamchatka Peninsula and Petropavlovsk, the only Soviet naval base with direct access to open seas. When the ships reached a designated point off the Kamchatka Peninsula, navy warplanes took off from the deck and flew west, racing across the Zeleny Islands in the Lesser Kurile Ridge, overflying the Soviet naval training base and several of its most sophisticated anti-aircraft radars.[19] Accompanying them were B-52 bombers and AWACS aircraft. US attack submarines and anti-submarine aircraft conducted operations in bastions where the Soviet Navy had stationed a large number of its nuclear-powered ballistic missile submarines (SSBNs). Several F-14 Tomcat fighters took off from the USS *Enterprise* and the USS *Midway* and overflew a Soviet military base on the Kurile Islands. The mission was to simulate a bombing raid which was a violation of Soviet airspace.

Fleet exercises demonstrated the US ability to deploy aircraft-carrier battle groups close to sensitive Soviet military and industrial sites, apparently without being detected or challenged.[20] Fleet Ex 83 comprised 'the largest fleet exercise conducted by the Pacific Fleet since World War II.'[21]

Later in May of 1983, Yuri Andropov—by then general secretary of the Soviet Union—met with the US envoy W. Averell Harriman. Harriman had been US ambassador to the Soviet Union during WWII. Four times during the meeting Andropov warned of a nuclear war. He morosely stated, 'It would seem that awareness of this danger should be precisely the common denominator with which statesmen of both countries would exercise restraint and seek mutual understanding to strengthen confidence, to avoid the irreparable. However, I must say that I do not see it on the part of the current administration, and they may be moving toward the dangerous "red line".'[22] At the meeting, Andropov expressed concerns about a conflagration far worse than the Second World War, in which the two nations had been allies. 'This war may perhaps not happen through evil intent,' he said, 'but could happen through miscalculation.'[23]

KAL 007

Just after midnight on 31 August 1983, following the Fleet Ex naval exercise, a US Air Force RC-135 SIGINT aircraft made slow eight loops in the international waters off the Kamchatka Peninsula. The RC-135s—packed with electronic recording systems and laden with antennae—could continuously record and intercept signals and electronic messages emanating from Soviet radars. The data collected from these flights were sent back to the National Security Agency (NSA) centre at Fort Meade, Maryland.

A day earlier, a Norwegian signals intelligence unit whose antenna coverage included the Soviet missile test range of Plesetsk had tipped the NSA about a possible Soviet missile launch. From the chatter it seemed like the Soviets were going to test-fire an SS-2S Sickle missile. It would land, as Soviet test missiles usually did, near Kamchatka.[24] The RC-135 aircraft was monitoring the missile launch.

The international passenger lounge at Anchorage airport, Alaska, was busy that night. Two Korean Air Lines 747 aircraft were parked up, en route to Seoul. One—KAL 007—had flown in from New York, the other—KAL 015—from Los Angeles.[25] The crew of the first leg on KAL 007 had reported a VHF radio malfunction. The new crew arrived on the flight deck while the engineers were fixing the faulty radio.[26] KAL 007 eventually took off at 0400 hours local time.

While the RC-135 was still in its monitoring position that night, flight KAL 007, by now more than 150 miles off course, flew into the same area, heading dangerously towards the Kamchatka.[27] It continued on directly into Soviet airspace, seemingly heading towards Petropavlosk, the site of a major Soviet air base and a nuclear submarine base. This would have caused immediate alarm as it was entering a prohibited area. The whole region had been tense since the Fleet Ex 83 exercises in April, after which Andropov himself had ordered Soviet defences to 'shoot to kill' any intruder over Soviet territory.[28]

Alarmed by an incoming aircraft, the radar controllers in Kamchatka contacted the Soviet Air Defence regional command at Kharbarovsk.[29] The deputy commander woke up Marshal Alexandr Kardunov, commander-in-chief of the Soviet Air Force and a deputy defence minister. After more than half an hour, at 0137 hours an SU 15 Flagon Soviet fighter aircraft—piloted by Lieutenant Colonel Ossipovich—was scrambled to intercept KAL 007.[30] He was instructed to lock his air-to-air missiles on the target.

He reported at 0312 hours: 'I see it. I'm locked on to the target.'[31] He could see its navigation lights flashing and moved in closer. Although he could not see the logo on the tail fin, he could see a row of windows on the side of the aircraft. The outline of a Boeing 747 aircraft was quite different to that of the

RC-135. But both had four engines below the wings and Ossipovich had never been trained in the identification of B-747s. He was absolutely sure that this must be some kind of spy plane disguised as a civilian airliner. He simply did not believe that a civil aircraft, with all its modern navigation technology, could possibly be so far off course[32]

Ossipovich tried to attract the attention of the intruder's pilots by flashing his lights, then by waggling his wings. When neither of these tactics worked, he was ordered to fire across the front of the aircraft to alert it. Having 'intercepted' an aircraft, he was then supposed to lead it down, and all aircraft had to follow an interceptor to the nearest airfield.[33] But KAL 007 did not respond.

Ossipovich was ordered by his ground controller to fire. He launched two air-to-air AA-3 missiles. One was a heat-seeking missile that latched on to the Boeing 747's engines and exploded in the left wing, starting a fire. The second missile hit the rear of the aircraft, immediately causing the lights to fail and the passenger cabin to depressurize. Ossipovich reported back, 'The target is destroyed.' Now running low on fuel, he peeled off and returned to base.[34]

It was another nine minutes before KAL 007 disappeared from radar screens and crashed into the sea. It was 365 miles off course when it was shot down.[35] Inadvertently, KAL 007 flew through the orbital path of the RC-135's 'Cobra Ball' mission monitoring the predicted Soviet intercontinental ballistic missile (ICBM) test launch. But when the ICBM launch didn't occur, the RC-135 returned to base, while the Korean 747 flew blithely on toward the Kamchatka Peninsula and Soviet airspace.

During the tense moments, a clandestine NSA SIGINT unit based in Wakkanai, Japan, was monitoring the activities. The unit detected bursts of encrypted communication from the Soviet regimental air defence posts. Suddenly, an American heard a Sukhoi Su-15 pilot name the 'Zapustkal' missile. The NSA team stopped what they were doing and re-racked the audiotape. They heard what appeared to be a chase through Soviet airspace of a large airplane, warnings given, and then the missile fired, along with the statement: 'The target is destroyed.'[36]

On 3 September 1983, two days after the shoot-down of KAL 007, Soviet Air Defence mistakenly judged a US Navy EP-3 SIGINT aircraft circling over the Flight 007 crash site as spying on the Soviet Union. Two Soviet MiG-23 fighters were dispatched to shoot the EP-3 down. General Charles L. Donnelly, commander of US forces in Japan and the 5th Air Force, ordered a flight of four F-15s to intercept the MiG-23s. Simultaneously, they warned the EP-3 of the threat. The pilot dove for the wave tops to evade the Russian fighters, and after a tense period, reached Japanese airspace, safe from Soviet attack. Donnelly ordered the F-15s to break off without engaging the Soviet fighters and to return to their combat air patrol orbit. When another general officer on the scene pointedly questioned Donnelly's decision not to engage the MiGs, Donnelly responded, 'I don't think I'll start World War III this afternoon.'

These and other global events leading up to Operation Able Archer led to widespread alert in the Soviet Union and ratcheted up tensions between the two superpowers. In Washington, the National Security Council was sorting through several crises situations such as Nicaragua, Grenada, Soviet invasion in Afghanistan, and the Iran-Iraq War. Andropov saw these events as the interconnected foundations of an aggressive US policy against the Soviet Union.[37]

Little did the public know that a few months later the Soviets would be preparing to launch a real nuclear attack on the West. It was just past midnight and Stanislav Petrov had barely settled into the commander's chair inside the secret bunker at Serpukhov-15 where the Soviet Union monitored its early-warning satellites over the US. The alarms all suddenly went off. On the panel before him was a red pulsating button. One word flashed: 'Start.' The warning system's computer concluded that an ICBM had been launched from a base in the US.[38]

Operation RYAN

There had been an increase in rhetorical speeches by US politicians which consolidated the crisis situation. During his 1980 US presidential campaign, George H.W. Bush, Reagan's eventual vice president, stated that the US could prevail in a nuclear conflict as long as it ensured the survival of a portion of its population and industrial capacity. 'That's the way you can have a winner.' Two months after Reagan took office, Richard Pipes—director of East European and Soviet Affairs at the National Security Council—told a reporter that 'Soviet leaders would have to choose between peacefully changing their Communist system in the direction followed by the West or going to war.' During his confirmation hearing three months later, Eugene Rostow, Reagan's nominee to head the US Arms Control and Disarmament Agency, was asked by Senator Claiborne Pell of Rhode Island if he believed the US could survive an all-out nuclear war. Rostow replied that the human race was very resilient. Some estimates predicted there would be 10 million casualties on one side and 100 million on another, but this did not represent the whole of the population.

By 1981, high-level Soviet officials had become seriously concerned that the US might be planning to start a nuclear war. In May 1981, four months after Reagan moved into the White House, Leonid Brezhnev stood before a closed meeting of KGB officers in an auditorium at their headquarters in Lubyanka and told them that détente was dead. President Reagan, he said, was bent on destroying the Soviet Union. Yuri Andropov, the head of the KGB and the future general secretary, explained that the Reagan administration was preparing for a possible pre-emptive nuclear strike against the Soviet Union. The situation was so dire that he was launching an intelligence programme, Operation RYAN—an acronym for *Raketno-Yadernoe Napadenie*, or 'nuclear missile attack'.[39] Andropov put 'strategic military intelligence' at the top of KGB collection priorities and created a special 'institute' within the organization to handle it.[40]

He announced that, by a decision of the Politburo, the KGB and GRU were—for the first time—to cooperate in the worldwide intelligence operation. A month later, Andropov dispatched a secret directive to all KGB station chiefs worldwide. RYAN was to be their top priority. 'Not since the end of World War II has the international situation been as explosive as it is now,' he wrote.[41] The Soviets had initiated the largest peace-time intelligence gathering operation in history to detect a US nuclear first strike before its launch.

The KGB's main objective was to monitor the military preparations of the enemy which could lead to the outbreak of a war. Operation RYAN was an exercise intended to help plan and prepare for a defensive, pre-emptive first strike, based on the premise that intelligence could be gathered on a range of military, economic and political indicators to signal that the West was preparing for nuclear war.

The KGB deployed a software programme named RYAN. Massive for its time, RYAN sought to compute the relative power of the two superpowers by modelling 40,000 military, political and economic factors reported by Soviet spies in US, Europe and Japan. The programme was designed to warn them when their country's relative strength had declined to a point that the US might launch a pre-emptive first strike on the Soviet Union. Its designers assigned a value of 100 to US economic, military and political power. They believed that as long as Soviet geopolitical power was 60 or higher, the USSR would be safe from attack. However, RYAN's conclusions indicated that Soviet power was declining rapidly relative to that of the US and was projected to fall to 45 by 1984.

By 1983, Soviet political and military leaders truly believed a nuclear war was coming. The RYAN programme told them that the odds favoured the US and the war indicators in Moscow were flashing red.[42] RYAN's slogan was '[D]o not miss the moment when the West is about to launch war.'[43] KGB Headquarters sent a new directive to its foreign residencies in February that re-emphasized the importance of detecting signs of an impending nuclear attack. The directive stated that the time between a NATO decision to strike and the actual onset of hostilities would likely be seven to 10 days. The GRU similarly advised its overseas military intelligence offices that war could break out at any moment.

Moscow's threat perceptions and Operation RYAN were influenced by Hitler's 1941 surprise attack on the USSR (Operation BARBAROSSA). Stalin received multiple, detailed and timely warnings of the impending invasion from a variety of open and clandestine sources. But he chose to interpret intelligence data with a best-case or not-so-bad-case hypothesis, assuming—incorrectly—that Hitler would not attack without issuing an ultimatum or fight a two-front war. The German counterintelligence misled the Soviet Union with an elaborate deception plan.[44] In 1981 Marshal Ogarkov, in particular, publicly expressed his concern over the readiness of Soviet society to respond to challenges. In his book *History Teaches Vigilance,* he mentioned that the element of surprise already played a certain role in World War II. It had only grown in strategic importance since then.[45]

Immediately following Brezhnev's death on 10 November 1982, KGB and GRU residencies in Soviet Embassies received orders to monitor installations for indications of any military mobilization. The KGB directive provided a detailed list of intelligence collection activities:[46]

Political

- Holding of extraordinary meetings by the NSC and the special crisis groups in the White House situation room
- The relocation of US president and the principal staff from the White House to protected command centres
- Evacuation of people close to the highest political leadership of the US from Washington, DC
- Holding of extraordinary consultations by the US political leadership and the NATO states
- Relocation of the most important people from NATO headquarters to places especially equipped to work under war conditions
- Arrival of former US presidents in Washington, DC
- Cancellations of travel, speeches and meetings by representatives of the military-political leadership of the country
- Early, unexpected returns by leading government representatives from vacation
- Unplanned visits by leading politicians from NATO states and US ambassadors from the capitals of NATO states to Washington, DC
- Work by a large number of employees on evenings, at night hours, and on non-workdays

Military

- Raising the level of combat readiness for the forward-deployed US nuclear forces in Europe
- Relocation of army corps, divisions and brigades to the forward command centres
- Distribution of nuclear missiles and bombs from missile depots to fighter aircraft and bombers
- Transfer of alert nuclear submarines with ballistic

missiles from daily patrol areas to patrol areas for extraordinary situations

- Mass delivery of conventional aerial bombs and guided missiles and fuels and lubricants from inventories to the airbases
- Preparation of warships for going to sea
- Implementation of planning documents, such as the US 'Single Integrated Operational Plan' for waging a nuclear war, the 'General Defence Plans' of the NATO strategic and subordinate joint commands, NATO's 'Nuclear Support Plans', and a number of NATO 'Contingency Operations Plans' (COPs)[47]
- Beginning of mass transports of forces by air from the US to Europe

Intelligence

- Activation of the adversary's technological intelligence operations
- Increased countermeasures against Soviet technological intelligence
- Introduction of additional travel restrictions in the country for USSR diplomats and business representatives
- Tightening of security in buildings of intelligence services and their offices
- Tightening of security in air, river and seaports, train stations and hubs, main roads and bridges
- Cancellation of amateur radio licenses for the territory of the US

Civil Defence

- Replenishment of food and water reserves
- Expansion of the network of medical institutions

- Preparation of roads for mass evacuations of population from large cities

Economic

- Evacuation of headquarters of leading US banks and corporations in areas designated for use under war conditions—particularly, the headquarters of the telecommunication branch of AT&T from Bedminster, New Jersey to the underground shelter in Netcong, New Jersey
- Transfer of financial and currency assets of the largest banks of the US and other NATO states to foreign banks (especially Swiss banks)
- Monitoring of the flow of money and gold on Wall Street

For two years prior to Able Archer 83, KGB spies had been scouring the world for evidence of what the Soviet leadership in general, and Andropov in particular, believed were US preparations for all-out nuclear war against the USSR.

At 1900 hours on 26 September 1983, Lieutenant Colonel Stanislav Petrov arrived at the Serpukhov-15 command centre, located about 60 miles south of Moscow. He spent an hour talking with colleagues whose shifts were ending, receiving latest reports and updates.[48] Then Petrov sat behind a console in the back of the room, sipping tea with an assistant who operated a switchboard which connected him to the Nuclear Command Centre in Moscow, consisting of the top military generals and the defence minister. The Soviet early warning satellites had a good coverage of the US, where it was early evening. Half the continent was bathed in sunlight; half was dark. He had just finished savouring his cheese and sausage sandwich when came the siren rose—an insistent, repeating *blaang*—'almost too loud'. Petrov stood up. Underneath the monitors, a huge electronic banner flashed in red and white. The radars were bombarded by the energy signature of what its computers interpreted as an ICBM launch from somewhere inside the US.[49]

Believing that a US ICBM was incoming, the base went into battle-station mode. However, some officers on duty were sceptical that the US would choose to send only one ICBM, knowing that it could not affect the Soviets' counter-strike capabilities. Petrov instructed his team to turn off the system for a few seconds and turn it back on again.[50] At first, the satellite reported that one missile had been launched, then another, and another. Soon, the system was 'roaring'. Now five Minuteman ICBMs had been launched.[51] Petrov checked the computer systems again. The main computer and the backup were functioning. The communication links were functioning. Other sensors were online. The confidence level, according to the satellites of these launches, was quite high.

Colonel Petrov had to figure out what to do. The estimate was that only 25 minutes would elapse between launch and detonation. The Soviet Union's military and political leadership needed to be informed without delay. The tension in the command centre was rising—as many as 200 pairs of eyes were trained on Petrov. He was situated at a critical point in the chain of command, overseeing a staff that monitored incoming signals from the satellites. He reported to superiors at warning-system headquarters; they, in turn, reported to the General Staff, who would consult with Soviet leader Yuri Andropov on the possibility of launching a retaliatory attack.[52]

Petrov remembered his military training. They had always been told that a nuclear war would start with the launch of a massive pre-emptive missile strike against the Soviet Union. Why would the Americans launch only a few missiles?[53] Petrov knew that ICBMs should have been visible to the Soviet reconnaissance satellites for at least 180 seconds after launch until the final stage of their rockets burned out. But there was nothing. No flashes, no fire, no contrails. The satellites picked up American test launches all the time. The analysts knew what to look for. This time, they just didn't see it.[54]

The interpreters of the optical satellite images continued to report that they could see no sign of a launch. But the computer analysts insisted there was no computer malfunction. The chief of the General Staff, Marshal Ogarkov, and Minister of Defence Ustinov had been informed of the incoming missiles. Those in charge of organizing a nuclear retaliation were preparing to receive their orders. Targets were being identified at the National Nuclear Command Centre.

On the night of the crisis, Petrov had little time to think. When the alarms went off, he recalled, 'for 15 seconds, we were in a state of shock. We needed to understand, what's next?' The responsibility fell to Petrov, then a 44-year-old lieutenant colonel, to decide—was it for real? Despite the electronic evidence, Petrov decided, and advised the others, that the satellite alert was a false alarm. He made the tense decision under enormous stress—electronic maps and consoles were flashing as he held a phone in one hand and juggled an intercom in the other, trying to take in all the information at once. Another officer at the early-warning facility was shouting into the phone—to remain calm and do his job. 'I had a funny feeling in my gut,' Petrov said. 'I didn't want to make a mistake. I made a decision, and that was it.'[55]

As part of Operation RYAN, there were undercover agents in the American Midwest who would have reported back had any missiles been launched. They were all silent. As the senior officers gathered around him, and as Moscow continued to clamour for information, it became clear that this was indeed a false alarm. Petrov had been right.[56] Another factor, he said, was that Soviet ground-based radar installations, which searched for missiles rising above the horizon, showed no evidence of an attack. The ground radar units were controlled from a different command centre, and because they cannot see beyond the horizon, they would not spot incoming missiles until some minutes after the satellites had.

Eventually, they concluded that a highly unusual set of atmospheric conditions over the northern tier of the US caused sunlight to be reflected off high clouds in such a way that the satellites' sensors mistook the reflections as ICBM launches. Petrov had to make an assessment in minutes, not months. Had the Kremlin ignored Petrov and instead acted on the phantom American ICBM attack, the world would have been plunged into global nuclear war. A hurried investigation by the Soviet General Staff would later determine that the Okos satellite picked up reflections from high clouds passing over F.E. Warren Air Force Base in Wyoming.[57]

Although virtually unknown to the West at the time, the false alarm at the heavily guarded military facility south of Moscow came during one of the tensest periods of the Cold War. The ICBM alarm came just weeks after Soviet pilots had shot down KAL 007.[58] Eleven days later, NATO forces in Brussels took part in a joint military exercise that simulated a response to a hypothetical Soviet nuclear attack. The exercise was code-named Able Archer 83. The primary purpose of the exercise was to test the command-and-control procedures for NATO's nuclear forces in the event of a global crisis. Unlike previous war games however, Able Archer 83 featured new elements specifically meant to confuse the Soviets.[59]

Operation Able Archer

November Nights over Europe

The zenith of the alarming global events started with the inauguration of the Reagan Presidency in 1983. In early November 1983, at the peak of the heightened level of tension between the Soviet Union and the West, NATO began the Able Archer 83 exercise. It was a part of a bigger group of

NATO exercises taking place in the autumn of 1983 under the umbrella name 'Autumn Forge 83'. It was made up of six exercises involving approximately 100,000 troops. Autumn Forge always culminated with Able Archer, an exercise which tested the command-and-control procedures for both conventional and nuclear weapons.[60] Able Archer included momentous preparations for a war in the face of a hypothetical Soviet invasion. It was a rehearsal for the nuclear attack by NATO upon Warsaw Pact.[61]

The NATO war game tested the alliance's ability to wage war on the Great European Plain in the event of the Warsaw Pact's invasion of West Germany. The Fulda Gap is the navigable expanse of land that stretched from the German border to Frankfurt. The Fulda Corridor furnished Napoleon with his escape route after Leipzig; it was the treeless plain along which American armies marched to secure Germany, late in World War II, and the focus of NATO strategy since the mid-1950s. Keeping the Fulda was essential to maintaining the integrity of nearly 700 miles of NATO's main lines. It was ground zero for World War III.[62]

The 1983 version of Operation Able Archer included crucial new changes. First, it was planned to involve high-level officials, including the US secretary of defense and the chairman of the joint chiefs of staff. The realism was such that among those involved were British prime minister Margaret Thatcher and West German chancellor Helmut Kohl.[63] Second, the exercise included a practice drill that took NATO forces through high-spectrum nuclear warfare and a full-scale simulated release of nuclear weapons against the Warsaw Pact. Moreover, the procedures and message formats used in the transition from conventional to nuclear war were different from those used before. In this exercise the NATO forces went through all of the alert phases—from normal readiness to war.[64] It was also more provocative in nature than its predecessors.

The exercise scenario began with the hypothetical enemy forces opening hostilities in Europe on 4 November, after which NATO went on general alert. The virtual enemy initiated the use of chemical weapons on 6 November. While this was all scripted, the exercise itself began on 7 November and ran over five days. It was based around a simulated transition from conventional and chemical warfare to a nuclear exchange. Above all, the exercises were designed to give NATO command posts and communication networks training in this kind of escalation.[65]

Leading up to Autumn Forge 83, Soviet officials were concerned that the West would launch a nuclear attack under the cover of a war game like Able Archer. KGB, in its memo—'*Instructions from the Centre* 87'—to spies stationed abroad, warned about indirect indications of preparation such as 'announcements of a military alert in units and at bases' and 'military exercises'.[66] Significantly, Soviet doctrine held that large exercises such as Autumn Forge 83 could be used to mask a pre-emptive attack. For this reason, after the Cold War's end, the Soviet chief of staff, Marshal Sergei F. Akhromeyev, described the Autumn Forge exercises as 'the most dangerous'.[67]

Able Archer 83 began on 2 November 1983. The war gamers invented a lively but credible scenario.

In the elaborate run-up to war in February of that year, prompted by a sense that the socialist bloc was losing power and influence due to the aggressive stance of the Western alliance, there has been a dramatic change of leadership in Moscow. Following this coup, a hard-line Kremlin leadership takes over and launches a new offensive against the West. In March, they send military supplies to Iran in its continuing war with Iraq. Military aid is also sent to Syria and South Yemen. The following month the Gulf States, threatened by the growing Soviet involvement in their region, seek US military aid, and the US Navy increases its presence in the Gulf.

In May and June the tension spreads from the Middle East

to Europe. There is increasing unrest in Eastern Europe as the Soviet Union fails to keep its promises of economic aid to its satellites. However, under instructions from Moscow, the Warsaw Pact nations carry out a series of training exercises and stockpile military supplies across Eastern Europe. In August, protests in Yugoslavia—caused by their financial difficulties—lead that nation to drop out of the Soviet bloc altogether and seek economic and military assistance from the West. In the Kremlin this seems to threaten a complete break-up of the Soviet dominated Eastern bloc. In response, the Warsaw Pact begins a full mobilization of its armed forces in September. By October these forces invade Yugoslavia to regain it for the socialist bloc. This leads to a major crisis in East-West relations.

At the end of the month, the Soviets invade Finland and Norway to open up the Atlantic for their fleet. Meanwhile, Soviet air and naval forces begin a massive attack on NATO bases. Soviet troops also invade Greece while its navy launches strikes in the Adriatic and the Mediterranean. On 4 November, Warsaw Pact uses their overwhelming superiority in ground and air forces to attack West Germany through the Fulda Gap. Soviet tanks and armour soon overpower NATO forces and rapidly begin to spread across the north German plain.

Operation Able Archer 83 began in real time.[68]

Around four potential indicators of Able Archer were reported by Operation RYAN: 170 flights; radio-silent airlift of 19,000 US soldiers to Europe; 1,500 tons of cargo which was sent to Europe over the course of 172 missions; the shifting of NATO commands to the alternate war headquarters that would be used for major military conflict; the practice of 'new nuclear weapons release procedures', including consultations with small cells of US Defense Department and UK Ministry of Defence war gamers; and numerous slips of the tongue in which NATO personnel called B-52 sorties nuclear 'strikes' during communications.[69] As Able Archer 83 was being conducted, a 'surge' of military personnel created a significant addition to the NATO footprint in Europe.[70]

This exercise uniquely involved differently coded messaging formats, a higher state of alert than previous iterations, and the incorporation of 'live mobilization exercises from US military forces in Europe'. Other non-routine elements included long radio silences, a shift of command to an Alternate War Headquarters,[71] and reports of 'nuclear strikes' on open radio frequencies that could have been interpreted as real.[72] And it was more realistic as well. US and NATO cargo planes maintained radio silence. B-52 bomber crews taxied their planes to their runways and loaded them with dummy bombs that looked remarkably real. The US Strategic Air Command raised its nuclear alert to the highest level. All this may have looked more realistic to Soviet spies, who were watching.

On 8 or 9 November, both the KGB and the GRU were ordered to report on increased alert at US bases in Europe and to check for other indications of an impending nuclear attack. Meanwhile, across the real Eastern bloc, in a series of listening stations, Soviet radio operators followed the Able Archer war game with increasing concern. In Moscow they began to ask if it was all a case of *maskirovka*, or deception. The Soviet military commanders knew that the Warsaw Pact had its own contingency plans to attack the West under the cover of military exercises.[73]

KGB spies had obtained a number of details about the Able Archer exercise scenario, one of which was striking. They learned that B-52s would participate for the first time, guided by an echelon of observers from the Strategic Air Command. The B-52 presence meant one thing to the Soviets: nuclear strikes.[74]

In London, Gordievsky received the first message from Moscow which warned that the Americans had a very important exercise, which could develop into something sinister. Gordievsky's boss, the KGB station chief Arkady Guk, asked Moscow for specifics: what signs should the London residency look for that might indicate NATO was within the seven- to 10-day window before a surprise attack? Vladimir Kryuchkov—chief of the KGB—dispatched the following instructions: 'Check for unusual activity at the Prime Minister's residence; observe whether large numbers of cars are parked around the Ministry of Defence in the evening; note the appearance in the streets of military detachments or the announcements of a military alert, at bases.'[75] The cable also noted that American bases around the world had beefed up their security.[76]

Soviet observers spotted planes carrying—what appeared to be—warheads taxiing out of their NATO hangars. Within days, KGB agents working on Operation RYAN reported changes in the movement of foreign officers in bases around Europe. An emergency telegram was sent to KGB residencies informing them that NATO forces had been placed on high alert. Soviet officials feared that a nuclear attack was imminent. Soviet aircraft in Poland and East Germany were immediately loaded with bombs, 70 SS-20 intermediate-range ballistic missiles were put on high alert, and nuclear submarines were sent under the Arctic ice, where they would be undetectable by American radar and sonar systems.[77] The realism of Able Archer was ironically effective: It was designed to simulate the start of a nuclear war.[78]

The growing alarm in the Kremlin was expressed to the Soviet people in many ways. There was a series of organized peace rallies and sponsored 'peace' classes in schools. There were closed briefings on the danger of war for party activists and military personnel. Civil defence measures were increased, including air raid drills that were held in factories across western Russia.[79]

On 8 November, the war gamers at Allied Command Europe in NATO decided to request authorization for a massive nuclear strike against the Warsaw Pact. Based on various assessments coming in from NATO stations across Europe, the planners started to calculate how many megatons of nuclear weapons would be needed, how they would be carried and where they would be directed. This time they would request permission to attack a whole range of targets inside the Soviet Union, including air bases, missile launch sites and communication and political centres. It would be a full nuclear strike.[80] All of this was being followed keenly at the Soviet listening posts.[81] It turned out, top Soviet leaders thought that the war game was real—that the US and NATO really were about to launch a nuclear first strike against the USSR—and top Soviet military commanders took steps to retaliate.

Soviet Response

The Soviet leadership was convinced that the Able Archer manoeuvres were a cover for a nuclear surprise attack by the US. This triggered a series of unparalleled Soviet military responses.[82] To the Kremlin, all incidents since 1981—such as Fleet Ex and KAL 007—fit in the RYAN pattern. They were particularly alarmed about the forces that stretched from Turkey to Britain.[83] Top Soviet leaders thought that the war game was real and top Soviet military commanders took steps to retaliate.

Defence Minister Ustinov wrote in the state-run *Pravda* newspaper that NATO's exercises 'are becoming increasingly difficult to distinguish from a real deployment of armed forces for aggression.'[84] A secret Soviet intelligence document prepared in October 1983 for General Ivashutin, chief of military intelligence, the GRU, stated that the US and NATO, rather than 'maintaining the approximate parity' that had developed, were trying to tip the strategic balance of forces in their favour. Vladimir Kryuchkov, then head of the KGB's foreign intelligence directorate, evidently shared this evaluation.[85]

The Soviet Union's fear of a nuclear attack also increased dramatically with the scheduled deployment of Pershing II missiles in West Germany. Soviet officials believed that the

Pershing II with a 1,500-mile range could strike command-and-control targets in the Moscow area with little or no warning. The KGB calculated that the flying time for the Pershing II from West Germany to Moscow was 10 minutes.[86] This apparent miscalculation increased the danger of war. As vice chairman of the National Intelligence Council, Herbert E. Meyer quipped in one classified memo, 10 minutes was 'roughly how long it takes some of the Kremlin's leaders to get out of their chairs, let alone to their shelters.'[87]

The Soviet nuclear strategy changed to include the option of pre-empting a 'decapitating first strike' by the West.[88] The Soviets developed their own strategy—'Launch Under Attack'. Knowing that time was so short to react during a nuclear assault, particularly with the Pershing IIs only minutes away from Moscow, the military recommended to the political leadership not to wait until the enemy's missiles had landed but to launch their own weapons as soon as evidence came in of a launch by the other side.[89]

The Soviet Union took unusual military and intelligence precautions at the time of Able Archer which had previously only been employed in actual crises. In Moscow a meeting was attended by Soviet leader Andropov, Defence Minister Ustinov, chief of the General Staff Ogarkov, KGB and GRU chiefs, commander of the Strategic Rocket Forces—including strategic missiles and nuclear weapons—and the chiefs of the army, navy and air force. In the meeting the highest level of alert was activated. This included the activation of the Cheggets suitcase codes. The Soviet's equivalent of the American football was called 'Cheggets'. The term referred to a hand-held bag containing the nuclear launch codes for the president to authorize a launch.[90]

Chief of the General Staff Marshal Nikolai Ogarkov, chief of Strategic Rocket Forces Marshal Vladimir Tolubko, Colonel General Victor Ivanovich Yesin, and the top military generals entered the Tagansky military command bunker outside Moscow from where they could securely monitor the exercise and launch the nuclear weapons should General Secretary Andropov be killed in a first strike.[91]

The commander of the Soviet 4th Army Air Force in Eastern Europe ordered all of his units to prepare for the immediate use of nuclear weapons. The Soviet military had already speeded up the response time of its nuclear forces. Nuclear weapons had been transported from storage sites to delivery units by helicopters. Some nuclear missiles had been deployed to Czechoslovakia and East Germany.[92] About 75 SS-20 missiles were moved to their wartime positions, hidden by camouflage, near mountains 60 miles from their bases. Special radar absorbing paint covered all of them. Each missile had three warheads with 200 kilotons of nuclear explosives on board which was 15 times more lethal than the one dropped on Hiroshima.[93]

The Soviet 16th Air Army, with its dozens of airbases scattered across East German territory, responded when the alarm was raised, being placed on a heightened state of alert on the evening of 2 November. Further to the east, the 4th Air Army in Poland was also put on alert on the orders of Marshal Pavel Kutakhov, the chief of the Soviet Air Forces.[94] All command posts were ordered to be manned around-the-clock by augmented teams.[95]

The NSA, which was intercepting Soviet military communications, sent a message to the CIA director stating that the Marshal Pavel S. Kutakhov had ordered all units of the Soviet 4th Air Army to be on alert 'which included preparations for immediate use of nuclear weapons.'[96] The intercepts were forwarded to US national security advisor Robert McFarlane. He became concerned and decided to collect intelligence through unofficial channels on the prevailing general environment in the Soviet Union. McFarlane arranged for Suzanne Massie, author of *Land of the Firebird: The Beauty of Old Russia* (1982) and amateur Sovietologist, to initiate unofficial contact between the

US and the Soviet Union. She was sent on an unofficial trip to Russia to open a channel for discussions. Suzanne Massie brought back a message to the president from senior Russians regarding how great the risk of nuclear war was at that time. Reagan was immediately intrigued by her commonplace approach to international relations and emphasis on the Russian people.

Soviet fighter aircraft were on strip alert. They were fully fuelled and armed, with pilots and crews on board, and engines running, waiting at the end of the runway for the order to take off. They could be scrambled within seconds of receiving an alarm. Their task was to keep the airspace clear of intruders by intercepting enemy aircraft. They also had the ability to make pre-emptive strikes against NATO nuclear delivery systems on the ground if it was thought they were about to launch missiles against the Soviet Union. US spy satellites picked up their presence at the end of runways during Operation Able Archer.[97]

Soviet fighter-bomber aircraft were armed and placed at 'readiness 3', meaning a 30-minute alert to destroy first-line enemy targets. Fighter-bomber divisions were ordered to load nuclear bombs on one squadron of aircraft in each regiment.[98] As the spearhead of the 16th Air Army, the fighter-bomber divisions, which primarily flew the ground attack MiG-27 Flogger, swing-wing Su-24 Fencers and Su-17 Fitter combat jets, were loaded with tactical nuclear weapons, such as the RN-40 and RN-41, which had an approximate yield of 30 kilotons—twice that of the 'Little Boy' bomb that the US dropped on Hiroshima.[99]

As well as the nuclear weapons themselves, NATO intelligence confirmed that at least one of the Su-17M4 Fitter-Ks at Neuruppin Air Base—home of the 730th Fighter-Bomber Aviation Regiment—was fitted with an electronic jamming pod for self-protection, more evidence that offensive missions were being planned.[100]

The Warsaw Pact also launched unprecedented reconnaissance flights over the Norwegian, North, Baltic and

Barents seas to determine whether US naval forces were deploying forward in support of Able Archer. The Warsaw Pact also imposed a suspension of all military flight operations between 4 and 10 November, except for the intelligence flights, 'probably to have available as many aircraft as possible for combat.'

The Soviet arsenal of medium-range nuclear missiles was also put on a similar state of heightened alert. The SS-20s were ready on full-combat alert in less than eight hours. The SS-20 could carry up to three MIRV warheads, each with the destructive yield of about 10 Hiroshima bombs. Its key distinguishing feature was that it could be launched from mobile launchers spread out across the countryside. In normal times, only about 10 per cent of all SS-20s were in the field on manoeuvres. However, in early November 1983, at least 50 per cent of the total SS-20 force was mobilized.[101]

The missiles were allocated targets such as political and economic infrastructure, airfields, ports and C3 (command, control and communication) facilities. Such an attack would prove to be an annihilating retaliatory nuclear strike. This meant that Washington and many other major cities would be hit in the first wave of a Soviet nuclear assault. Only six weeks before, the Soviet early warning system had malfunctioned by interpreting reflections of the sun on clouds in the Midwest of the US as a sign that missiles had been launched.[102]

Captain Viktor Tkachenko was in charge of one of the ICBM missile silos. On 8 November he had dinner with his wife and two young sons, who lived nearby on the base, and said goodbye, knowing that he would have to miss the ongoing celebrations at the base as he was on combat duty. He departed and descended to his bunker command post where he received a special order—to immediately raise combat alert. He was ordered to stay in his bunker in constant radio communication, on the highest state of alert, and await orders to launch. He was in contact with Marshal Nikolai Ogarkov. Unusually, there was a third man present that night. This man explained that as they were now on heightened alert he was there to ensure there was no breakdown in communication with Moscow. He was from the KGB.[103]

Meanwhile, the Soviet Navy began to implement steps to reduce the missile launch readiness of 'duty status' submarines. Prior to 1980, submarines were required to be able to launch their missiles within four hours of receiving orders. During Able Archer the submarines were able to launch missiles within 20 minutes.[104]

The admiral of Fleet Gorskhov issued instructions for the Soviet naval warships to leave ports and take up offensive positions. Typhoon-class submarines left the port for undisclosed positions. They were among the largest submarines ever built at 25,000 tons with a length of 171 metres (560 feet). The crew enjoyed an unusual level of luxury for a Soviet ship with plenty of space and facilities that included both a swimming pool and a sauna. This was because the Typhoon was intended to spend most of its patrols sitting at the bottom of oceans for long periods of time. It could sit out a nuclear exchange and only fire its 20 huge SS-N-20 missiles months after war had broken out in a final assault on enemy territory.[105]

A letter was issued to all Soviet first secretaries in all regions and territories, and the heads of all military districts and departments, instructing them to increase border protection and internal preventative activities.[106] Leningrad became a closed city to Western diplomats, with US and European diplomats being kept under surveillance.[107] Soviet citizens were ordered to participate in civil defence exercises, including evacuations to nuclear fallout shelters in Moscow and other major cities. Factories, offices and schools conducted civil defence drills.

Lieutenant General Leonard Perroots was assistant chief of staff for Intelligence at the Ramstein Air Force Base in Germany while the Soviets were preparing for a nuclear conflict. At the beginning of the second week of November, Perroots started to receive reports of unparalleled Soviet military activity. He spoke with the commander-in-chief of the US Air Forces in Europe, General Billy Minter. When Minter asked Perroots whether the USAF should increase its real force generation, Perroots advised that there was insufficient evidence to justify doing so and that the situation should instead be closely monitored for any changes. As a result, neither the US nor NATO decided to increase real force generation and later the Soviet Union lowered the state of alert of its missiles and forces.[108]

On 9 November in Brussels, a top-level West German NATO employee, Rainer Rupp, who was also a covert agent of East German intelligence, used a burst transmitter and a public payphone to reassure his handlers in East Berlin that NATO was not planning a pre-emptive nuclear attack. Rupp passed on the information through a Bond-like gadget resembling a calculator. The device would transform coded message into a short burst of static. Then he went to a phone booth and dialled a number. From HVA headquarters in the Lichtenberg district of Berlin, the communication Rupp had sent was immediately passed on to the KGB Centre in Moscow. It was as though the Centre was getting a message direct from the command headquarters of NATO that nothing untoward was happening.[109]

Oleg Gordievsky—a KGB spy—was the protégé of Andropov. He had the suave looks of a KGB operative—square jaw, pursed lips, narrow eyes—except his hair was so blond as to be conspicuous. He looked Nordic. It helped his cover at previous postings, in places like Copenhagen.[110] Gordievsky was trained in spy craft at the KGB's Red Banner elite training academy, deep in the woods 50 miles north of Moscow. The academy was code-named School 101, an echo of George Orwell's Room 101 in *1984*.[111]

Gordievsky liked the British culture: whisky, cigars, cricket, gentlemen's clubs, tailored tweed, billiards, strolling on boulevards ensconced by medieval architecture, sipping Glenlivet in panelled clubrooms, and gossip. In London Gordievsky immersed himself in the artistic life of the British capital, in gallery openings and theatrical performances. He enjoyed listening to the classical works of Bach and Handel played by the London Philharmonic Orchestra in the spectacular surroundings of Royal Albert Hall. He loved London's parks and pubs and the little Middle Eastern restaurants of Kensington with their exotic, spicy fragrances. Perhaps that is why he was working as a double agent for the British intelligence.

Gordievsky was providing his British handlers in MI6 with documents revealing that Soviet officials were viewing the exercise as a prelude to an attack by the US and NATO.[112] On 8 November, a telegram duly arrived at the KGB's London station, addressed to Arkadi Guk (under his alias 'Yermakov'), labelled 'strictly personal' and 'top secret'. The telegram from the KGB warned that once the US and NATO decided to launch a first strike, their missiles would be airborne in seven to 10 days. It also contained the details of Operation RYAN. In the evening Gordievsky smuggled it out of the embassy in his pocket. It was seven in the evening. Snow had fallen overnight and the temperature was minus six. Gordievsky left his apartment and drove his unheated car on a deserted, tree-lined street. The telegram was handed over by Gordievsky to John Scarlett of MI6.[113]

MI6 passed on the details to the cabinet secretary Sir Robert Armstrong. He briefed British PM Margaret Thatcher that the Soviets' response did not appear to be an exercise because it 'took place over a major Soviet holiday, it had the form of actual military activity and alerts, not just war-gaming, and it was limited geographically to the area, central Europe, covered by the NATO exercise which the Soviet Union was monitoring.' Armstrong told Thatcher that Moscow's response 'shows the concern of the Soviet Union over a possible NATO surprise attack mounted under cover of exercises.' Later, during a lengthy meeting with Thatcher, Gordievsky supplied a fuller report on the Soviet war preparations, including details of Operation RYAN.[114] He described the leadership's worries of a 'decapitating' strike from the Pershing missiles.[115]

Gordievsky became a close advisor to Thatcher on Soviet matters. Thatcher travelled the short distance from 10 Downing Street to give a talk to her party's youth leadership—the Young Conservatives. Entering the ballroom at the High Cliff Hotel, she was introduced to a number of visitors from the diplomatic core. One of the first hands she grasped belonged to a man with close-cropped blonde hair and a thin smile, Oleg Gordievsky.[116] Probably no British prime minister has ever followed the case of a British agent with as much personal attention as Mrs Thatcher devoted to Gordievsky.[117]

Thatcher was so alarmed by the briefings that she ordered her officials to 'consider what could be done to remove the danger that, by miscalculating western intentions, the Soviet Union would over-react.' She ordered her officials to 'urgently consider how to approach the Americans on the question of possible Soviet misapprehensions about a surprise Nato attack.'[118] Margaret Thatcher's government urgently warned Washington of the danger.

The Foreign Office and Ministry of Defence drafted a joint paper for discussion with the US that proposed 'NATO should inform the Soviet Union on a routine basis of proposed NATO exercise activity involving nuclear play.' MI6 forwarded a memo containing the details of the Soviet military preparations for war provided by Gordievsky to CIA director William Casey. William Casey sent the alarming message to Reagan about the war events. Reagan 'expressed surprise upon reading the Casey memorandum and described the events as "really scary".'[119]

US-Soviet backchannel contacts warned that the tense atmosphere in the Soviet Union was not just propaganda. The NSC Soviet expert Jack Matlock had a lunch meeting with

Sergei Vishensky, a columnist for *Pravda,* at The Buck Stops Here cafeteria. Vishensky, who Matlock believed was 'conveying a series of messages someone in the regime wants us to hear,' warned that 'the state of U.S.-Soviet relations has deteriorated to a dangerous point. Many in the Soviet public are asking if war is imminent.' He also told Matlock that 'the leadership is convinced that the Reagan Administration is out to bring their system down and will give no quarter; therefore they have no choice but to hunker down and fight back.'[120]

All this while, Able Archer was being played out in Europe. The United Kingdom came next in its imagined scenario: On 10 November, attacks on UK airfields disrupted B-52 and KC-135 operations as well as destroyed some aircraft. Unable to stop the Soviets' conventional advance, the NATO had requested initial limited use of nuclear weapons against pre-selected fixed targets on the morning of 8 November. Because this initial nuclear response did not stop the Warsaw Pact's aggression, the Supreme Allied Commander Europe (SACEUR) requested follow-on use of nuclear weapons the next day. Washington approved this request within 24 hours, and on 11 November the follow-on attack was executed. Then, with nothing left to destroy, the exercise ended.[121] They had practised the release of nuclear weapons. That was it. The exercise did not follow on with what would have happened next. Some who had been working through the night probably went for a celebratory drink. Farewells were said. Backs were patted. Departures made. Able Archer 83 was over.[122]

In Kremlin, all the senior members of the Politburo and the leadership had vivid memories of the Second World War. They knew the savage destruction that war could bring. The Soviet Union had lost an estimated 27 million soldiers and citizens during that conflict. Ogarkov, deep in the central military command bunker, and Ustinov in the Ministry of Defence did not want to push the nuclear button—unless they absolutely had to—and bring down on an even worse catastrophe on a new generation of their people. But no alarm was received of enemy launches, and the leaders refrained from launching their own nuclear weapons in anticipation of an assault. Probably the most dangerous moment of the Cold War passed. As dawn came up on another day, the world had survived.[123]

Conclusion

At the Commonwealth heads of government conference in New Delhi later that month, less than two weeks after the Able Archer 83 exercise had ended, there was a discussion with the Tanzanian president Julius Nyerere and others. Nyerere then cited a Swahili proverb: 'When the elephants fight, it is the grass that suffers.' Listening in, the prime minister of Singapore Lee Kuan Yew added, 'So too when the elephants make love!' 'I would prefer that,' replied Nyerere, 'for at least it would enhance the prospects for peace.'[124]

The Day After is an American film which portrays a tale of a nuclear exchange between America and the Soviet Union set in the American Midwest. The film postulates a fictional war between the NATO forces and the Warsaw Pact that rapidly escalates into a full-scale nuclear exchange between the US and the Soviet Union. More than 100 million people watched the film during its initial broadcast.

The film was first aired on 20 November 1983, days after the worst real nuclear standoff in Cold War Europe began to wind down. Ronald Reagan screened the film in the White House. It seems evident that *The Day After*, along with a nuclear war briefing he received at the Pentagon that fall, affected Reagan's view of nuclear weapons and the need for serious arms control. Reagan later sent the film's director Nicholas Meyer a telegram after the summit: 'Don't think your movie didn't have any part of this, because it did.' He was adamant—'That will not happen on my watch.' Four years after the film aired, Reagan and Soviet leader Mikhail Gorbachev signed the Intermediate-Range Nuclear Forces Treaty, reducing both countries' stockpiles.

Thatcher met Gorbachev in London and assented to 'doing business' together. Reagan wanted to start with a private talk. He began by saying that they had both come from humble beginnings but now were the only two men in the world who 'could start WWIII or bring peace to the world'. Gorbachev spoke about the various events that culminated in Able Archer which nearly brought the world to a Third World War. Both agreed to work towards peace.

Robert Gates was the deputy director for intelligence at the CIA during Able Archer. He described 1983 as 'the most dangerous year'. He would go on to become the director of the CIA and later the defense secretary. In retrospect, the 'miscalculation' that Andropov had feared five months earlier seemed plausible.[125] Paul Dibb, the former director of the Australian Joint Intelligence Organization, recalled, 'Able Archer could have triggered the ultimate unintended catastrophe, and with prompt nuclear strike capacities on both the US and Soviet sides, orders of magnitude greater than in 1962.' Soviet general secretary Mikhail Gorbachev likewise affirmed, 'Never, perhaps, in the post-war decades has the situation in the world been as explosive as in the first half of the eighties.'[126]

Petrov was awarded the Dresden Peace Prize and became the subject of a 2014 film, a docu-drama titled *The Man Who Saved the World*. Massie became a frequent unofficial advisor to the president on the Soviet Union. She met Reagan 22 times over the next four years, where he engaged her in dialogues about Russia. Massie was Reagan's window into the Soviet Union and provided the personal insight he needed to guide him as he tried to reduce tensions with Moscow. She passed on to Reagan the peasant saying 'Trust but verify.'[127] Leonard Harry Perroots Sr went on to direct the Defense Intelligence Agency from 1985 to 1988 under

President Reagan. Len Perroots Jr said his father's momentous decision in 1983 had personal ramifications: 'The bottom line was, he put his career on the line by not doing anything.' The chairman of KGB Vladimir Aleksandrovich Kryuchkov would be one of the chief plotters in the abortive coup of August 1991.[128]

The famous whistle song 'Wind of Change' was performed by singer Klaus Meine at the Moscow Music Peace Festival in 1989. Months after the song's release, the Berlin Wall came down. A grand finale to the end of the Cold War.

SEVEN

One Minute to Accuracy: The Silent Strike on Yamamoto

An intelligence message began: 'On April 18, 1943 CINC Combined Fleet will visit RXZ, R–, and RXP in accordance with the following schedule . . .'

> **TO**: COMMANDER, 1ST BASE FLOTILLA COMMANDER, 11TH AIR FLOTILLA COMMANDER, 26TH AIR FLOTILLA COMMANDER, 958TH AIR DETACHMENT CHIEF, BALLALE DEFENSE UNIT
>
> **FROM**: C-IN-C, 8TH FLEET, SOUTH-EASTERN AREA FLEET
>
> **INFORMATION**: C-IN-C, COMBINED FLEET C-IN-C, COMBINED FLEET WILL INSPECT RXZ, RXE, AND RXP ON 'SETSUA' AS FOLLOWS: 1. AT 0600 LEAVES RR BY 'CHUKO', A LAND-BASED MEDIUM BOMBER (6 FIGHTERS ESCORTING) AT 0800 ARRIVES AT RXZ
>
> DEPART RR AT 0600 IN A MEDIUM ATTACK PLANE ESCORTED BY 6 FIGHTERS. ARRIVE RXZ AT 0800. IMMEDIATELY DEPART FOR R- ON BOARD SUBCHASER (1ST BASE FORCE TO READY ONE BOAT), ARRIVING AT 0840. DEPART R- 0945 ABOARD SIAD SUBCHASER, ARRIVING RXZ AT 1030. (FOR

TRANSPORTATION PURPOSES, HAVE READY AN ASSAULT BOAT AT R- AND A MOTOR LAUNCH AT RXZ.) 1100 DEPART RXZ ON BOARD MEDIUM ATTACK PLANE, ARRIVING RXP AT 1110. LUNCH AT 1 BASE FORCE HEADQUARTERS (SENIOR STAFF OFFICER OF AIR FLOTILLA 26 TO BE PRESENT). 1400 DEPART RXP ABOARD MEDIUM ATTACK PLANE; ARRIVE RR AT 1540.

The dispatch bore the signature of Vice Admiral Tomoshige Samejima, commander of the Japanese 8th Fleet, with headquarters at Shortland, an island off the southern tip of Bougainville. The admiral was a newcomer to the South Pacific theatre; until lately Samejima had served as naval aide to Emperor Hirohito in Tokyo.[1]

On its face, it was an innocuous administrative message providing notification of an inspection of some outposts by a senior officer. Yet it contained time and location details of Admiral Isoroku Yamamoto's itinerary as well as the number and types of planes that would transport and accompany him on the journey.

The message NTF131755 was sent by the Japanese Foreign Ministry to diplomatic personnel in the South Pacific. The Japanese diplomatic code, known by the US code name 'Purple', had been broken by the State Department's secret communications intelligence section in 1940. The first message completely decoded was the November 1940 text of the Tripartite Treaty between Germany, Italy and Japan which contained an agreement that if any one signatory became involved in war with the United States, the others would declare war in support. The value of this code was so great that when Filipino guerrillas saved a copy of the 1944 codebook from Admiral Fukodome's crashed aircraft that March, the Japanese Army slaughtered several thousand Filipinos in an effort to force the guerrillas to return it.

The Japanese coded message concerning the forthcoming itinerary of Yamamoto was simultaneously intercepted by NEGAT (code name), a US Navy radio intercept station in Washington, DC, FRUMEL (Fleet Radio Unit, Melbourne, Australia), and FRUPAC (Fleet Radio Unit, Pacific), the communications intelligence unit for the US Navy's Pacific Fleet at Pearl Harbor.[2] Cryptanalysts at Pearl Harbor and in Washington immediately appreciated that they had intercepted a communication of critical significance. Marine Major Alva B. 'Red' Lasswell at FRUPAC leaped to his feet and shouted, 'We've hit the jackpot!'

The decrypted text revealed that on 18 April 1943 Yamamoto would fly from Rabaul to Balalae Airfield, on an island near Bougainville in the Solomon Islands. He and his staff would depart in two medium bombers (Mitsubishi G4M Bettys of the Kōkūtai 705), escorted by six navy fighters (Mitsubishi A6M Zero fighters of the Kōkūtai 204), from Rabaul at 0600 hours and arrive at Balalae at 0800, Tokyo time.

The key aces of WWII intelligence agencies were seldom mysterious operatives lurking in the back streets of Tokyo or Singapore. More often they were the unshaven cryptologists or photo reconnaissance analysts deep in a basement or windowless room, surrounded by the clack of IBM sorters and tabulator machines, or the stench of darkroom chemicals. Far from the fighting fronts, in Pearl Harbor, Melbourne, New Delhi and Washington, small groups of relentlessly driven men and women laboured over the greatest intelligence feat of the war: the recovery, decryption, and analysis of coded messages.[3]

Another wartime day had dawned at Hawaii as the morning colours had just been sounded and echoes of navy bugles still hung in the air. Flags had been raised on the ground and on ships in the harbour some 500 feet below. The port and airfields were busy, and heavy traffic snaked along roads to and from Honolulu. A little more than 16 months earlier, Japanese planes had struck here, plunging the United States into war—a strike launched by Admiral Isoroku Yamamoto, the most daring and formidable of Japan's naval strategists.[4]

Station Hypo (the H stood for Hawaii) was one of the branches of the navy's cryptologic programme—the largest signals intelligence programme of any of the US military services. Lasswell wore a green eyeshade to block the glare of fluorescent lighting and smoked Cuban cigars as he huddled over his work at a tidy, grey, metal desk. Lasswell had worked it out in every minute detail before he dispatched the Japanese message to the US Pacific Task Force commanders. He had plotted the itinerary and measured times and distances on maps. Everything checked out.[5] The contents that Lasswell shared began:

> The Commander in Chief Combined Fleet will inspect Ballale, Shortland, and Buin in accordance with the following: 0600 depart Rabaul on board medium attack plane (escorted by 6 fighters) 0800 arrive Ballale. Immediately depart for Shortland on board subchaser (1st Base Force to ready one boat), arriving at 0840. 0945 depart Shortland aboard said subchaser, arriving Ballale at 1030. (For transportation purposes, have ready an assault boat at Shortland and a motor launch at Ballale.) 1100 depart Ballale on board medium attack plane, arriving Buin at 1110. Lunch at 1st Base Force Headquarters (Senior Staff Officer of Air Flotilla 26 to be present). 1400 depart Buin aboard medium attack plane. Arrive Rabaul at 1540.[6]

Two US cryptanalysts took the message from Lasswell and rushed into the office of Pacific Fleet intelligence officer Commander Edwin Layton, Admiral Chester W. Nimitz's intelligence officer, and delivered the deciphered message in his hands.[7]

After reading the message Layton raced out of his office, into the bright light of dawn, and hurried across the grounds to the headquarters of the commander-in-chief, Pacific Fleet (CINCPAC), Admiral Chester Nimitz.[8] He passed the marine sentry posted outside his suite. Inside, a Samurai sword hung on a wall, taken from the body of the commander of a Japanese midget submarine sunk off Pearl Harbor on 7 December 1941. 'Zero Zero is in, and will see you now,' the aide said. It was 0802 hours. Layton was on time. He entered the office of Admiral Nimitz, who gave him a friendly greeting in his soft, Texas drawl. The office was so still that the footfalls of the marine sentry in the corridor could be heard. The room was oddly reminiscent of a Hawaiian cottage on the hills. Drapes of a gaudy flower print matched the chairs of split bamboo—furnishings left behind by evacuated navy families. The Admiral's desk was cluttered with souvenir ashtrays. Under the glass top were several stern mottoes and a signed photograph of General Douglas MacArthur.[9]

Layton handed him the dispatch and said, 'Our old friend Yamamoto.'[10] Nimitz pressed his wide mouth in anticipation as he began to read, passing a hand through his thinning, sun-bleached hair as he scanned the sheets of the enemy dispatch.[11] He sat rigidly erect and looked lean and fit. He had been up for two or more hours, and had hiked a couple of miles in the hills before breakfast.

They discussed several four-star Japanese admirals, men known to them for years; Layton's view was that no other Japanese admiral had Yamamoto's stature, experience, innovative thought, or charisma. Other Japanese admirals had technical ability and leadership skill, but none on par with Yamamoto; his loss would be a major blow to the Japanese Navy's strategy and planning, already reeling from defeats at Midway and Guadalcanal.[12] Nimitz walked towards Layton and narrated an anecdote that Commander Mitsuo Fuchida, leader of the planes during the Pearl Harbor attack, wrote: 'If, at the start of the Pacific War a poll had been taken among Japanese naval officers to determine their choice of the man to lead them as

Commander in Chief Combined Fleet, there is little doubt that Admiral Yamamoto would have been selected by an overwhelming majority.'[13] Aside from the emperor there was no one held in higher regard by the public than Yamamoto.

The intercepted enemy message laid out a detailed itinerary of Yamamoto's movements in the South Pacific islands, some 4,000 miles from Honolulu.[14] Nimitz walked to a huge wall chart of the Pacific Ocean and checked the distances between Guadalcanal—where there were army and navy fighters under Admiral William F. 'Bull' Halsey's command—and Yamamoto's possible destinations on Bougainville. This revelation of the hour-by-hour movements of a key Japanese commander presented a rare opportunity. Nimitz smiled slightly. 'What do you say? Do we try to get him?'[15]

'You know, Admiral Nimitz, it would be just as if they shot you down,' Layton said. 'There isn't anybody to replace you.' Nimitz smiled but didn't reply to the compliment. 'It's down in Halsey's bailiwick. If there's a way, he'll find it. All right, we'll try it.'[16]

Layton had been an assistant naval attaché at the American Embassy in Tokyo in the late 1930s, and had socialized with Yamamoto, then a navy vice minister.[17] They had met and spoken at official embassy functions, diplomatic dinners, formal cocktail parties, and theatre parties hosted by Yamamoto.

At the emperor's hunting preserve, Isoroku Yamamoto had played host on a duck hunt to a group of Japanese, American, British and Dutch naval officers. Layton could still smell the rich odours of soy sauce, ginger and wild duck that had boiled up from the *sukiyaki* pans. It was a Yamamoto Layton hadn't seen before—charming, friendly, courteous and dignified. He presided over the serving dishes to urge generous portions upon each guest, a short, trim, athletic figure striding about with bottles of sake and Old Parr Scotch, interjecting hospitably, 'Drink up! Drink up! Good friends must be kept warm.' Layton had played bridge against the admiral, who played with skill and confidence; Yamamoto had won both rubbers. At the hunt's end, with ceremonial care, the admiral had presented each officer with some of the emperor's ducks.[18] Layton regarded Yamamoto as the real deal, 'An official friend of mine.'

Layton and Rochefort led a little band of analysts who operated Station Hypo in what was known as the 'Dungeon', for the offices were chilly even in Hawaii's tropical heat. A few desks were jammed into a larger room that was festooned with maps, while IBM punch-card sorting machines clanked away in the smaller room. Rochefort padded about in carpet slippers and wore a tattered, red, smoking jacket over his uniform. He lived off sandwiches and coffee, caught a few hours of sleep on a small cot when he was about to collapse, and was occasionally expelled from the Dungeon and told to take a bath.[19]

Earlier in 1942, an intelligence game had been planned by Layton and his team. The radio traffic they intercepted in May 1942 suggested that Admiral Isoroku Yamamoto was preparing a major invasion involving four Japanese aircraft carriers of the Kido Butai, Akagi, Kaga, Hiryu and Soryu classes, along with many other ships, at a location designated with the initials 'AF'. It referred to the US naval and air base on Midway Atoll, two tiny islands located in the central Pacific, around 1,200 miles northwest of Pearl Harbor. Back in March, a Japanese plane reporting weather conditions near the islands had also mentioned 'AF', suggesting strongly that the designator referred to Midway. Rochefort's team famously devised a ruse. Via submarine, they sent a message to the base on Midway instructing personnel there to radio Pearl Harbor that the salt-water evaporators on the base had broken down. Two days later, a Japanese message was intercepted that reported AF was running out of fresh drinking water.

Later, Edwin T. Layton and Rochefort were summoned to headquarters to give a briefing on Japanese naval plans. Layton mentioned, 'They will come in from the northwest on bearing

325 degrees and they will be sighted at about 175 miles from Midway, and the time will be about 0600 HRS Midway time.' Rarely can one side have entered battle so entirely aware of the enemy's strengths and plans. When the sighting reports of the Japanese fleet arrived at CINCPAC headquarters, Nimitz went to his operations plot room to fix the location on the maps. Once this was established, he immediately turned to Layton. 'Well,' he said, 'you were only five miles, five degrees, and five minutes off.' Forewarned is forearmed; the battle of Midway was a triumph for the US Navy and a disaster for the IJN, which lost all four of its carriers in exchange for just one American flat top, the Yorktown.[20] It was a prediction of stunning accuracy.[21]

Victory at Midway was in no small part the result of the extraordinary work done by US naval intelligence. The Battle of Midway's success was a team effort that also involved Pacific Fleet intelligence officer Lieutenant Commander Edwin T. Layton; the gutsy fleet commander-in-chief Admiral Chester W. Nimitz, who directed U.S. carrier deployments; and Rochefort's skilled team of cryptanalysts.

In 1943, the information about the coded message immediately went from Chester W. Nimitz to secretary of the navy Frank Knox who delivered the news to President Franklin D. Roosevelt. The President's response was 'Get Yamamoto.' Frank Knox dispatched a 'TOP SECRET' message to Nimitz on 17 April 1943 that the designated 339th Squadron's P-38s must reach and destroy their target at all costs. 'President attaches extreme importance to mission.'

Yamamoto had organized the surprise attack on Pearl Harbor in 1941. The raid had enraged the American people and initiated war between the two countries. As a target, he was a high priority. Nimitz signed off on an operation to shoot Yamamoto out of the sky; he asked Admiral Bull Halsey to design and execute the mission. Halsey, in turn, tasked Admiral Marc Mitscher with orchestrating the strike.[22]

Isoroku Yamamoto

Yamamoto had been part of the Japanese fleet that delivered a crushing defeat on the Russian Navy in Tsushima Strait in 1905. Japan's foremost admiral, Heihachiro Togo, lured the Russian fleet into a decisive battle in the waters between Japan and Korea. He remained the most famous admiral in Japanese history until Isoroku Yamamoto attacked Pearl Harbor.[23]

The IJN had opened the war against the Russian fleet on the night of 8 February, with a surprise torpedo boat attack on the Russian ships anchored inside Port Arthur in Manchuria. Thus a weaker power began a war against a stronger power through a surprise attack—a tactic Yamamoto would use again 37 years later.[24] He had been assigned to the cruiser *Nisshin*.

In a single day—27 May 1905—the Russians lost 23 of their ships with 4,480 sailors killed in action and another 5,917 captured.[25] Against this the Imperial Navy lost three torpedo boats, 117 dead, and 583 wounded, including Ensign Takano. When Nisshin's forward eight-inch gun barrel overheated during the battle, the weakened metal burst, and the flying fragments severed the index and middle fingers from Yamamoto's left hand.[26] Thereafter, he became known in the Shimbashi geisha district as 'Eighty Sen' because the regular charge for a manicure of all 10 fingers was one yen and his favourite geisha charged him for only eight.[27]

A year after his wedding, he left his new bride behind and headed for Washington, DC, as the new assistant naval attaché at the Japanese Embassy.[28] He spent only a week there as a tourist visiting the White House, the monuments and the centre of US government. Then he travelled to his true duty assignment in Boston, crossing the Charles River to study at Harvard University from 1919 to 1921.[29]

In Washington, he concentrated his considerable skills on getting to know the US Navy—its ships, planes and influential officers—on an intimate basis. In off hours, he gambled in Cuba—where he also bought fine cigars to give to his visitors—attended White House receptions, played poker and bridge with US officers and watched the Washington senators play baseball.[30]

One of Yamamoto's special interests in his economic studies was the petroleum industry, which he realized was of utmost importance to any navy, especially his own because Japan had minimal oil resources and was greatly dependent on imports. As a result, most of the fleet's training during WWI was restricted mainly to the waters off the Pacific shores of Japan.[31] The clattering production lines in Detroit and the thumping pumps that pulled oil from the Texas dirt worried Yamamoto greatly.[32]

Yamamoto was enamoured by Hector C. Bywater. His favourite book was *The Great Pacific War: A History of the American-Japanese Campaign of 1931-33*, in which Bywater postulated a sneak attack by the Japanese on the US fleet in Manila Bay.[33] Bywater was a naval correspondent for the *London Daily Telegraph* and, it was later learned, led a double life as a spy for the British Secret Service. He was a prodigious writer who was fascinated with Japan's navy and, by the 1920s, had become a leading voice on naval science. The novel forecast a massive war that begins when the Japanese fleet launches an attack in the Pacific against the US Navy—a sneak attack, no less, a plot-point that was certain to catch Yamamoto's interest. In Bywater's imagined conflict, the Japanese surprise attack at sea is coupled with invasions of Guam and the Philippines, the goal being to create an invincible Japanese Empire in the western Pacific. Bywater's plot then takes a turn—after Japan's initial hard-hitting blow, the United States recovers, counterattacks, and eventually crushes its enemy. This was exactly the plan Yamamoto would implement, ironically paving the path to Japan's disastrous eventual defeat as well.[34]

Yamamoto welcomed Bywater into his hotel suite at Grosvenor House. They settled into easy chairs, and a butler served Johnnie Walker Black, the high-quality blended Scotch whisky that was a favourite not only among officers of the Imperial Japanese Navy but also of Great Britain's prime minister Winston Churchill.

In the early 1930s, he played a crucial role in developing new attack planes, most notably the speedy, single-engine Zero fighter. He persuaded leading aircraft manufacturers such as Mitsubishi and Nakajima to design new fighters, torpedo planes and long-range bombers.[35] A twin-engine bomber with an incredibly long range was also needed because Yamamoto saw the need to be able to cover the vast distances between islands in the Pacific. Mitsubishi manufactured the G4M Betty which—if fully loaded—could fly a 2,000-mile mission. A dozen years later, Yamamoto would be shot down aboard a Betty.[36]

Yamamoto argued for airpower as being central to the navy's future while his superiors still measured sea strength in tonnage, big guns and larger ships.[37] Admiral Yamamoto's fleets sailed from one impressive victory to another, and Allied leaders had no problem envisioning the Rising Sun flag being hoisted in a vast semicircle from the cold shores of Russia all the way down to New Zealand.[38]

The Planning

The mission had been approved by Pearl Harbor and Washington.[39] The high command met to prepare a plan to assassinate Yamamoto on 18 April 1943 at Bougainville Island when his transport bomber aircraft was to be intercepted by the US Army Air Force's (USAAF) fighter aircraft operating from Kukum Field on Guadalcanal. It was on the same date a year before that a 16-ship task force—under the command of Admiral William F. Halsey—had launched Lieutenant Colonel James H. 'Jimmy' Doolittle and his fleet of 16 B-25 medium bombers on their morale-boosting raid against Tokyo and four other major Japanese cities. Doolittle and his raiders had departed the carrier *Hornet*—then under the command of Captain Marc A. Mitscher, now assigned as commander of air forces in the Solomon Islands (COMAIRSOL) with the rank of rear admiral. The interception would be assigned to his command.[40] Admiral Nimitz gave the go-ahead for Operation Vengeance on 17 April. Admiral Nimitz was the commanding officer of the operation in which 16 P-38 Lightnings of US Air Force 339th Fighter Squadron—equipped with long-range fuel tanks—flew about 400 miles (700 kilometres) from Guadalcanal, at 66.6 feet (20 metres) over open sea to avoid radar and Japanese coast watchers. Major John W. Mitchell—the 339's commander—was assigned to lead the mission. He already had eight victories to his credit.[41]

The telephone rang in the pilots' operations room. Lieutenant Colonel Henry Viccellio answered and had a brief conversation. As Mitchell drowsed, Vicellio, the 347's commander, poked his head under the tent flap. 'Mitch, they want you over at the "Opium Den" [the pilots' name for the fighter command dugout] at Henderson.[42] They're cooking up something for your guys. Take Tom along and see what's up.' 'What is it, Vic?' 'Some mission or other. You'll like it.'[43] Rolling out of his sweaty cot on that steamy Saturday afternoon, Mitchell left with Vicellio, picking up Captain Tom Lanphier and Major Lou Kittel—the bearded commander of the 70th Fighter Squadron—on their slow, two-mile drive to Henderson Field, over pockmarked coral roads.

Mitchell, Vicellio and Lanphier entered the small, stuffy and poorly lit command dugout crowded with navy, marine and army officers. Lanphier recalled that every 'brass hat' on the island was there and they had to elbow their way in. A clear sign that something big was in the works. The dugout, unsophisticated as it was, was the operations centre for Admiral Marc Mitscher—a raw-boned veteran of several naval battles.[44] 'It was mass confusion…lots of smoke, and everyone was talking.' A marine major held out a sheet from a teletype machine—'A little job for you, Mitchell.' Lanphier looked over his shoulder, and both pilots glanced first to the signature. The message was signed 'Knox'. The text detailed the movements of Yamamoto and his staff on the visit to Bougainville.[45]

Major Mitchell, USAAF, found himself looking across the table at Admiral Marc Mitscher and all the 'senior leadership' present on Guadalcanal that day. In the close confines of the admiral's tent he read the 'TOP SECRET' message from the US president, and signed by the secretary of the navy Frank Knox, again:

> SQUADRON 339 P-38 MUST AT ALL COSTS REACH AND DESTROY. PRESIDENT ATTACHES EXTREME IMPORTANCE TO MISSION.

The Team

Mitscher asked, 'Who should lead the strike?' Viccellio did not hesitate: 'Major John W. Mitchell, commander of the 339th Fighter Squadron.'[46]

Pilots' names came up. Mitscher mentioned how impressed he'd been with the Tom Lanphier's recent flying feats alongside Rex Barber, Joe Moore and Lim McLanahan—a reference to the four pilots successfully strafing an enemy ship.[47] But ultimately, Mitchel was chosen as the commander of the strike.[48]

Mitchell scoured the list of about 40 available pilots and chose 18. They were men he had flown with from Fiji and New Caledonia with the 12th and 70th Fighter Squadrons and who were now assigned to the newly activated 339th under his command. All three squadrons were assigned to the 347th Fighter Group headed by Lieutenant Colonel Vicellio.[49] Mitchell let Major Louis Kittel select seven other men, besides himself, to fly in the cover.[50] That ended the briefing.

The army pilots who would lead the flight were summoned to the admiral's tent with less than 24 hours remaining before they would have to take off on the Yamamoto intercept. Mitchell conferred with Kittel, and together, they settled on a pilot roster for the mission. In the cover flight were Kittel and lieutenants Roger J. Ames, Everett H. Anglin, Doug Canning, D.C. Goerke, Lawrence A. Graebner, Raymond K. Hine, Besby Holmes, Jack Jacobson, Albert R. Long, William E. Smith, Eldon E. Stratton and Gordon Whitaker. Mitchell designated four pilots as 'the hunters' in the attack/killer flight: Captain Tom Lanphier and First Lieutenant Rex Barber as one pair; First Lieutenant Jim McLanahan and First Lieutenant Joe Moore as another. Mitchell, as mission leader, would fly the first Lightning in formation and be in charge of the cover group as well.[51]

The War Room

The target, Mitchell confirmed, would be the top man in the Imperial Japanese Navy, Admiral Isoroku Yamamoto. The admiral would be flying down to Ballale in a Betty. The P-38s would intercept the flight and shoot him down. While Mitchell would take most of the Lightnings up high to provide a covering shield for the attack, the four-plane killer flight would hit the admiral's bomber; then everybody would highball out of there.[52]

Admiral Mitscher called in several officers and began probing the problems of the mission. They talked of the route, the enemy coast watchers on intervening islands, the difficulty of navigating over open water, the range of the Lightnings, the probable defence of the visiting admiral arranged by Japanese planes on Bougainville. Mitscher was convinced by his survey that only a meticulously planned and superbly flown mission could make an interception across such a long course.[53]

Mitchell knew Yamamoto's arrival time at Ballale, but did not know which side of Bougainville his bomber would fly over. He predicted that Yamamoto would fly the direct route from Rabaul down the western coast, and calculated the best intercept point to be about 30 miles—approximately 10 minutes' flying time—for the bomber, which would be approaching the airfield at that time, descending from 5,000 feet. Since the admiral was due in Ballale at 0945 hours, the interception should take place at 0935 hours Guadalcanal time. Mitchell divided his flight plan into five legs. Working backward from 0935, he calculated that take-off from Guadalcanal would have to be at 0720. Allowing 15 minutes for join-up in formation, the flight should depart the island area at 0735 Guadalcanal time.[54]

The target lay almost precisely midway between Mitchell's base and Rabaul. Bougainville, an irregularly shaped island—somewhat larger than Guadalcanal—was about 320 miles northwest of Henderson Field by the most direct route. Since numerous islands lay between, most of them in enemy hands, Mitchell must fly a longer route, an arc over the open sea.[55] There were obvious problems with this. Navigation, for one. There were no landmarks at sea; one wave looked just like another. The fighters would be too far out for visual checkpoints, and far too low to see anything anyway. Pilot fatigue would be another concern. And the margin of error at 50 feet was nil.[56]

Mitchell estimated that once they arrived over Buin, his fighters would have no more than 15 minutes in which to target Yamamoto's plane and complete the mission. At the time, 'I figured the odds at about a thousand to one that we could make a successful intercept at that distance,' Mitchell later confessed. 'Today, after years of thinking about it, I'd make that a million to one.'[57] There were no guarantees that Yamamoto wouldn't change his mind at the last minute to delay his departure, change the itinerary, or cancel the trip altogether. The only assurance came from Captain Morrison, the army intelligence officer who had lived in Japan for a number of years. He reiterated multiple times that the Japanese were noted for their punctuality and that Yamamoto was publicly known for keeping precise schedules.

He assured that Yamamoto being on time was the one thing that could be counted upon.[58]

Joined by Morrison and Lieutenant Joseph E. McGuigan, a navy intelligence officer, Mitchell laid out a map of the Solomon Islands on a table in the mess tent and studied it by lamp light. There were many concerns: What tactics should they use at the interception point? Would Yamamoto's flight be flying direct from Rabaul to Ballale or on a dogleg course to avoid possible interception? How long could the P-38s loiter in the area if Yamamoto was late?[59] What about the hundred or so Zero fighters at Kahili? Would a number of them be sent up from Kahili to escort their leader to Ballale?[60]

The P-38s

Arguments ensued—navy and marine officers on Mitscher's staff came and went, each giving their opinions. The team considered the true determining factor of the mission, the distance between Guadalcanal and their target—about 450 miles. They went through the inventory of navy and marine planes and concluded that none, not even the formidable F4U Corsairs, were suitable.

Thus, consensus emerged on only one point: the P-38s of the USAAF's 339th Fighter Squadron—based on the Fighter Two strip two miles away—were the only available fighter aircraft that could fly the distance, make the intercept, engage in combat for a short time, and return. And that was possible only if at least one large 310-gallon belly fuel tank was installed alongside the regular 165-gallon tanks on each aircraft.[61] They were the only birds on Guadalcanal that could be modified with extra fuel tanks to reach the probable attack area and have a chance of making it back.[62] Mitchell decided to use all 18 of the available P-38s on the raid.

The mission would be executed by the US Army. The team was advised by US Navy pilots who had fought at Midway and were experts in Japanese air combat tactics. The pilots also showed Viccellio's men how they had used their Wildcats in dogfights against the Japanese. The navy fighters made tighter turns and climbed higher and faster than the cumbersome Airacobras and bested them in mock dogfights in the Fiji skies. The carrier pilots taught them how to fight in pairs, scissoring back and forth in the Thach weave, a pattern which would keep the agile Zeros off their tails.[63]

The planners sent an emergency request to 5th Air Force Headquarters on New Guinea to ferry up some of the larger fuel tanks—to be used for the auxiliary load—as soon as possible. Mitchell said that even with the bigger tanks the Lightnings would only have enough time for a couple of passes at the intercept point before being forced to leave for Guadalcanal.[64]

The P-38 Lightning had a superior altitude performance. They were always assigned high cover, leading to other pilots dubbing the plane a 'high altitude foxhole'. It boasted the highest altitude, longest range and most powerful armament. The twin-engine plane was said to combine speed, versatility and shooting power greater than any other plane. It could supposedly reach speeds of nearly 400 miles per hour—50 miles per hour faster than Japan's premier fighter plane, the Mitsubishi Zero—and could undertake longer-range missions of more than 500 miles.

Mitchell was told that the 310-gallon drop tanks were being flown in that night from Port Moresby, New Guinea. That evening, the long-range drop tanks arrived at Henderson aboard B-24 heavy bombers from the 90th Bomb Group.[65]

On 17 April 1943, Mitchel ordered all 339th pilots to wake up at 0500 hours, get breakfast, and report to the operations tent at 0600 for a briefing. Everybody retired to their tents that night. They could hear music coming from Doug Canning's tent—Glenn Miller's 'Serenade in Blue', with its easy-listening lyrics, 'When I hear a serenade in blue I'm somewhere in another world, alone with you'—and Lanphier actually fell asleep.[66] The night passed without an enemy air raid. Crew worked around the fighter strip, fitting the new tanks to the wings of the Lightnings, connecting fuel lines, loading the 20 mm cannons with incendiary shells and the four .50 cal. machine guns, and testing controls of the improvised long-range system. The welding torches had barely sputtered out when dawn shone upon the island. The 18 planes were ready.[67]

The Operation

The Airfield

The weather was fine when Mitchell woke up at 0430, ate a light breakfast, and rechecked his flight plan. The pilots straggled into the mess tent in the first rays of daylight, drawn by the aroma of the coffee. The morning was fresh and the sky sparkled. As the weather forecast had promised, there was only the slightest breeze.[68] When the pilots assembled, Mitchell told them the essentials of the task the squadron had been assigned, confirmed who the target was, and reminded them the mission was highly classified.[69] The 18 P-38s were checked and ready. Take-off time for the more-than-450-mile trip was set for a little after 0700 hours. Their target was scheduled to fly from Rabaul an hour after they were airborne, at 0800 hours Guadalcanal time.[70]

Alongside the core team of the killer flight—including Tom Lanphier, Rex Barber, Jim McLanahan, and Joe Moore—Mitchell chose Besby Holmes and Ray Hine as designated spares. He reminded the squadron that '[n]o one was to touch that mike button from the time we took off until we engaged the enemy planes.'[71]

Mitchell hustled down to the airfield, climbed onto the wing of his plane and into the cockpit. He wore a lightweight khaki flying suit and the snug-fitting rawhide marine boots that would not slip off during a parachute drop. He adjusted his helmet, goggles, radio headset and throat mic, then checked the instrument panel, fuel mixture control, prop and rudder settings, and control yoke. Satisfied, he positioned the strip map he'd drawn on lined white paper on his knees.[72]

Cockpits closed all along the flight line The crew stood away as 36 Allison engines shattered the morning stillness. The P-38s came to life and rolled heavily towards their take-off positions on the metalled runway.[73] The engines of the first four planes fired in unison, coughing dark smoke and throttling into a vast roar. Lanphier and Barber were wheels-up. McLanahan and Moore released their brakes, increased the throttles, and headed down the strip following Mitchell's lead. The planes had never been loaded so heavily and trundled near the very end of the runway, using flaps for extra lift, before rising into the air.[74] To the left, coconut trees and parked planes began to fade while jeeps, trucks and people vanished to the right as the big P-38 rolled faster down the strip. All that remained was for Admiral Yamamoto to do his part. So, at 0710 hours of 18 April 1943, the longest aerial interception mission of World War II commenced.[75]

Mitchell lifted off at precisely 0710, as planned. Men on the ground stood in groups, waving and cheering them on.[76] They zoomed over the coconut stumps and Mitchell led them in a slow overhead circle, turning to allow the next planes to cut the arc and join him. He was followed by his wingman, Jack Jacobson, then by Canning and Goerke. Admiral Mitscher had come over to see them off and sat alone in his jeep on the apron of the strip, buffeted by the prop washes as he waved a hand to each plane, crinkling the seamed face with 'The Guadalcanal Smile'. Mitch and Jacobson circled the airfield at an altitude of about 4,000 feet, waiting for the others to join them and form up.[77] The killer group was next, with Lanphier leading the fray.[78]

McLanahan bounced along behind them, but close to taking off, his Lightning lurched off the runway, veering wildly; McLanahan had blown a tire on a loose spike in the matting. There was no time to wait for him. The killer flight was down to three planes.[79]

The pilots switched to the new wing tanks as soon as they were in formation, and only Joe Moore had trouble. His engines sputtered as he switched from his main tanks to the drop tanks. He switched back and forth, unable to start the flow from the new tanks, and caught the engines once more from the internal tanks by frantically working the handle of his fuel pump. He pulled abreast of Lanphier and made dejected gestures to indicate that he was getting no fuel from the drop tanks. Lanphier motioned to him: 'Turn back. You'd never make it.' Moore grimaced and pulled his plane out of formation and wheeled to the east. The killer flight was down to two.[80]

Mitchell set his power to give him an air speed of 200 miles per hour. The 32 big engines hummed steadily. The swift shadows of the planes skimmed over the water, bearing almost due west.[81]

In Rabaul

Japanese officers at Rabaul tried to convince Yamamoto to cancel the Bougainville visit out of fear of an ambush, being so close to the Americans. But he insisted that he wanted to thank his men in person for their courage during the bombing raids of the previous week, first at Guadalcanal and then at other US-held islands. Admiral Joshima urged him to change the plan. 'Please. This is dangerous. We no longer have rear bases there; it is the front line. I know the conditions.' Yamamoto smiled. 'There is no cause for alarm. Even if it were dangerous, I could not turn back now. I've told all these people, here, there and everywhere, all over the place. They will be waiting for me.' He threw an arm around Joshima's shoulders. 'I will be back, all right. We leave in the morning, quite early, and return in the evening. You must have dinner with me tomorrow night.'[82] He cheerfully reassured the concerned Joshima, 'This is no cause for concern… I have to go.'[83]

Yamamoto felt safe travelling with a cover escort of six Zero fighters, one of them flown by one of the navy's best pilots,

Shoichi Sugita. Sugita was considered a wild man in the sky, a *gekitsui-o*—'Shoot Down King'. He was barely 19 years old when he brought down his first enemy plane, an American B-17 bomber. He somehow survived the Battle of Midway and never slowed down. Over the next three years, Sugita would stack up more than 70 confirmed aerial victories and share in another 40 before he was shot down and killed over Japan.[84]

Late on the afternoon of 17 April, the final arrangements were being made for Yamamoto's trip. As always, he would not allow his entire staff to fly aboard a single plane owing to the risk of all of them losing their lives in case of a mishap or attack. Therefore, a pair of brand new Betty bombers of the 705th Naval Air Group were carefully prepared. Admiral Yamamoto and three members of his staff would travel in bomber No. 323. They would take off at 0800 hours and the trip would last an hour and 45 minutes, from Rabaul to the coastal town of Buin on the eastern coast of Bougainville Island.

Dawn broke bright and mild on 18 April. It was a clear spring morning and Rabaul was loud with birdsong. The admiral was adhering to his schedule. He had woken up early, preparing, as briskly as ever, for his journey. Aides had convinced him that he should wear a new dark-green field uniform. US intelligence would go to any lengths to find him in this forward area, his officers said; the admiral had to change uniforms both for the good of the service and his own safety.[85] Making last-minute adjustments, he stuck a handkerchief into one pocket, some folded toilet paper into another, and his diary containing the poems he had copied from the works of Emperor Meiji into a breast pocket.

The man who emerged from the residence that morning, dressed in the green uniform and black boots, hardly looked like the commander-in-chief of the Combined Fleet. He better resembled a determined soldier ready for a fight.[86] As they left headquarters, Yamamoto and his chief of staff Matome Ugaki met rear admirals Takada and Kitamura—the fleet medical and finance officers who were to fly with them—both wearing dress whites.[87]

His car drove down the hill, into thick green forests, until it broke out onto the flat coastal roads that traced through black volcanic ash. Other automobiles bearing members of his staff followed. Thirty minutes after the US aircraft had taken off—and 650 miles to the northeast—Yamamoto and Ugaki arrived by car at the east airfield at Rabaul. Because they were scheduled to return by day's end, they travelled light, taking only items that fit into their pockets.[88] Two Betty bombers that had flown in from an air strip seven miles away were waiting.[89]

Three staff cars pulled up near the parked aircraft. Admirals Kusaka and Ozawa clambered from the first car to see off the commander-in-chief. Captain Watanabe, who had given up his seat on the plane, was also there to say farewell. Nine passengers emerged from the other two cars to see that, surprisingly, Yamamoto had forsaken his customary starched white uniform for the plain, green tropical tunic.[90]

After greetings and mutual bows, the admiral handed a special gift to the newly appointed commander of the Eighth Fleet, two scrolls of his copied Meiji poetry. Then he climbed aboard the bomber with the number '323' painted on its tail and settled into a seat right behind the pilots. The flight was commanded by Flight Warrant Officer Takeo Kotani with Chief Flight Seaman Akiharu Ohsaki as co-pilot and six additional aircrew personnel. The chief surgeon of the Combined Fleet Rear Admiral Rokuro Takada, naval air force staff officer Commander Toibana, and Yamamoto's secretary found places farther back in the plane.[91]

Ugaki boarded the second plane—No. 326—with Rear Admiral Motoharu Kitamura, chief paymaster; Commander Rinji Tomono, the fleet weather officer; Commander Kaoru Imanaka, communications staff officer; and Commander Suteji Muroi, a naval air force staff officer. Flight Petty Officer Hiroshi Hayashi was the pilot and Chief Flight Seaman Fumikatsu Fujimoto was co-pilot. There were also five air crewmen aboard No. 326.[92] The Japanese communication about the trip that the US code breakers had intercepted had mentioned only one Betty bomber. But the final travel plan had the two high-ranking officials flying separately for security purposes.[93]

Six experienced combat veterans had been picked for the escort. The first flight would be led by Lieutenant Takeshi Morizaki—the commander of the escort. Flying on his wings would be Flight Petty Officer First Class Toyomitsu Tsujinoue and Assistant Flight Petty Officer Shoichi Sugita. Chief Petty Officer Yoshimi Hidaka would lead the second flight with Petty Officer Second Class Yasuji Okazaki on one wing and Assistant Flight Petty Officer Kenji Yanagiya on the other. They were old friends who had graduated from the same flight school and survived numerous combat missions.[94]

Precisely at 0800 hours, Isoroku Yamamoto's plane rose from Rabaul's Lakunai Airfield. The engines roared to life, and the two bombers hurried down the empty runway and lifted easily into the air. Behind them came the six Zero fighters of the 309th Fighter Squadron, churning up a cloud of dust. As they climbed, the escort planes broke into two groups of three and slid into position on the flanks of the lead bomber.[95] From the sky they looked down upon the volcanoes towering over Rabaul.[96]

Several officers saw the departure, among them Kukada and one of his staff, Commander Masatake Okumiya, who personally waved the two bombers off the starting line this morning. Several officers watched glumly as the commander's bomber picked up speed—Admiral Joshima and General Imamura, uneasy over their failure to halt Yamamoto's flight, and Captain Watanabe, disappointed at being left behind.[97]

As a concession to security, and to permit the Combined Fleet commander to see something of his deployed forces, the flight path made its first landfall at the southern tip of New Ireland, then turned south along the east coast of Bougainville, past the Japanese bases at Buka and Kieta, on to Buin.[98] As the Japanese held air superiority at Buin, they did not anticipate enemy action. Ugaki recorded that his plane was flying in excellent formation to the left and slightly to the rear of Yamamoto's aircraft—so excellent that at times the wingtips seemed almost in danger of touching. He could clearly see the profile of the c-in-c in the captain's seat, and the forms of people moving inside the plane. It was a comfortable flight as he sat listening to explanations, with reference to flight maps, of objects visible on the ground below.[99]

The new Bettys were remarkable planes with a range of almost 2,300 miles. Only a few months earlier, when Americans met them west of the Gilbert Islands, far from the nearest Japanese base, they thought the bombers had flown from carriers. However, the Mitsubishi designers had sacrificed the Betty's armour for range, and it was vulnerable under fire; Japanese crews knew the ship as '*hamaki*' or 'flying cigar'.[100] They could not get up and stretch, and flying such a long mission was like sitting in a bathtub for hours on end.

When not scanning the skies, Officer Yanagiya would occasionally check on the twin-engine bombers. With a wingspan of almost 82 feet, and about 65 feet in length, they were cumbersome beasts. They seemed powerful enough and bristled with machine guns for defence, but the big planes were mostly flying fuel tanks. They were gaining a terrible reputation among pilots for turning into torches when hit by enemy fire. Yanagiya preferred his Zero anytime.[101]

Meanwhile, Mitchell and his band of fighter pilots were on their way to the target location. The sun on the big windows of the Lightning gondolas made them feel like overheated green houses, and the shirts of the pilots were already drenched with sweat. The fighters had been designed for high altitudes and had no coolers; ventilation was poor. Mitchell thought that it must be 95 degrees in his cockpit.[102] They were two hours out, and had flown about 396 miles—only 40 or so miles to go. The pilots missed the radios; they had never flown so long without using them. The close quarters made them uncomfortable.[103]

A bead of sweat rolled down Mitchell's face. Gathering momentum, it furrowed a light stripe over his cheekbone, down around his mouth, and—when it could go no farther—hung suspended from the end of his stubbled chin. Stretching until gravity triumphed, the bead dropped onto the narrow strip map on the man's left thigh and splattered across a blue area marked 'SOLOMON SEA'. Condensation made the metal surfaces of the cockpit clammy; the control wheel was slick with moisture.[104]

Mitchell tried to hold them at 30 feet, but they were sometimes as low as 10 feet and sometimes as high as 50. He looked around and saw one of the planes lurch downward, too near the water; it was drenched with a froth of spray over the windscreen. As Mitchell watched helplessly, the pilot struggled, then eased upward to safety once more. The water raced beneath them at dizzying speed and the pilots were forced to look outward into the sunlit depths.[105]

Canning noted that the sea was as still as a mill pond—without whitecaps—and much clearer than the Atlantic. He spotted a huge shark, and when he saw another one, began counting; he would see 48 of the big fish on the flight, and one manta ray, which he thought must have weighed a ton or more. Holmes, who had so often fished in the Pacific, saw even more—schools of sharks so numerous that he did not think of counting them.[106] The prop blast of their planes created little feathery wakes in the moving sea as they sped along. The pilots test fired their guns, creating brief rolls of thunder. They might be in combat in less than 10 minutes.[107]

The Japanese formation of two bombers and six Zeros hummed along at a steady altitude of 6,500 feet. From Rabaul, they had flown east for a few minutes, then banked southeast, crossed the Saint George Channel and gone over the lighthouse at the edge of New Ireland. Then, flying in a straight line, they crossed the water again and found the long coastline of the violin-shaped island of Bougainville.[108]

The planes flew without incident over the open sea until they reached the western tip of Bougainville and followed its coastline southeast-ward. Ugaki had dozed off soon after departing Rabaul. They had been in flight an hour and a half.[109] The pilots were relaxed, chatting with their crews. No one was studying the sky ahead with any particular rigour since the preflight briefing had not included any mention or warning of possible enemy activity in the area. The northwestern tip of Bougainville Island was visible, and the plane carrying Yamamoto began a slow and unremarkable descent from its cruising altitude of 6,500 feet to about 4,500 feet. It was nearly 0930 hours and the island's coastline and thickly jungled lowlands were clearly in sight—mile upon mile of mangrove swamps, palm trees and inlets. To the north lay the Emperor Range, whose tallest peak, Mount Balbi, trailed smoke from its 10,000-foot cone.

Yamamoto, right on schedule, began to prepare for landing in 15 minutes as his aircraft continued its steady descent. Neither he or Ugaki, nor any of the pilots of the eight Japanese planes were aware that a few thousand feet below—off to their right—16 P-38 Lightnings were emerging from the haze over the ocean's surface.[110] But his ordeal was just beginning.[111]

Air Combat

A compactly built, intense combat veteran with eight aerial kills to his name, Mitchell was the army's leading ace on Guadalcanal. He had managed to navigate entirely by dead-reckoning on the longest interception mission of the war. Their flight had completed an incredible journey of 494 miles. His navigation was so skilful that the formation arrived at the intercept point at 0934 hours—one minute early.[112] The 16 primary planes—plus two spares—were divided into two groups: three flights of four fighters who would provide top cover against any Japanese fighters, and one flight of four fighters—led by Captain Tom Lanphier—who would do the hunting. Part of this latter four-ship flight, Rex's job was to break through whatever opposition existed, which promised to be heavy, and kill the target. A target that was the solitary, vital objective of this raid; one so critical that 18 officers were cheerfully volunteering their own lives to destroy it at all costs.[113] Several pilots of the killer section had been here before. Mitchell had often flown bomber escort in the region. Lanphier and Barber had sunk a Japanese destroyer off Fauro Island and blasted the float planes at Shortland, both just off the southwestern toc of Bougainville.[114]

The 16 planes had climbed to a height of 2,000 feet and were in a tight formation—Mitchell's four, Lanphier's four, with Kittle's two sections in the rear. They flew towards the island on a course almost perpendicular to the beach.[115] The planes rose abruptly from haze which lay like an enormous, invisible pool over the water. Mitchell was exhilarated: 'All of a sudden it jumped up at me and I saw Bougainville.' A towering mountain range thrust above the jungle, a bay and the coastline. He had hit Bougainville precisely as he had planned.[116] They began climbing to 10,000 feet, where they would wait in ambush. All that was needed now was the arrival of Yamamoto, but Mitchell only saw an empty sky for miles around.[117]

He thought: Here we are one minute ahead of schedule. Where is he? He should be about three miles back to the west. He peered to his left but saw no planes. At that moment Doug Canning broke radio silence and said, 'Bogeys! Eleven o'clock high!' Mitchell looked up and there they were, five miles away at about 4,500 feet—two Betty bombers instead of one and six Zeros behind them about a thousand feet higher.[118] The US fighters were over Bougainville exactly as the commander-in-chief of the

Combined Fleet happened to be descending to land.

Mitchell saw them against the mountains. He counted quickly: eight planes, two of them bombers. Two, he thought, and not one. Something's wrong. He glanced back toward the enemy. 'Roger,' he called to Canning. 'I have 'em.' He counted the six Zeroes again and was reassured; it must be Yamamoto. But could Lanphier's four planes take on both bombers? There was no way to know which plane carried the admiral—but there they were, just where he had planned to jump them. Mitchell felt a surge of exultation.[119] The admiral, true to his reputation, was on time.[120] It was almost as if the affair had been pre-arranged with the mutual consent of friend and foe.

Mitchell led his squadron of 16 P-38s into the attack As Mitchell had told his men before take-off, he led the high-cover planes in a rapid climb while the killer flight went after the two bombers.[121]

All six Zeros turned sharply to take on the two P-38 Lightnings that were fast approaching. Simultaneously, Yamamoto's pilot did two things: he pushed the throttle to accelerate rapidly and dived toward the jungle's treetops where it would be far more difficult for an attacker to hit them. Most machine guns in fighter planes pointed slightly upward, making the best firing position a tad beneath a target, and an attack plane trying to slip under Yamamoto flying across the treetops might easily end up in the jungle.[122]

The Zeros dropped their belly tanks and peeled down in a string to intercept Lanphier. When he saw that he could not reach the bomber, he turned up and into the Zeros, exploding the first, and firing into the others as they passed. By then he had reached 6,000 feet, so he nosed over and went down to the treetops after his absconding target. He came into it broadside and fired his bursts. A wing flew off and the plane went off-course. The Zeros were now pursuing him and had the benefit of altitude. His mission seemingly accomplished, he hedgehopped the treetops and made desperate manoeuvres to escape. He kicked rudders, slipped and skidded as tracers flew past his plane. Nonetheless, he managed to outrun them.[123]

As the Zeros fell on Barber's tail, Holmes whipped up and around, and shot one down in flames. Their attempt to draw away ended in another dogfight during which Barber exploded one more Zero fighter. Barber and Holmes were forced to use extreme evasive measures to successfully escape from the enemy hotbed and their course out, like Lanphier's, was further complicated by a huge cloud of dust fanning out from a swarm of planes taking off from Kahili Airfield.[124]

Mitchell was calling Lanphier from above—unheeded in the din—'Leave the Zeros, Tom. Bore in on the bombers. Get the bombers. Damn it, all the bombers!'[125]

Plane 1

Hayashi noticed that his plane was vibrating slightly because an antenna pole had come loose and was shaking in the wind stream. When the engines changed their sound, Ugaki awoke suddenly, sensing something was wrong. He recalled: 'Suddenly Hayashi, at the controls, saw a red tracer flash past. Tanimoto jabbed Hayashi on the shoulder and shouted, "Enemy aircraft!" Hayashi glanced up and saw a P-38 flash by overhead. He jammed the throttles to the stops, pushed the control wheel forward, kicked right rudder, and headed toward the sea. The lead bomber, still flying about two and a half miles to the right, had also nosed down toward the jungle treetops.'[126]

When Hayashi rolled out of the bank, he quickly lined up on one P-38 directly in front of him, not knowing if it was the lead bomber or not. The Japanese pilot steepened his dive, and Barber rammed his throttles up again as the bomber accelerated. Barber's turn had carried him slightly to the left of the Betty and he closed to approximately 50 yards behind it.[127] Dipping his left wing, Rex slid left past the tail, lined up on the Betty's other engine and sent in another burst as it levelled off over the jungle. Barber simultaneously began firing into him and saw the bomber shudder at each burst. He was so close now he could see its rear cannon and realized no one was manning it, which explained why he wasn't receiving any fire. He centred his fire on the fuselage—the vertical fin and rudder—of the Betty one more time. The bomber did a quarter snap to its left, 'the kind of a stall that would come from the pilot being killed.'[128] As he moved right, he continued firing into the right engine which began to emit heavy, black smoke from around the cowling. Continuing to rake the bomber with his guns, Barber shifted his fire back along the wing root into the fuselage, then onto the left engine.[129]

They were on the treetops now. As Barber drifted sideways again, he put another three-second burst into the fuselage from the left side and the Betty staggered.[130] It slowed down suddenly and he flew past it as it started to smoke. He saw the bomber level off while continuing to drop, less than a hundred yards from the tops of the trees.[131] Then, engulfed in flames, the plane brushed the jungle canopy before plunging into it, the left wing ripped off against the trees. Upon impact it exploded into flames and broke up—the biggest chunks being the tail assembly, engines and parts of the wings.[132] Looking back, Barber only saw a black plume rising.[133]

In the second bomber, Admiral Ugaki looked up in alarm out of the window during the hectic evasive action. He grasped Rear Admiral Motoharu Kitamura by the shoulder and pulled him to the window, pointing to the admiral's burning plane. 'I caught a last glimpse myself, an eternal farewell to this beloved officer.' The plane of the commander-inchief had crashed. It was the same spot where General Imamura had escaped enemy interception two months before.

The Betty's remaining wing, snagged by the upper branches of trees, was ripped from the burning ship, which careened from trunk to trunk and fell to the forest floor. Explosions flung flaming debris for hundreds of feet. A greasy pall of smoke rose above the gash in the green tangle, and through it flew thousands of terrified parrots and cockatoos in gaudy flocks of scarlet, blue, yellow, green and white. Soon after the planes had broken off the battle, the Ako villagers conferred in the region; some of them ran to peer at the smoking wreckage of the downed bomber, and a small man trotted the downhill trail, carrying news of the lost plane to the Japanese. On his way down the mountain, the villager met a native road-building crew under guard of Japanese soldiers. He explained with emphatic gestures that a great plane had fallen near his village, and a young army officer, Lieutenant Tsuyoshi Hamasuna, abandoned the roadwork and marched his crew after the villager on the upward trail.[134]

Approaching from the northeast, Hamasuna saw a large, white '323' stencilled on the tail. In the gap between the rear and forward sections the lieutenant found the bodies of two high-ranking officers, both admirals. One man was on the ground, his dress white uniform a stark contrast against the green foliage. Flat on his back, the officer bore the gold epaulettes of a rear admiral. The other officer wore a green uniform with ribbons on the chest. He had no cap covering his close-cropped hair and was wearing black flying boots. The epaulettes on his shoulder had three cherry blossoms. He was a *kaigun-taishō*—a full admiral—and was clutching a samurai sword with his white-gloved left hand, holding it upright next to his thigh. The right hand rested on his lap. As Hamasuna stared at the left glove, he saw the middle and index fingers tied back with thread—a full admiral who was missing two fingers. The lieutenant knew who this man was. It was Admiral Isoroku Yamamoto.[135]

Plane 2

Once Yamamoto's plane had plunged into the jungle, those aboard the second Betty could see the US fighter planes turning towards them. One P-38 pursued Hayashi as he flew over the ocean, skimming about a 100 feet above the wave tops.[136] He had brought the bomber down, trying to dodge the P-38's attacks, until the propellers almost dug holes in the ocean.[137]

Meanwhile, Besby Holmes and Ray Hine witnessed the strange sight of a bomber being chased by a P-38 that was itself being chased by three Zeros. It was not until much late that Holmes determined its pilot to be Rex Barber. He and Hine dived to the rescue.[138]

'I told Hine to take the Zero on Barber's right, and I slid over to get the two crowding him from the left… I let the first Zero have a long burst in his tail. I was firing straight ahead, without deflection, the range about 400 yards. The little Japanese fighter…exploded …' Holmes claimed a second Zero: 'I touched my triggers and watched the bullets nibble at the Zero's tail. The airplane fell off into the sea.'[139]

Tracers flashed past the wings, and the plane weaved back and forth violently as Hayashi tried to evade the fire of the pursuing Lightning. Holmes saw that he was moving at 425 miles per hour, much faster than the Lightning's red-line speed. He zoomed past Barber's plane. The bomber's gunners shot at Holmes. He fired back a short burst to get his range, then another; his bullets kicked up the water behind the bomber, but he held the Betty in his sight.[140] Holmes touched the trigger again and the .50 cal. machine gun chattered and vibrated, shaking the whole airplane. Bullets tore into the Betty. Then he pressed the button to fire the 20 mm cannon and listened to the dull 'POM-POM-POM' of the shells exploding. It was the longest burst he had ever fired. Lanphier also fired at the second Betty. The bullets ripped into the right wing and the engine burst into flames. Then the wing caught fire.

Despite the damage, the rear gunner in the Betty was pumping a steady stream of bullets at the US aircraft.[141] Ugaki saw that the 7.7 machine guns of the Betty were not reaching the Lightning, which came in swiftly, and opened fire while remaining beyond the bomber's range. He realized that he was firing cannon shells as well as machine gun bullets.[142] Suddenly, the bomber shook from the impact of the enemy's machine gun bullets and cannon shells. One by one, the answering 7.7 mm machine guns aboard the Betty fell silent. The Japanese gunners no longer returned fire. Ugaki saw that several of the crew were already dead as bullets continued to stream through the airplane: 'Abruptly our crew chief, who had been shouting orders to his men, fell from our view. Commander Muroi sprawled over the chair and table in the fuselage compartment, his hands thrown out before him, his head rolling lifelessly back and forth as the plane shuddered.'[143]

Just as Holmes was pulling up to make another pass, he saw the Betty crash: 'The whole aft section flew apart from the bomber and tumbled into the sea with terrific force, broke into pieces and scattered. Barber bored in and fired at the wreckage. The spot was covered instantly by a blaze that swept over the surface of the ocean. The Betty sank from sight.'[144] Holmes continued shooting until there was a puff of smoke and a flash of orange flame. We had completed the mission—both Bettys had been shot down.[145]

For Ugaki, 'everything turned black.' He felt the crushing force of salt water pouring into the fuselage and almost immediately they were below the surface. Ugaki and Hayashi were thrown out of the plane through the canopy of the cockpit.[146] Both started swimming for the shore. A rescue boat picked them up, along with Rear Admiral Motoharu Kitamura. They were rushed to shore for treatment.[147] Ugaki's injuries were severe, including a severed radial artery and compound fracture of the right arm.[148]

After the Betty went down into the sea, Barber pulled up to get some altitude and noticed Hine's left engine was smoking. 'Another Zero came under me and rolled and I shot him down. Hine disappeared. I could not locate him, nor spot a place he could have crashed.' Barber looked for a tell-tale circle of bubbles, which were usually visible for miles, but saw nothing—Ray Hine was gone.[149] It is believed that he also shot a Zero down as a total of three enemy fighters were seen falling into the sea during this part of the combat.

After the Attack

John Mitchell and Jack Jacobson circled over the eastern tip of Bougainville at 15,000 feet. They were pointing towards home when Mitchell saw a Lightning in trouble far below, smoking from an engine, with a Zero on its tail. Mitchell went into a dive followed by Jacobson; they reached 400 miles an hour until the planes were dangerously near buffeting. Mitchell fired on the Zero, which turned back towards the airfield at Kahili.[150]

Mitchell spoke into the radio: 'Head back at once. We're under orders to evade further action—we've done the job.' He had outrun the enemy and knew that he was safe: 'No Zero in the Pacific was a match for the P-38 in a high-speed climb; the Japs knew it as well as I did.'[151] With the mission accomplished, the P-38 flight broke up as each pilot headed for home individually. All but one made it back to Guadalcanal. Operating at the limit of their range, the other pilots sweated out their return flights.

Checking his fuel gauges, Holmes realized that he could not make it back to Guadalcanal. From the standard cruising speed of 260 mph he throttled back to 170 mph, just enough power to keep his fighter from stalling, and set course for the newly constructed airfield on the Russell Islands. With Doug Canning alongside him, Holmes kept switching back and forth between his tanks to squeeze every last drop of gasoline into his fuel lines. Finally, the Russell Islands appeared on the horizon. The airfield was still cluttered with steamrollers and other heavy construction equipment. Holmes set down hard and his Lightning came to a skidding halt near the far end of the track. When he opened the canopy his flying suit was soaked through.[152] He scrambled from the cockpit and did a war dance on the wing of his plane above gaping working crews. 'We got him!' Holmes yelled. 'We got him!' 'Got who?' 'Yamamoto—the Admiral—the Pearl Harbor guy!'[153]

Canning landed about 10 minutes after noon: he had been in the air about four hours and 45 minutes. He was welcomed by a marine who trotted down the runway beside him and handed him a cold bottle of beer as he emerged.[154] Later that day, a navy PT boat arrived. Since the PTs also had Allison engines installed and burned high-octane fuel, they furnished Holmes with about 120 gallons in 5-gallon cans, enough to return to Guadalcanal in a few hours.

Commander Read of Mitscher's staff first realized that Yamamoto had been downed when he saw some of these first arrivals doing barrel rolls over the fighter strip. It was a little after 1100 hours then. Within a matter of minutes, most of the mission's survivors had returned.[155] Lanphier was the first of the killer section to land. He put down on the bumpy runway and was astonished to see his parking crew rush out to meet him. He quickly cut both propellers.[156]

Barber also returned to Guadalcanal, sweating out his own gas supply in the final few minutes: 'I landed at Fighter Two almost out of gas,' he recalled. 'My crew chief showed me four bullet holes through the blades of my left prop and three in the right prop. There were 104 in-and-out bullet holes in the wings, tail section, and fuselage, probably 52 hits, all from the rear to front.'[157]

Pilots leaped from their planes and excitedly gathered to greet the next one to land, and when their mission leader touched ground at about 1130, a bunch of them began jumping up and down and cheering Mitch, 'like it was a football game that we had won.' He unstrapped his parachute and climbed down from the cockpit to a hero's welcome from all the crew chiefs.[158] The men who ran towards him were shouting and laughing—they were the familiar faces of his crew, with a mixture of strangers, mechanics, pilots, marines and soldiers, charging the plane before he could clamber from the gondola. They swarmed about the plane and pulled him out, thumping him on the back. 'It felt like a halfback who had just scored the winning touchdown.'[159] Two cases of 'Combat Whiskey'—the best in the navy's stock—were to go up to the pilots.[160]

A message was sent to Admiral Halsey:

> POP GOES THE WEASEL. P-38's LED BY MAJOR JOHN W. MITCHELL USA VISITED KAHILI AREA ABOUT 0930. SHOT DOWN TWO BOMBERS ESCORTED BY ZEROS FLYING CLOSE FORMATION. ONE SHOT DOWN BELIEVED TO BE TEST FLIGHT. THREE ZEROS ADDED TO THE SCORE SUM TOTAL SIX. ONE P-38 FAILED RETURN.[161]

Another military cable was sent notifying the chief of the Naval General Staff and the navy minister in Tokyo of Yamamoto's crash and disappearance. The secret cable prompted an emergency gathering of the country's top naval officials. The devastated Vice Admiral Shigeru Fukudome, a longtime friend of Yamamoto, spoke for many when he lamented, 'There could be only one Yamamoto, and nobody could take his place.'[162]

In both Tokyo and Washington, it was felt that the course of the war had changed with the death of Yamamoto. As an audacious strategist, he had no peer in the Imperial Navy and no true successor. As the chief designer and builder of Japan's naval air arm in the years of peace, he had used carriers and their planes with an easy intimacy other senior officers could not match.[163]

Emperor Hirohito addressed the Japanese people by radio; Ugaki heard the thin, quavering voice in his headquarters, a cave near Oita Airbase, far southwest of Tokyo. He announced the demise of Admiral Yamamoto. Millions of listeners sobbed, but Ugaki drank a ceremonial cup of sake, said goodbye to friends, stripped his uniform of its braid and insignia, and went from his cave toward his plane on the runway. At his side he wore a short sword that had been presented to him by Yamamoto.[164] One of his young officers, Captain Tamashi Miyazaki, trotted at his side, begging to be allowed to fly with him. The admiral refused, ordering him to his duty. But when he reached his plane, Ugaki was astounded to find 10 fighter bombers ready for take-off, with their crewmen standing rigidly alongside. 'Are you so willing to die with me?' Ugaki asked. The young men raised their hands in salute, and Ugaki led them into the hot August sky.[165] About two hours later, when the flight should have been near Okinawa, Oita Airbase heard Ugaki's last words as his radio crackled a message to his planes: 'I alone am to blame for our failure to defend the homeland and destroy the arrogant enemy…' Ugaki and his flight disappeared. The US Navy reported no Kamikaze attack on the fleet that day, but the eleven planes did not return.[166]

The Aftermath

Mitchell and Lanphier, who had shot down 11 Japanese planes between them, were feted as heroes.[167] Congressional Medals of Honor, the nation's highest decoration for bravery, were recommended for Major John Mitchell, Captain Tom Lanphier, and first lieutenants Rex Barber and Besby Holmes.[168] Each pilot was promoted a grade as soon as they reached the US, and Mitchell, Lanphier, Barber and Holmes were awarded Navy Crosses for 'extraordinary heroism…in the longest planned interception mission ever attempted.' Ray Hine also received a posthumous Navy Cross.[169]

Having been promoted to captain, after his tour of duty ended in June 1943, Rex Barber served in China as commander of the 449th Fighter Squadron, Fourteenth Air Force, flying 28 combat missions before being shot down in enemy territory. Although seriously injured, he evaded capture thanks to the efforts of local civilians. In 1950, Barber was sent to Korea on a special assignment during which he flew three combat missions. Subsequent posts included duty with the Air Defense Command and as air attaché in Colombia and Ecuador. He retired as a full colonel in 1961 after 21 years of active duty and died in July 2001.[170]

John Mitchell would return to combat during the Korean War in 1952, after assuming command of the famed 51st Fighter-Interceptor Wing based at Suwon. Flying the legendary F-86 Sabre from January through May 1953, Mitch downed four North Korean MiG-15 fighters, bringing his career total to 15 enemy aircraft destroyed.

Only two men have ever been targeted as individuals for their roles in planning attacks on the US. Osama bin Laden was hunted down and assassinated for organizing and directing 'America's second Pearl Harbor', the attacks on the World Trade Center and the Pentagon on 11 September 2001. Admiral Isoroku Yamamoto, architect of the actual Pearl Harbor, was killed in an act revealed by the codename for the event—Operation *Vengeance.*

Endnotes

Chapter 1: A Duel at Close Quarters

1 The continental powers were Germany, Italy, and Japan while the Allied powers primarily included the United Kingdom, the Soviet Union, and the United States.
2 Frame, Tom, *HMAS Sydney: Australia's Greatest Naval Tragedy*, Hachette Australia, 2018, pp. 41–4.
3 Olson, Wesley, *Bitter Victory: The Death of HMAS Sydney*, Naval Institute Press, Maryland, 2003, p. 136.
4 *Report on the loss of HMAS Sydney to the Senate*, Vol. 1, Chapter 3, p. 110.
5 Frame, Tom, *HMAS Sydney: Australia's Greatest Naval Tragedy*, Hachette Australia, 2018, p. 26.
6 Detmers, Theodor, *The Raider Kormoran: The exploits of a German 'mystery ship' in World War II*, Tandem, 1975, p. 25.
7 Frame, Tom, *HMAS Sydney: Australia's Greatest Naval Tragedy*, Hachette Australia, 2018, pp. 275–7.
8 Mearns, David L., *The Sinking of HMAS Sydney: How Australia's Greatest Maritime Mystery Was Solved*, HarperCollins, 2018, p. 25.
9 Stevenson, Jason, 'The Last Fight of the HMAS Sydney', *Webatomics*, 2008, https://tinyurl.com/3mc37mbn. Accessed on 26 August 2025.
10 *Report on the loss of HMAS Sydney to the Senate*, Vol. 1, Chapter 4, p. 193.
11 Stevenson, Jason, 'The Last Fight of the HMAS Sydney', *Webatomics*, 2008, https://tinyurl.com/3mc37mbn. Accessed on 26 August 2025.
12 Frame, Tom, *HMAS Sydney: Australia's Greatest Naval Tragedy*, Hachette Australia, 2018, p. 46.
13 Ibid.
14 Stevenson, Jason, 'The Last Fight of the HMAS Sydney', *Webatomics*, 2008, https://tinyurl.com/3mc37mbn. Accessed on 26 August 2025.

15 Ibid., p. 3.
16 Cassells, Vic, *The Capital Ships: Their Battles and Their Badges*, Regimental Books, 2000, p. 151.
17 Olson, Wesley, *Bitter Victory: The Death of HMAS Sydney*, Naval Institute Press, Maryland, p. 144.
18 Detmers, Theodor, *The Raider Kormoran: The exploits of a German 'mystery ship' in World War II*, Tandem, 1975, p. 26.
19 Ibid., Chapter 4, p. 194.
20 *Report on the loss of HMAS Sydney to the Senate*, Vol. 1, Chapter 3, p. 170.
21 Ibid., Chapter 4, p. 196.
22 Ibid., Chapter 3, p. 119.
23 Ibid., p. 108.
24 Ibid., p. 110.
25 Ibid., p. 109.
26 Personal communication with Heinz Messerschmidt, 2008.
27 Olson, Wesley, *Bitter Victory: The Death of HMAS Sydney*, Naval Institute Press, Maryland, p. 1.
28 Public Records Office: ADM 1/18899.
29 *Report on the loss of HMAS Sydney to the Senate*, Vol. 1, Chapter 1, p. 1.
30 Public Records Office: ADM 1/18899, Operation and Tactics, Evaluation of Important Events in the Naval War, Book 10.
31 Olson, Wesley, *Bitter Victory: The Death of HMAS Sydney*, Naval Institute Press, Maryland, p. 356.
32 Detmers, Theodor, *The Raider Kormoran: The exploits of a German 'mystery ship' in World War II*, Tandem, 1975, p. 177.
33 *Report on the loss of HMAS Sydney to the Senate*, Vol. 2, Chapter 9, p. 42.
34 Mearns, David L., *The Sinking of HMAS Sydney: How Australia's Greatest Maritime Mystery Was Solved*, HarperCollins, 2018, p. 26.
35 Ibid., p. 27.
36 Detmers, Theodor, *The Raider Kormoran: The exploits of a German 'mystery ship' in World War II*, Tandem, 1975, p. 178.
37 Olson, Wesley, *Bitter Victory: The Death of HMAS Sydney*, Naval Institute Press, Maryland, p. 178.
38 Gill, Hermon G., *Royal Australian Navy, 1939–1942*, Naval and Military Press, p. 453.
39 Detmers, Theodor, *The Raider Kormoran: The exploits of a German 'mystery ship' in World War II*, Tandem, 1975, p. 18.
40 *Report on the loss of HMAS Sydney to the Senate*, Vol. 2, Chapter 9, p. 13.
41 Stevenson, Jason, 'The Last Fight of the HMAS Sydney', *Webatomics*, 2008, https://tinyurl.com/3mc37mbn. Accessed on 26 August 2025.

42 Mearns, David L., *The Sinking of HMAS Sydney: How Australia's Greatest Maritime Mystery Was Solved*, HarperCollins, 2018, p. 28.
43 Ibid., p. 30.
44 Detmers, Theodor, *The Raider Kormoran: The exploits of a German 'mystery ship' in World War II*, Tandem, 1975, p. 182.
45 Mearns, David L., *The Sinking of HMAS Sydney: How Australia's Greatest Maritime Mystery Was Solved*, HarperCollins, 2018, p. 28.
46 *Report on the loss of HMAS Sydney to the Senate*, Vol. 1, Summary, p. xv.
47 *Report on the loss of HMAS Sydney to the Senate*, Vol. 2, Chapter 19, p. 402.
48 Stevenson, Jason, 'The Last Fight of the HMAS Sydney', *Webatomics*, 2008, https://tinyurl.com/3mc37mbn. Accessed on 26 August 2025.
49 Detmers, Theodor, *The Raider Kormoran: The exploits of a German 'mystery ship' in World War II*, Tandem, 1975, p. 181.
50 Ibid., p. 184.
51 Stevenson, Jason, 'The Last Fight of the HMAS Sydney', *Webatomics*, 2008, https://tinyurl.com/3mc37mbn. Accessed on 26 August 2025.
52 *Report on the loss of HMAS Sydney to the Senate*, Vol. 1, p. 389.
53 Mearns, David L., *The Sinking of HMAS Sydney: How Australia's Greatest Maritime Mystery Was Solved*, HarperCollins, 2018, p. 31.
54 *Report on the loss of HMAS Sydney to the Senate*, Vol. 2, Chapter 9, p. 13.
55 Olson, Wesley, *Bitter Victory: The Death of HMAS Sydney*, Naval Institute Press, Maryland, p. 241.
56 Stevenson, Jason, 'The Last Fight of the HMAS Sydney', *Webatomics*, 2008, https://tinyurl.com/3mc37mbn. Accessed on 26 August 2025.
57 Mearns, David L., *The Sinking of HMAS Sydney: How Australia's Greatest Maritime Mystery Was Solved*, HarperCollins, 2018, p. 31.
58 *Report on the loss of HMAS Sydney to the Senate*, Vol. 1, Summary, p. xvii.
59 Gill, Herman G., *Royal Australian Navy 1939–1942*, Volume 1, *Australia in the War of 1939–1945*, Naval and Military Press, Australia, 1957, p. 454.
60 *Report on the loss of HMAS Sydney to the Senate*, Vol. 1, Summary, p. xvii.
61 Detmers, Theodor, *The Raider Kormoran: The exploits of a German 'mystery ship' in World War II*, Tandem, 1975, p. 185.
62 Ibid., p. 18.
63 Olson, Wesley, *Bitter Victory: The Death of HMAS Sydney*, Naval Institute Press, Maryland, p. 248.
64 Mearns, David L., *The Sinking of HMAS Sydney: How Australia's Greatest Maritime Mystery Was Solved*, HarperCollins, 2018, pp. 37, 205.
65 Ibid., p. 37.
66 Olson, Wesley, *Bitter Victory: The Death of HMAS Sydney*, Naval Institute Press, Maryland, p. 233.

67 Mearns, David L., *The Sinking of HMAS Sydney: How Australia's Greatest Maritime Mystery Was Solved*, HarperCollins, 2018, p. 34.
68 *Report on the loss of HMAS Sydney to the Senate*, Vol. 1, Summary, p. xvii.
69 Ibid., Vol. 2, Chapter 9, p. 42.
70 Ibid., p. xvii.
71 Ibid., p. 389.
72 Olson, Wesley, *Bitter Victory: The Death of HMAS Sydney*, Naval Institute Press, Maryland, p. 267.
73 Winter, B., *H.M.A.S. Sydney: Fact, Fantasy and Fraud*, Boolarong Publications, Brisbane, Australia, 1984.
74 *Report on the loss of HMAS Sydney to the Senate*, Vol. 2, Chapter 9, p. 42.
75 Olson, Wesley, *Bitter Victory: The Death of HMAS Sydney*, Naval Institute Press, Maryland, p. 267.
76 *Report on the loss of HMAS Sydney to the Senate*, Vol. 1, Chapter 8, p. 389.
77 Ibid., p. 370.
78 Ibid., p. 389.
79 Detmers, Theodor, *The Raider Kormoran: The exploits of a German 'mystery ship' in World War II*, Tandem, 1975, p. 188.
80 *Report on the loss of HMAS Sydney to the Senate*, Vol. 1, Chapter 8, p. 389.
81 Ibid.
82 Mearns, David L., *The Sinking of HMAS Sydney: How Australia's Greatest Maritime Mystery Was Solved*, HarperCollins, 2018, p. 35.
83 Stevenson, Jason, 'The Last Fight of the HMAS Sydney', *Webatomics*, 2008, https://tinyurl.com/3mc37mbn. Accessed on 26 August 2025.
84 Detmers, Theodor, *The Raider Kormoran: The exploits of a German 'mystery ship' in World War II*, Tandem, 1975, p. 191.
85 Gill, Herman G., *Royal Australian Navy 1939–1942*, Volume 1, *Australia in the War of 1939–1945*, Naval and Military Press, Australia,1957, p. 456.
86 Mearns, David L., *The Sinking of HMAS Sydney: How Australia's Greatest Maritime Mystery Was Solved*, HarperCollins, 2018, p. 35.
87 Frame, Tom, *HMAS Sydney: Loss & Controversy*, Hodder & Stoughton, 1993, p. 224.
88 *Report on the loss of HMAS Sydney to the Senate*, Vol. 1, Chapter 8, p. 389.
89 Ibid., p. xiv.
90 Detmers, Theodor, *The Raider Kormoran: The exploits of a German 'mystery ship' in World War II*, Tandem, 1975, p. 191.
91 Stevenson, Jason, 'The Last Fight of the HMAS Sydney', *Webatomics*, 2008, https://tinyurl.com/3mc37mbn. Accessed on 26 August 2025.
92 Detmers, Theodor, *The Raider Kormoran: The exploits of a German 'mystery ship' in World War II*, Tandem, 1975, p. 191.

93 Mearns, David L., *The Sinking of HMAS Sydney: How Australia's Greatest Maritime Mystery Was Solved*, HarperCollins, 2018, p. 36.
94 Detmers, Theodor, *The Raider Kormoran: The exploits of a German 'mystery ship' in World War II*, Tandem, 1975, p. 187.
95 *Report on the loss of HMAS Sydney to the Senate*, Vol. 2, Chapter 9, p. 373.
96 Ibid., Vol. 1, Chapter 8, p. 370.
97 Detmers, Theodor, *The Raider Kormoran: The exploits of a German 'mystery ship' in World War II*, Tandem, 1975, p. 187.
98 Olson, Wesley, *Bitter Victory: The Death of HMAS Sydney*, Naval Institute Press, Maryland, p. 274.
99 Detmers, Theodor, *The Raider Kormoran: The exploits of a German 'mystery ship' in World War II*, Tandem, 1975.
100 Ibid., p. 201.
101 Gill, Herman G., *Royal Australian Navy 1939–1942*, Volume 1, *Australia in the War of 1939–1945*, Naval and Military Press, Australia,1957, p. 456.
102 Mearns, David L., *The Sinking of HMAS Sydney: How Australia's Greatest Maritime Mystery Was Solved*, HarperCollins, 2018, p. 34.
103 Olson, Wesley, *Bitter Victory: The Death of HMAS Sydney*, Naval Institute Press, Maryland, p. 34.
104 Ibid., p. 35.
105 Ibid., p. 77.
106 Ibid., p. 37.
107 Stevenson, Jason, 'The Last Fight of the HMAS Sydney', *Webatomics*, 2008, https://tinyurl.com/3mc37mbn, Accessed on 26 August 2025.
108 Olson, Wesley, *Bitter Victory: The Death of HMAS Sydney*, Naval Institute Press, Maryland, p. 356.
109 Ibid., p. 77.
110 Ibid., p. 78.
111 Ibid., p. 53.
112 Ibid., p. 79.
113 Ibid., p. 44.
114 Ibid., p. 82.
115 Ibid., p. 83.
116 Ibid., p. 51.
117 Ibid., p. 84.
118 Ibid., p. 79.
119 Ibid., p. 80.
120 Ibid., p. 73.
121 Stevenson, Jason, 'The Last Fight of the HMAS Sydney', *Webatomics*, 2008, https://tinyurl.com/3mc37mbn. Accessed on 26 August 2025.

122 Olson, Wesley, *Bitter Victory: The Death of HMAS Sydney*, Naval Institute Press, Maryland, p. 109.

Chapter 2: A Pearl Harbor on India's Doorstep

1 Ferris, John R., 'Student and Master: The United Kingdom, Japan, Airpower and the Fall of Singapore, 1920–1941', Brian Farrell and Sandy Hunter (eds.), *A Great Betrayal?: The Fall of Singapore Revisited,* Marshall Cavendish, Singapore, 2009, p. 80.

2 Heavily escorted convoys are groups of ships which are traveling together with significant protective measures in place, often including armed escorts from naval destroyers.

3 Clancy, John, *The Most Dangerous Moment of the War, Japan's Attack on the Indian Ocean, 1942,* Casemate Publishers, Pennsylvania, 2015, p. 36.

4 Jain, Sandip C., 'Hisao Kimura', *Sikkim Express*, 21 January 2023, https://tinyurl.com/5n8sbx97. Accessed on 28 August 2025.

5 *Armed Aircraft Carriers in World War 2*, 'Trial By Fire', n.d., https://tinyurl.com/mp7n3c7v. Accessed on 25 August 2025.

6 Jeff, 'Japanese Indian Ocean Raid on Ceylon in April, 1942', *Naval Matters of World War II*, 14 January 2012, https://tinyurl.com/5b5jy8r7. Accessed on 25 August 2025.

7 Ceylon Command, 'Battle Summaries, No.15 Naval Operations off Ceylon Mar.-Apr. 1942; No.16 Naval Operations at the capture of Diego Suarez (Operation "Ironclad")', p. 2.

8 Suciu, Peter, 'Japan's Indian Ocean "Pearl Harbor" in 1942 Was the Stuff of Legends', *The National Interest*, 1 June 2020, https://tinyurl.com/33a7c854. Accessed on 25 August 2025.

9 Leighton, Richard M. and Robert W. Coakley, *United States Army in World War II. The War Department: Global Logistics and Strategy 1940–1943*, Center Of Military History United States Army, Washington, DC, 1995, p. 170.

10 Lewin, Ronald, *Slim: the Standard Bearer. A Biography of Field-Marshal Viscount Slim*, Wordsworth Editions, Hertfordshire, 1999, p. 99.

11 'Battle Summaries, No.15 Naval Operations off Ceylon Mar.-Apr. 1942 (Also) No.16 Naval Operations at the capture of Diego Suarez (Operation "Ironclad")', p. 1.

12 Jackson, Ashley, *War and Empire in Mauritius and the Indian Ocean*, Palgrave Macmillan, 2001, p. 11.

13 Clancy, John, *The Most Dangerous Moment of the War, Japan's Attack on the*

Indian Ocean, 1942, Casemate Publishers, Pennsylvania, 2015, p. 36.

14 'Battle Summaries, No.15 Naval Operations off Ceylon Mar.-Apr. 1942 (Also) No.16 Naval Operations at the capture of Diego Suarez (Operation "Ironclad")', p. 2.

15 Clancy, John, *The Most Dangerous Moment of the War, Japan's Attack on the Indian Ocean, 1942*, Casemate Publishers, Pennsylvania, 2015, p. 36.

16 Ibid., p. 20.

17 Ibid., p. 59.

18 Zimmerman, Dwight Jon, 'Vice Adm. Chuichi Nagumo's Indian Ocean Raid', *Defense Media Network*, 25 May 2017, https://tinyurl.com/hjhvn46p. Accessed on 28 August 2025.

19 Clancy, John, *The Most Dangerous Moment of the War, Japan's Attack on the Indian Ocean, 1942*, Casemate Publishers, Pennsylvania, 2015, p. 12.

20 Elphick, Peter, *Far Eastern File: Intelligence War in the Far east, 1930-45*, Hodder & Stoughton, p. 31.

21 Clancy, John, *The Most Dangerous Moment of the War, Japan's Attack on the Indian Ocean, 1942*, Casemate Publishers, Pennsylvania, 2015, p. 9.

22 'The Saviour of Ceylon', *HistoricWings.com: A Magazine for Aviators, Pilots and Adventurers*, 04 April, 2013, https://tinyurl.com/bdddvrdx. Accessed on 28 August 2025.

23 Ibid.

24 Clancy, John, *The Most Dangerous Moment of the War, Japan's Attack on the Indian Ocean, 1942*, Casemate Publishers, Pennsylvania, 2015, p. 26.

25 Ibid., p. 26.

26 'AIR22/74 AID Weekly Intelligence Summary 17 April 1941 no. 85'; and 'AIR40/1448 Warburton (AA Chungking) to DAI 22 April 1941 no. 19'.

27 'CAB81/102 JIC(41)175 (Revise) "Future Strategy of Japan", JIC memorandum, 1 May 1941. For assessments of 'Japanese strategy see CAB69/2 DO12(41) Defence Operations Committee meeting 9 April 1941', p. 167.

28 Gunawardene, Nalaka, 'The Japanese Air Raids on Ceylon in April 1942', *Thuppahi's Blog*, 02 April, 2012, https://tinyurl.com/rub6y73n, Accessed on 28 August 2025.

29 Zimmerman, Dwight Jon, 'Vice Adm. Chuichi Nagumo's Indian Ocean Raid', *Defense Media Network*, 25 May 2017, https://tinyurl.com/hjhvn46p. Accessed on 28 August 2025.

30 Clancy, John, *The Most Dangerous Moment of the War, Japan's Attack on the Indian Ocean, 1942*, Casemate Publishers, Pennsylvania, 2015, p. 38.

31 Ibid., p. 35.

32 Evans, David C. (ed.), *The Japanese Navy in WW II: In the Words of Former*

Japanese Naval Officers, Naval Institute Press, Maryland, 2017, p. 98.

33 Kolinsky, Martin, *Britain's War in the Middle East: Strategy and Diplomacy, 1936–42*, Palgrave Macmillan, 1999.

34 Suciu, Peter, 'Japan's Indian Ocean "Pearl Harbor" in 1942 Was the Stuff of Legends', *The National Interest*, 1 June 2020, https://tinyurl.com/33a7c854. Accessed on 28 August 2025.

35 RHL, 'Debates of the Mauritius Council of Government', 19 June 1945. Stuart, Rob, 'Leonard Birchall and The Japanese raid on Colombo', *Canadian Military Journal*, Winter 2006–2007, pp. 65–74, https://tinyurl.com/47abbpak. Accessed on 28 August 2025.

36 Ball, Desmond, *SIGNALS INTETLIGENCE (SIGINT) IN SOUTH ASIA: India, Pakistan, Sri Lanka (Ceylon)*, Strategic and Defence Studies Centre, Research School of Pacific Studies, Australian National University.

37 Elphick, Peter, *Far Eastern File: Intelligence War in the Far east, 1930–45*, Hodder & Stoughton, 1997, p. 396.

38 RHL, FCB Papers, 'Inaugural Meeting of the Central Development and Welfare Committee', 1 March 1945, p. 6.

39 Clancy, John, *The Most Dangerous Moment of the War, Japan's Attack on the Indian Ocean, 1942*, Casemate Publishers, Pennsylvania, 2015, p. 18.

40 Boyd, Andrew Jonathan Corrie, 'Worthy of better Memory: The Royal Navy and the defence of the Eastern Empire 1935 – 1942', University of Buckingham, PhD Dissertation, 2015, p. 407.

41 Stuart, Rob, 'Air Raid Colombo, 5 April 1942: The Fully Expected Surprise Attack', *The Royal Canadian Air Force Journal*, Vol. 3, No. 4, 2014, https://tinyurl.com/mrxwvp4e. Accessed on 28 August 2025.

42 Ibid.

43 'Trial By Fire', *Armoured Aircraft Carriers in World War II*, https://tinyurl.com/mp7n3c7v. Accessed on 25 August 2025.

44 Clancy, John, *The Most Dangerous Moment of the War, Japan's Attack on the Indian Ocean, 1942*, Casemate Publishers, Pennsylvania, 2015, p. 9.

45 Ibid., p. 36.

46 Ibid., p. 12.

47 Ibid., p. 81.

48 Ibid., p. 51.

49 'Trial By Fire', *Armoured Aircraft Carriers in World War II*, https://tinyurl.com/mp7n3c7v. Accessed on 25 August 2025.

50 Richmond, Admiral Sir Herbert, *Statesmen and Sea Power*, Clarendon Press, Oxford, 1947, p. 328.

51 Clancy, John, *The Most Dangerous Moment of the War, Japan's Attack on the Indian Ocean, 1942*, Casemate Publishers, Pennsylvania, 2015, p. 40.

52 Ibid., p. 59.
53 Ibid., p. 56.
54 Ibid., p. 12.
55 Devarajah, Lloyd Rajaratnam, 'Ceylon's Pearl Harbour Attack: How allied forces thwarted the Japanese attempt to invade Lanka 68 Easters ago', *Sunday Times*, 11 April 2010, https://tinyurl.com/5bxuwp3j. Accessed on 28 August 2025.
56 Somasundaram, Jayantha, 'The Most Dangerous Moment', *Colombo Telegraph*, 18 April 2019, https://tinyurl.com/ybj4ps2v. Accessed on 28 August 2025.
57 Stuart, Rob, '"a raid of the Pearl Harbour type": The Japanese Attack on Colombo', *Combined Fleet*, 2022, p. 3, https://tinyurl.com/yec87jxt. Accessed on 6 November 2025.
58 Clancy, John, *The Most Dangerous Moment of the War, Japan's Attack on the Indian Ocean, 1942*, Casemate Publishers, Pennsylvania, 2015, p. 41.
59 Simpson, Michael, *The Somerville Papers: Selections from the Private and Official Correspondence of Admiral of the Fleet Sir James Somerville, GCB, GBE, DSO*, Routledge, 1996, p. 403.
60 Clancy, John, *The Most Dangerous Moment of the War, Japan's Attack on the Indian Ocean, 1942*, Casemate Publishers, Pennsylvania, 2015, p. 41.
61 Ibid., p. 43.
62 Ibid., p. 41.
63 Ibid., p. 43.
64 Battle Summaries, 'No.15 Naval Operations off Ceylon Mar.-Apr. 1942 (Also) No.16 Naval Operations at the capture of Diego Suarez (Operation "Ironclad")', p. 3.
65 Remmelink, Willem, *The Operations of the Navy in the Dutch East Indies and the Bay of Bengal*, 'War History' Series (Vol. 26), Leiden University Press, 2018, p. 569.
66 Ibid., p. 604.
67 Stuart, Rob, '"a raid of the Pearl Harbour type": The Japanese Attack on Colombo', *Combined Fleet*, 2022, p. 12, https://tinyurl.com/yec87jxt. Accessed on 6 November 2025.
68 Somasundaram, Jayantha, 'The Most Dangerous Moment', *Colombo Telegraph*, 18 April 2019, https://tinyurl.com/ybj4ps2v. Accessed on 28 August 2025.
69 Clancy, John, *The Most Dangerous Moment of the War, Japan's Attack on the Indian Ocean, 1942*, Casemate Publishers, Pennsylvania, 2015, p. 12.
70 Ibid., p. 12.
71 Ibid., p. 63.

72 Ibid., p. 69.

73 Stuart, Rob, 'Leonard Birchall and The Japanese raid on Colombo', *Canadian Military Journal*, Winter 2006–2007, pp. 65–74 https://tinyurl.com/47abbpak. Accessed on 28 August 2025.

74 Matt, P.E., 'The Indian Ocean Raid: Bay of Bengal and Trincomalee', *Pacific Eagles*, 24 February 2017, https://tinyurl.com/3xyxxrh3. Accessed on 28 August 2025.

75 Raghavan, Srinath, *India's War: World War II and the Making of Modern South Asia*, Basic Books, New York, 2016, pp. 268–9.

76 Matt, P.E., 'The Indian Ocean Raid: Bay of Bengal and Trincomalee', *Pacific Eagles*, 24 February 2017, https://tinyurl.com/3xyxxrh3. Accessed on 28 August 2025.

77 Clancy, John, *The Most Dangerous Moment of the War, Japan's Attack on the Indian Ocean, 1942*, Casemate Publishers, Pennsylvania, 2015, p. 69.

78 Matt, P.E., 'The Indian Ocean Raid: Bay of Bengal and Trincomalee', *Pacific Eagles*, 24 February 2017, https://tinyurl.com/3xyxxrh3. Accessed on 28 August 2025.

79 Somasundaram, Jayantha, 'The Most Dangerous Moment', *Colombo Telegraph*, 18 April 2019, https://tinyurl.com/ybj4ps2v. Accessed on 28 August 2025.

80 Devarajah, Lloyd Rajaratnam, 'Ceylon's Pearl Harbour Attack: How allied forces thwarted the Japanese attempt to invade Lanka 68 Easters ago', *Sunday Times*, 11 April 2010, https://tinyurl.com/5bxuwp3j. Accessed on 28 August 2025.

81 Clancy, John, *The Most Dangerous Moment of the War, Japan's Attack on the Indian Ocean, 1942*, Casemate Publishers, Pennsylvania, 2015, p. 64.

82 'The Saviour of Ceylon', *HistoricWings.com: A Magazine for Aviators, Pilots and Adventurers*, 4 April, 2013, https://tinyurl.com/bdddvrdx. Accessed on 28 August 2025.

83 Clancy, John, *The Most Dangerous Moment of the War, Japan's Attack on the Indian Ocean, 1942*, Casemate Publishers, Pennsylvania, 2015, p. 64.

84 Weerasinghe, Asoka, 'World War II – The Battle of the Indian Ocean (5 April 1942 – over Colombo, Ceylon) Interview with Commodore Leonard Birchall, OBE, DFC, CD (Retd) "The Saviour of Ceylon"', *Lankaweb*, 24 October 2021, https://tinyurl.com/4w8ayphz. Accessed on 28 August 2025.

85 Devarajah, Lloyd Rajaratnam, 'Ceylon's Pearl Harbour Attack: How allied forces thwarted the Japanese attempt to invade Lanka 68 Easters ago', *Sunday Times*, 11 April 2010, https://tinyurl.com/5bxuwp3j. Accessed on 28 August 2025.

86 Clancy, John, *The Most Dangerous Moment of the War, Japan's Attack on the*

Indian Ocean, 1942, Casemate Publishers, Pennsylvania, 2015, p. 43.

87 Clancy, John, *The Most Dangerous Moment of the War, Japan's Attack on the Indian Ocean, 1942*, Casemate Publishers, Pennsylvania, 2015, p. 48.

88 Clancy John, *The Most Dangerous Moment of the War, Japan's Attack on the Indian Ocean, 1942*, Casemate Publishers, Pennsylvania, 2015, p. 81.

89 Ibid., p. 71.

90 Ibid.

91 Ibid., p. 61; The Air Raid on Colombo; the Sinking of Two [Enemy] Heavy Cruisers ('Dai-go Kōkū Sentai Sentō Shōhō' (「第五航空戦隊戦闘詳報」['Action report of the 5th Carrier Division']).

92 Clancy, John, *The Most Dangerous Moment of the War, Japan's Attack on the Indian Ocean, 1942*, Casemate Publishers, Pennsylvania, 2015, p. 73.

93 Remmelink, Willem, *Operations of the Navy in the Dutch East Indies and the Bay of Bengal*, Leiden University Press, Leiden, 2018, p. 621.

94 Stuart, Rob, '"a raid of the Pearl Harbour type": The Japanese Attack on Colombo', *Combined Fleet*, 2022, https://tinyurl.com/yec87jxt, p. 48.

95 Clancy John, *The Most Dangerous Moment of the War, Japan's Attack on the Indian Ocean, 1942*, Casemate Publishers, Pennsylvania, 2015, p. 73.

96 Ibid., p. 79.

97 Ibid.

98 Ibid., p. 73.

99 Ibid., p. 76.

100 Stuart, Rob, 'Leonard Birchall and The Japanese raid on Colombo', *Canadian Military Journal*, Winter 2006–2007, pp. 65–74, https://tinyurl.com/47abbpak. Accessed on 28 August 2025.

101 Clancy, John, *The Most Dangerous Moment of the War, Japan's Attack on the Indian Ocean, 1942*, Casemate Publishers, Pennsylvania, 2015, p. 129.

102 Clancy, John, *The Most Dangerous Moment of the War, Japan's Attack on the Indian Ocean, 1942*, Casemate Publishers, Pennsylvania, 2015, p. 89.

103 Ibid., p. 101.

104 The Operations of the Navy in the Dutch East Indies and the Bay of Bengal, p. 624.

105 Clancy, John, *The Most Dangerous Moment of the War, Japan's Attack on the Indian Ocean, 1942*, Casemate Publishers, Pennsylvania, 2015, p. 89.

106 Ibid., p. 89.

107 Ibid., p. 85.

108 Ibid., p. 101.

109 Ibid., p. 86.

110 Ibid., p. 86.

111 Battle Summaries, 'No.15 Naval Operations off Ceylon Mar.-Apr. 1942

(Also) No.16 Naval Operations at the capture of Diego Suarez (Operation "Ironclad")', p. 8.

112 Clancy, John, *The Most Dangerous Moment of the War, Japan's Attack on the Indian Ocean, 1942*, Casemate Publishers, Pennsylvania, 2015, p. 86.

113 Battle Summaries, 'No.15 Naval Operations off Ceylon Mar.-Apr. 1942 (Also) No.16 Naval Operations at the capture of Diego Suarez (Operation "Ironclad")', p. 9.

114 Ibid., p. 101.

115 Ibid.

116 Ibid., p. 89.

117 Battle Summaries, 'No.15 Naval Operations off Ceylon Mar.-Apr. 1942 (Also) No.16 Naval Operations at the capture of Diego Suarez (Operation "Ironclad")', p. 10.

118 Matt, P.E., 'The Indian Ocean Raid: Bay of Bengal and Trincomalee', *Pacific Eagles*, 24 February 2017, https://tinyurl.com/3xyxxrh3. Accessed on 28 August 2025.

119 Ibid.

120 Stuart, Rob, 'Leonard Birchall and The Japanese raid on Colombo', *Canadian Military Journal*, Winter 2006–2007, pp. 65–74, https://tinyurl.com/47abbpak. Accessed on 28 August 2025.

121 Battle Summaries, 'No.15 Naval Operations off Ceylon Mar.-Apr. 1942 (Also) No.16 Naval Operations at the capture of Diego Suarez (Operation "Ironclad")', p. 14.

122 Clancy, John, *The Most Dangerous Moment of the War, Japan's Attack on the Indian Ocean, 1942*, Casemate Publishers, Pennsylvania, 2015, p. 114.

123 Ibid., p. 114.

124 Ibid., p. 121.

125 Ibid.

126 Matt, P.E., 'The Indian Ocean Raid: Bay of Bengal and Trincomalee', *Pacific Eagles*, 24 February 2017, https://tinyurl.com/3xyxxrh3. Accessed on 28 August 2025.

127 Remmelink, Willem, *The Operations of the Navy in the Dutch East Indies and the Bay of Bengal*, 'War History' Series (Vol, 26), Leiden University Press, Leiden, 2018, p. 630.

128 Clancy, John, *The Most Dangerous Moment of the War, Japan's Attack on the Indian Ocean, 1942*, Casemate Publishers, Pennsylvania, 2015, p. 121.

129 Ibid., p. 121

130 Battle Summaries, 'No.15 Naval Operations off Ceylon Mar.-Apr. 1942 (Also) No.16 Naval Operations at the capture of Diego Suarez (Operation "Ironclad")', p. 15.

131 Clancy, John, *The Most Dangerous Moment of the War, Japan's Attack on the Indian Ocean, 1942*, Casemate Publishers, Pennsylvania, 2015, p. 121.

132 Matt, P.E., 'The Indian Ocean Raid: Bay of Bengal and Trincomalee', *Pacific Eagles*, 24 February 2017, https://tinyurl.com/3xyxxrh3. Accessed on 28 August 2025.

133 Clancy, John, *The Most Dangerous Moment of the War, Japan's Attack on the Indian Ocean, 1942*, Casemate Publishers, Pennsylvania, 2015, p. 124.

134 Matt, P.E., 'The Indian Ocean Raid: Bay of Bengal and Trincomalee', *Pacific Eagles*, 24 February 2017, https://tinyurl.com/3xyxxrh3. Accessed on 28 August 2025.

135 Battle Summaries, 'No.15 Naval Operations off Ceylon Mar.-Apr. 1942 (Also) No.16 Naval Operations at the capture of Diego Suarez (Operation "Ironclad")', p. 16.

136 Matt, P.E., 'The Indian Ocean Raid: Bay of Bengal and Trincomalee', *Pacific Eagles*, 24 February 2017, https://tinyurl.com/3xyxxrh3. Accessed on 28 August 2025.

137 Hobbs, David, 'Chapter 7: Hermes', *British Aircraft Carriers*, Seaforth Publishing, 2013.

138 Clancy, John, *The Most Dangerous Moment of the War, Japan's Attack on the Indian Ocean, 1942*, Casemate Publishers, Pennsylvania, 2015, p. 124.

139 Devarajah, Lloyd Rajaratnam, 'Ceylon's Pearl Harbour Attack: How allied forces thwarted the Japanese attempt to invade Lanka 68 Easters ago', *Sunday Times*, 11 April 2010, https://tinyurl.com/5bxuwp3j. Accessed on 28 August 2025.

140 Clancy, John, *The Most Dangerous Moment of the War, Japan's Attack on the Indian Ocean, 1942*, Casemate Publishers, Pennsylvania, 2015, p. 124.

141 Gunawardene, Nalaka, 'The Japanese Air Raids on Ceylon in April 1942', *Thuppahi's Blog*, 2 April 2012, https://tinyurl.com/rub6y73n. Accessed on 28 August 2025.

142 Clancy, John, *The Most Dangerous Moment of the War, Japan's Attack on the Indian Ocean, 1942*, Casemate Publishers, Pennsylvania, 2015, p. 134.

143 Field Marshal The Viscount Wavell, 'Operations In Eastern Theatre, Based On India, From March 1942 To December 31, 1942', in The Supplement To The London Gazette Of Wednesday, 18 September, 1946, pp. 4664–6.

144 Clancy, John, *The Most Dangerous Moment of the War, Japan's Attack on the Indian Ocean, 1942*, Casemate Publishers, Pennsylvania, 2015, p. 139.

145 Ibid., p. 14.

146 Somasundaram, Jayantha, 'The Most Dangerous Moment', *Colombo Telegraph*, 18 April 2019, https://tinyurl.com/ybj4ps2v. Accessed on 28 August 2025.

Chapter 3: Neutral Territory, Hidden Wars and Espionage Beneath Goan Skies

1 Leasor, James. *Boarding Party: The Last Action of the Calcutta Light Horse*, Houghton Mifflin Harcourt, 1978, p. 1.

2 Ibid., p. 1.

3 Ibid., p. 3.

4 Ibid., p. 2.

5 Ibid., p. 4; Zimmerman, Dwight Jon, 'Operation Creek: SOE Enlists an "Over the Hill Gang" for a Mission', *Defense Media Network*, 10 August 2013, https://tinyurl.com/acen5drv. Accessed on 28 August 2025.

6 Miller, David, 'Operation Longshanks', *Revista Portuguesa de História Militar - Dossier: Portugal no Contexto da Segunda Guerra Mundial, 1939-1945*, Vol. III, No. 4, June 2023, https://tinyurl.com/3tfkm9zp. Accessed on 28 August 2025.

7 Miller, David, *Special Operations Forces in South East Asia 1942-1945: Minerva Baldhead & Longshank/Creek*, Pen & Sword Military, 2020, p. 135.

8 Miller, David, 'Operation Longshanks', *Revista Portuguesa de História Militar - Dossier: Portugal no Contexto da Segunda Guerra Mundial, 1939-1945*. Vol. III, No. 4, June 2023, https://tinyurl.com/3tfkm9zp. Accessed on 28 August 2025.

9 Miller, David, *Special Operations Forces in South East Asia 1942-1945: Minerva Baldhead & Longshank/Creek*, Pen & Sword Military, 2020, p. 154.

10 The Naval Archives, *Audacious Missions of WWII: Daring Acts of Bravery Revealed Through letters and Documents from the Time*, Osprey Publishing, 2020, p. 138.

11 Sardesai, Sanjeev V., 'Goa's first tryst with World War II – Attack on Gemran Ships', *The Navhind Times*, 24 March 2018, https://tinyurl.com/4d665cb4. Accessed on 28 August 2025.

12 Miller, David, *Special Operations Forces in South East Asia 1942-1945: Minerva Baldhead & Longshank/Creek*, Pen & Sword Military, 2020, p. 126.

13 Ibid., p. 158.

14 Leasor, James. *Boarding Party: The Last Action of the Calcutta Light Horse*, Houghton Mifflin Harcourt, 1978, p. 5.

15 Sardesai, Sanjeev V., 'Goa's first tryst with World War II – Attack on Gemran Ships', *The Navhind Times*, 24 March 2018, https://tinyurl.com/4d665cb4. Accessed on 28 August 2025.

16 Miller, David, 'Operation Longshanks', *Revista Portuguesa de História Militar - Dossier: Portugal no Contexto da Segunda Guerra Mundial, 1939-1945*, Vol. III, No. 4, June 2023, https://tinyurl.com/3tfkm9zp. Accessed on

28 August 2025.

17 Leasor, James. *Boarding Party: The Last Action of the Calcutta Light Horse*, Houghton Mifflin Harcourt, 1978, p. 3.

18 Ibid., p. 4.

19 Miller, David, *Special Operations Forces in South East Asia 1942-1945: Minerva Baldhead & Longshank/Creek*, Pen & Sword Military, 2020, p. 149; UK National Archives. WO 106/3685. General A. P. Wavell: Cables. 21627 Cipher 23/12. 'Personal for CIGS from General Wavell' 24.12.41.

20 Leasor, James. *Boarding Party: The Last Action of the Calcutta Light Horse*, Houghton Mifflin Harcourt, 1978, p. 5.

21 Ibid., p. 6.

22 Ibid., p. 13.

23 O'Sullivan, Adrian, 'German Covert Initiatives and British Intelligence in Persia (Iran), 1939-1945', DLitt et Phil diss., UNISA, 2012.

24 Miller, David, *Special Operations Forces in South East Asia 1942-1945: Minerva Baldhead & Longshank/Creek*, Pen & Sword Military, 2020, p. 159.

25 Zimmerman, Dwight Jon, 'Operation Creek: SOE Enlists an "Over the Hill Gang" for a Mission, Part 1', *Defense Media Network*, 10 August 2013, https://tinyurl.com/acen5drv. Accessed on 28 August 2025.

26 Miller, David, *Special Operations Forces in South East Asia 1942-1945: Minerva Baldhead & Longshank/Creek*, Pen & Sword Military, 2020, p. 159.

27 Zimmerman, Dwight Jon, 'Operation Creek: SOE Enlists an "Over the Hill Gang" for a Mission, Part 1', *Defense Media Network*, 10 August 2013, https://tinyurl.com/acen5drv. Accessed on 28 August 2025.

28 Miller, David, 'Operation Longshanks', *Revista Portuguesa de História Militar - Dossier: Portugal no Contexto da Segunda Guerra Mundial, 1939-1945*. Vol. III, No. 4, June 2023, https://tinyurl.com/3tfkm9zp. Accessed on 28 August 2025.

29 Zimmerman, Dwight Jon, 'Operation Creek: SOE Enlists an "Over the Hill Gang" for a Mission, Part 1', *Defense Media Network*, 10 August 2013, https://tinyurl.com/acen5drv. Accessed on 28 August 2025.

30 Leasor, James. *Boarding Party: The Last Action of the Calcutta Light Horse*, Houghton Mifflin Harcourt, 1978, p. xi.

31 Ibid., p. 13.

32 Ibid., p. 14.

33 Ibid., p. 15.

34 Ibid., p. 16.

35 Ibid., p. 18.

36 Ibid., p. 19.

37 Ibid., p. 21.

38 Ibid., p. 22.
39 Miller, David, 'Operation Longshanks', *Revista Portuguesa de História Militar - Dossier: Portugal no Contexto da Segunda Guerra Mundial, 1939-1945*, Vol. III, No. 4, June 2023, https://tinyurl.com/3tfkm9zp. Accessed on 28 August 2025.
40 The Naval Archives, *Audacious Missions of WWII: Daring Acts of Bravery Revealed Through letters and Documents from the Time*, Osprey Publishing, 2020, p. 138.
41 Ibid., p. 137.
42 Cruz, Bruno Henrique Manfrim, 'Uma Missão em Goa', in *Revista De Villegagnon*, Vol. V, No. 5, 2010, pp. 70–5.
43 Leasor, James. *Boarding Party: The Last Action of the Calcutta Light Horse*, Houghton Mifflin Harcourt, 1978, p. 36.
44 Ibid., p. 36.
45 Ibid., p. 39.
46 Ibid., p. 45.
47 Ibid., p. 48.
48 Ibid., p. 51.
49 Ibid., p. 48.
50 Ibid., p. 51.
51 Ibid., p. 46.
52 Ibid., p. 54.
53 Ibid., p. 55.
54 Ibid., p. 56.
55 Ibid., p. 58.
56 O'Sullivan, Adrian, 'German Covert Initiatives and British Intelligence in Persia (Iran), 1939-1945', DLitt et Phil diss., UNISA, 2012.
57 The Naval Archives, *Audacious Missions of WWII: Daring Acts of Bravery Revealed Through letters and Documents from the Time*, Osprey Publishing, 2020, p. 139.
58 Miller, David, 'Operation Longshanks', *Revista Portuguesa de História Militar - Dossier: Portugal no Contexto da Segunda Guerra Mundial, 1939-1945*. Vol. III, No. 4, June 2023, https://tinyurl.com/3tfkm9zp. Accessed on 28 August 2025.
59 Leasor, James, *Boarding Party: The Last Action of the Calcutta Light Horse*, Houghton Mifflin Harcourt, 1978, p. 72.
60 Elphick, Peter, *Far Eastern File: Intelligence War in the Far east, 1930-45*, Hodder & Stoughton, p. 403.
61 Miller, David, *Special Operations Forces in South East Asia 1942-1945: Minerva Baldhead & Longshank/Creek*, Pen & Sword Military, 2020, p. 173.

62 The Naval Archives, *Audacious Missions of WWII: Daring Acts of Bravery Revealed Through letters and Documents from the Time*, Osprey Publishing, 2020, p. 139.
63 Miller, David, 'Operation Longshanks', *Revista Portuguesa de História Militar - Dossier: Portugal no Contexto da Segunda Guerra Mundial, 1939-1945*, Vol. III, No. 4, June 2023, https://tinyurl.com/3tfkm9zp. Accessed on 28 August 2025,
64 Leasor, James, *The Sea Wolves*, Corgi, London, 1980, p. 31.
65 Zimmerman, Dwight Jon, 'Operation Creek: SOE Enlists an "Over the Hill Gang" for a Mission, Part 1', *Defense Media Network*, 10 August 2013, https://tinyurl.com/acen5drv. Accessed on 28 August 2025.
66 Leasor, James, *Boarding Party: The Last Action of the Calcutta Light Horse*, Houghton Mifflin Harcourt, 1978, p. 94.
67 Ibid., p. 130.
68 Ibid., p. 131.
69 Ibid., p. 95.
70 Ibid., p. 101.
71 Ibid., p. 107.
72 Ibid., p. 114.
73 Ibid., p. 148.
74 Ibid., p. 151.
75 Zimmerman, Dwight Jon, 'Operation Creek: SOE Enlists an "Over the Hill Gang" for a Mission, Part 1', *Defense Media Network*, 10 August 2013, https://tinyurl.com/acen5drv, accessed on 28 August 2025.
76 Miller, David, 'Operation Longshanks'. *Revista Portuguesa de História Militar - Dossier: Portugal no Contexto da Segunda Guerra Mundial, 1939-1945*, Vol. III, No. 4, June 2023, https://tinyurl.com/3tfkm9zp. Accessed on 28 August 2025.
77 Ibid.
78 Leasor, James, *Boarding Party: The Last Action of the Calcutta Light Horse*, Houghton Mifflin Harcourt, 1978, p. 87.
79 Ibid., p. 90.
80 Zimmerman, Dwight Jon, 'Operation Creek: SOE Enlists an "Over the Hill Gang" for a Mission, Part 1', *Defense Media Network*, 10 August 2013, https://tinyurl.com/acen5drv. Accessed on 28 August 2025.
81 Miller, David, *Special Operations Forces in South East Asia 1942-1945: Minerva Baldhead & Longshank/Creek*, Pen & Sword Military, 2020, p. 189.
82 Ibid., p. 192.
83 Ibid., p. 192.
84 Leasor, James, *Boarding Party: The Last Action of the Calcutta Light Horse*,

Houghton Mifflin Harcourt, 1978, p. 116.

85 Ibid., p. 117.

86 Zimmerman, Dwight Jon, 'Operation Creek: SOE Enlists an "Over the Hill Gang" for a Mission, Part 1', *Defense Media Network*, 10 August 2013, https://tinyurl.com/acen5drv. Accessed on 28 August 2025.

87 Leasor, James, *Boarding Party: The Last Action of the Calcutta Light Horse*, Houghton Mifflin Harcourt, 1978, p. 123.

88 Miller, David, 'Operation Longshanks', *Revista Portuguesa de História Militar - Dossier: Portugal no Contexto da Segunda Guerra Mundial, 1939-1945*. Vol. III, No. 4, June 2023, https://tinyurl.com/3tfkm9zp. Accessed on 28 August 2025.

89 Leasor, James, *Boarding Party: The Last Action of the Calcutta Light Horse*, Houghton Mifflin Harcourt, 1978, p. 120.

90 Ibid., p. 129.

91 Miller, David, 'Operation Longshanks', *Revista Portuguesa de História Militar - Dossier: Portugal no Contexto da Segunda Guerra Mundial, 1939-1945*. Vol. III, No. 4, June 2023, https://tinyurl.com/3tfkm9zp. Accessed on 28 August 2025.

92 Leasor, James, *Boarding Party: The Last Action of the Calcutta Light Horse*, Houghton Mifflin Harcourt, 1978, p. 161.

93 Miller, David, 'Operation Longshanks', *Revista Portuguesa de História Militar - Dossier: Portugal no Contexto da Segunda Guerra Mundial, 1939-1945*, Vol. III, No. 4, June 2023, https://tinyurl.com/3tfkm9zp. Accessed on 28 August 2025.

94 Leasor, James. *Boarding Party: The Last Action of the Calcutta Light Horse*, Houghton Mifflin Harcourt, 1978, p. 161.

95 Ibid.

96 Ibid., p. 167.

97 Ibid.

98 Miller, David, *Special Operations Forces in South East Asia 1942-1945: Minerva Baldhead & Longshank/Creek*, Pen & Sword Military, 2020, p. 198.

99 Leasor, James, *Boarding Party: The Last Action of the Calcutta Light Horse*, Houghton Mifflin Harcourt, 1978, p. 170.

100 Miller, David, 'Operation Longshanks', *Revista Portuguesa de História Militar - Dossier: Portugal no Contexto da Segunda Guerra Mundial, 1939-1945*, Vol. III, No. 4, June 2023, https://tinyurl.com/3tfkm9zp. Accessed on 28 August 2025.

101 Ibid.

102 Leasor, James. *Boarding Party: The Last Action of the Calcutta Light Horse*, Houghton Mifflin Harcourt, 1978, p. 173.

103 Ibid., p. 174.
104 Ibid., p. 171.
105 Ibid., p. 172.
106 Ibid., p. 178.
107 Ibid., p. 179.
108 Ibid., p. 181.
109 Ibid., p. 182.
110 Ibid., p. 174.
111 Ibid., p. 181.
112 Miller, David, *Special Operations Forces in South East Asia 1942-1945: Minerva Baldhead & Longshank/Creek*, Pen & Sword Military, 2020, p. 201.
113 Leasor, James. *Boarding Party: The Last Action of the Calcutta Light Horse*, Houghton Mifflin Harcourt, 1978, p. 180.
114 Ibid., p. 183.
115 Ibid., p. 184.
116 Miller, David, *Special Operations Forces in South East Asia 1942-1945: Minerva Baldhead & Longshank/Creek*, Pen & Sword Military, 2020, p. 201.
117 Leasor, James. *Boarding Party: The Last Action of the Calcutta Light Horse*, Houghton Mifflin Harcourt, 1978, p. 186.
118 Ibid., p. 185.
119 Ibid., p. 187.
120 Ibid., p. 188.
121 Ibid., p. 186.
122 Ibid., p. 189.
123 Ibid., p. 192.
124 Ibid., p. 193.
125 Miller, David, 'Operation Longshanks'. *Revista Portuguesa de História Militar - Dossier: Portugal no Contexto da Segunda Guerra Mundial, 1939-1945*. Vol. III, No. 4, June 2023, https://tinyurl.com/3tfkm9zp. Accessed on 28 August 2025.
126 Leasor, James. *Boarding Party: The Last Action of the Calcutta Light Horse*, Houghton Mifflin Harcourt, 1978, p. 197.

Chapter 4: Drama on the High Seas in 1975

1 Essen, Michael Fredholm Von, *The Hunt for Storozhevoy: The 1975 Soviet Navy Mutiny in the Baltic*, Helio & Company, 2022, p. 3.
2 Yefremenko, V.G., 'Razvitiye i sovershenstvovaniye protivolodochnykh sil i ikh taktiki', *Morskoy sbornik*, Vol. 10, 1970, pp.16–23; Essen, Michael

Fredholm Von, 'Chapter 1', *The Hunt for Storozhevoy: The 1975 Soviet Navy Mutiny in the Baltic*, Helio & Company, 2022, p. 5.

3 Ibid., p. 10.

4 Hagberg, David and Boris Gindin, *Mutiny: The True Events That Inspired The Hunt for Red October*, Forge Books, 2009, p. 20.

5 Ibid., p. 125.
Young, Gregory D., 'Mutiny on the *Storozhevoy*: A Case Study of Dissent in the Soviet Navy', *All World Wars*, https://tinyurl.com/yyjwd99c. Accessed on 28 August 2025.

6 Essen, Michael Fredholm Von, *The Hunt for Storozhevoy: The 1975 Soviet Navy Mutiny in the Baltic*, Helio & Company, 2022, p. 9.

7 Hagberg, David and Boris Gindin, *Mutiny: The True Events That Inspired The Hunt for Red October*, Forge Books, 2009, p 126.
Young, Gregory D., 'Mutiny on the *Storozhevoy*: A Case Study of Dissent in the Soviet Navy', *All World Wars*, https://tinyurl.com/yyjwd99c. Accessed on 28 August 2025.

8 Essen, Michael Fredholm Von, *The Hunt for Storozhevoy: The 1975 Soviet Navy Mutiny in the Baltic*, Helio & Company, 2022, p. 8.

9 Young, Gregory D. and Nate Braden, *The Last Sentry: The True Story That Inspired The Hunt for Red October*, Naval Institute Press, 2005, p. 3.

10 Essen, Michael Fredholm Von, *The Hunt for Storozhevoy: The 1975 Soviet Navy Mutiny in the Baltic*, Helio & Company, 2022, p. 10.

11 Young, Gregory D. and Nate Braden, *The Last Sentry: The True Story That Inspired The Hunt for Red October*, Naval Institute Press, 2005, p. 86.

12 Young, Gregory D., 'Mutiny on the *Storozhevoy*: A Case Study of Dissent in the Soviet Navy', *All World Wars*, https://tinyurl.com/yyjwd99c. Accessed on 28 August 2025.

13 Reuters, 'US MAGAZINE CHRONICLES MUTINY ON A SOVIET WARSHIP IN '75', *New York Times*, 10 February 1935, https://tinyurl.com/bc9uvhjj. Accessed on 28 August 2025.

14 Young, Gregory D., 'Mutiny on the *Storozhevoy*: A Case Study of Dissent in the Soviet Navy', *All World Wars*, https://tinyurl.com/yyjwd99c. Accessed on 28 August 2025.

15 A Decembrist was a member of a group of Russian revolutionaries.

16 Young, Gregory D., 'Mutiny on the *Storozhevoy*: A Case Study of Dissent in the Soviet Navy', *All World Wars*, https://tinyurl.com/yyjwd99c. Accessed on 28 August 2025.

17 Young, Gregory D. and Nate Braden, *The Last Sentry: The True Story That Inspired The Hunt for Red October*, Naval Institute Press, 2005, p. 7.

18 Ibid., p. 8.

19 Braden, Nate, 'Mutiny on the Sentry', *HistoryNet*, 29 May 2018, https://tinyurl.com/5x62vvxs. Accessed on 28 August 2025. Woods, Alan, 'A Leninist Hero of our Times – In Memory of Valery Sablin: The true story of Red October', *In Defence of Marxism*, 05 February 2007, https://tinyurl.com/pr72a832. Accessed on 28 August 2025.

20 Hagberg, David and Boris Gindin, *Mutiny: The True Events That Inspired The Hunt for Red October*, Forge Books, 2009, p. 20.

21 Ibid., p. 21.

22 Egorov, Boris, 'How did a Navy officer organize one more revolution in the USSR in 1975?', *Russia Beyond*, 09 November 2018, https://tinyurl.com/2p9uwb8x. Accessed on 28 August 2025.

23 Young, Gregory D., 'Mutiny on the *Storozhevoy*: A Case Study of Dissent in the Soviet Navy', *All World Wars*, https://tinyurl.com/yyjwd99c. Accessed on 28 August 2025.

24 Hagberg, David and Boris Gindin, *Mutiny: The True Events That Inspired The Hunt for Red October*, Forge Books, 2009, p. 71.

25 Braden, Nate, 'Mutiny on the Sentry', *HistoryNet*, 29 May 2018, https://tinyurl.com/5x62vvxs. Accessed on 28 August 2025.

26 Essen, Michael Fredholm Von, *The Hunt for Storozhevoy: The 1975 Soviet Navy Mutiny in the Baltic*, Helio & Company, 2022, p. 10.

27 Braden, Nate, 'Mutiny on the Sentry', *HistoryNet*, 29 May 2018, https://tinyurl.com/5x62vvxs. Accessed on 28 August 2025.

28 Essen, Michael Fredholm Von, *The Hunt for Storozhevoy: The 1975 Soviet Navy Mutiny in the Baltic*, Helio & Company, 2022, p. 12.

29 Ibid., p. 2.

30 Ibid., p. 13.

31 Young, Gregory D. and Nate Braden, *The Last Sentry: The True Story That Inspired The Hunt for Red October*, Naval Institute Press, 2005, p. 87.

32 Ibid., p. 87.

33 Ibid., p. 97.

34 Ibid., p. 100.

35 Young, Gregory D. and Nate Braden, *The Last Sentry: The True Story That Inspired The Hunt for Red October*, Naval Institute Press, 2005, p. 97.

36 Essen, Michael Fredholm Von, *The Hunt for Storozhevoy: The 1975 Soviet Navy Mutiny in the Baltic*, Helio & Company, 2022, p. 13.

37 Braden, Nate, 'Mutiny on the Sentry', *HistoryNet*, 29 May 2018, https://tinyurl.com/5x62vvxs. Accessed on 28 August 2025.

38 Ibid.

39 Young, Gregory D. and Nate Braden, *The Last Sentry: The True Story That Inspired The Hunt for Red October*, Naval Institute Press, 2005, p. 87.

40 Braden, Nate, 'Mutiny on the Sentry', *HistoryNet*, 29 May 2018, https://tinyurl.com/5x62vvxs. Accessed on 28 August 2025.
41 Essen, Michael Fredholm Von, *The Hunt for Storozhevoy: The 1975 Soviet Navy Mutiny in the Baltic*, Helio & Company, 2022, p. 14.
42 Hagberg, David and Boris Gindin, *Mutiny: The True Events That Inspired The Hunt for Red October*, Forge Books, 2009, p. 192.
43 Ibid., p. 216.
44 Essen, Michael Fredholm Von, *The Hunt for Storozhevoy: The 1975 Soviet Navy Mutiny in the Baltic*, Helio & Company, 2022, p. 14.
45 Hagberg, David and Boris Gindin, *Mutiny: The True Events That Inspired The Hunt for Red October*, Forge Books, 2009, p. 216.
46 Young, Gregory D. and Nate Braden, *The Last Sentry: The True Story That Inspired The Hunt for Red October*, Naval Institute Press, 2005, p. 6.
47 Braden, Nate, 'Mutiny on the Sentry', *HistoryNet*, 29 May 2018, https://tinyurl.com/5x62vvxs. Accessed on 28 August 2025.
48 Essen, Michael Fredholm Von, *The Hunt for Storozhevoy: The 1975 Soviet Navy Mutiny in the Baltic*, Helio & Company, 2022, p. 14.
49 Hagberg, David and Boris Gindin, *Mutiny: The True Events That Inspired The Hunt for Red October*, Forge Books, 2009, p. 197.
50 Braden, Nate, 'Mutiny on the Sentry', *HistoryNet*, 29 May 2018, https://tinyurl.com/5x62vvxs. Accessed on 28 August 2025.
51 Young, Gregory D. and Nate Braden, *The Last Sentry: The True Story That Inspired The Hunt for Red October*, Naval Institute Press, 2005, p. 5.
52 Ibid., p. 6.
53 Braden, Nate, 'Mutiny on the Sentry', *HistoryNet*, 29 May 2018, https://tinyurl.com/5x62vvxs. Accessed on 28 August 2025.
54 Essen, Michael Fredholm Von, *The Hunt for Storozhevoy: The 1975 Soviet Navy Mutiny in the Baltic*, Helio & Company, 2022, p. 14.
55 Young, Gregory D. and Nate Braden, *The Last Sentry: The True Story That Inspired The Hunt for Red October*, Naval Institute Press, 2005, p. 99.
56 Essen, Michael Fredholm Von, *The Hunt for Storozhevoy: The 1975 Soviet Navy Mutiny in the Baltic*, Helio & Company, 2022, p. 14.
57 Young, Gregory D. and Nate Braden, *The Last Sentry: The True Story That Inspired The Hunt for Red October*, Naval Institute Press, 2005, p. 99.
58 Braden, Nate, 'Mutiny on the Sentry', *HistoryNet*, 29 May 2018, https://tinyurl.com/5x62vvxs. Accessed on 28 August 2025.
59 Young, Gregory D., 'Mutiny on the *Storozhevoy*: A Case Study of Dissent in the Soviet Navy', *All World Wars*, https://tinyurl.com/yyjwd99c. Accessed on 28 August 2025.
60 Hagberg, David and Boris Gindin, *Mutiny: The True Events That Inspired*

The Hunt for Red October, Forge Books, 2009, p. 216.

61 Braden, Nate, 'Mutiny on the Sentry', *HistoryNet*, 29 May 2018, https://tinyurl.com/5x62vvxs. Accessed on 28 August 2025.

62 Essen, Michael Fredholm Von, *The Hunt for Storozhevoy: The 1975 Soviet Navy Mutiny in the Baltic*, Helio & Company, 2022, p. 14.

63 Young, Gregory D., 'Mutiny on the *Storozhevoy*: A Case Study of Dissent in the Soviet Navy', *All World Wars*, https://tinyurl.com/yyjwd99c. Accessed on 28 August 2025.

64 Essen, Michael Fredholm Von, *The Hunt for Storozhevoy: The 1975 Soviet Navy Mutiny in the Baltic*, Helio & Company, 2022, p. 20.

65 Hagberg, David and Boris Gindin, *Mutiny: The True Events That Inspired The Hunt for Red October*, Forge Books, 2009, p. 237.

66 Ibid., p. 239.

67 Ibid., p. 249.

68 Braden, Nate, 'Mutiny on the Sentry', *HistoryNet*, 29 May 2018, https://tinyurl.com/5x62vvxs. Accessed on 28 August 2025.

69 Essen, Michael Fredholm Von, *The Hunt for Storozhevoy: The 1975 Soviet Navy Mutiny in the Baltic*, Helio & Company, 2022, p. 20.

70 Ibid., p. 14.

71 Ibid.

72 Ibid., p. 265.

73 Ibid., p. 256.

74 Ibid., p. 265.

75 Ibid., p. 15.

76 Ibid., p.16.

77 Hagberg, David and Boris Gindin, *Mutiny: The True Events That Inspired The Hunt for Red October*, Forge Books, 2009, p. 253.

78 Young, Gregory D. and Nate Braden, *The Last Sentry: The True Story That Inspired The Hunt for Red October*, Naval Institute Press, 2005, p. 101.

79 Essen, Michael Fredholm Von, *The Hunt for Storozhevoy: The 1975 Soviet Navy Mutiny in the Baltic*, Helio & Company, 2022, p. 35.

80 Young, Gregory D. and Nate Braden, *The Last Sentry: The True Story That Inspired The Hunt for Red October*, Naval Institute Press, 2005, p. 100.

81 Hagberg, David and Boris Gindin, *Mutiny: The True Events That Inspired The Hunt for Red October*, Forge Books, 2009, p. 255.

82 Young, Gregory D. and Nate Braden, *The Last Sentry: The True Story That Inspired The Hunt for Red October*, Naval Institute Press, 2005, p. 101.

83 Hagberg, David and Boris Gindin, *Mutiny: The True Events That Inspired The Hunt for Red October*, Forge Books, 2009, p. 275.

84 Young, Gregory D. and Nate Braden, *The Last Sentry: The True Story That*

Inspired The Hunt for Red October, Naval Institute Press, 2005, p. 101.

85 Ibid., p. 102.

86 Hagberg, David and Boris Gindin, *Mutiny: The True Events That Inspired The Hunt for Red October*, Forge Books, 2009, p. 275.

87 Essen, Michael Fredholm Von, *The Hunt for Storozhevoy: The 1975 Soviet Navy Mutiny in the Baltic*, Helio & Company, 2022, p. 16.

88 Ibid., p. 28.

89 Ibid., p. 29.

90 Hagberg, David and Boris Gindin, *Mutiny: The True Events That Inspired The Hunt for Red October*, Forge Books, 2009, p. 287.

91 Essen, Michael Fredholm Von, *The Hunt for Storozhevoy: The 1975 Soviet Navy Mutiny in the Baltic*, Helio & Company, 2022, p. 29.

92 Hagberg, David and Boris Gindin, *Mutiny: The True Events That Inspired The Hunt for Red October*, Forge Books, 2009, p. 301.

93 Essen, Michael Fredholm Von, *The Hunt for Storozhevoy: The 1975 Soviet Navy Mutiny in the Baltic*, Helio & Company, 2022, p. 29.

94 Young, Gregory D. and Nate Braden, *The Last Sentry: The True Story That Inspired The Hunt for Red October*, Naval Institute Press, 2005, p. 103.

95 Essen, Michael Fredholm Von, *The Hunt for Storozhevoy: The 1975 Soviet Navy Mutiny in the Baltic*, Helio & Company, 2022, p. 25.

96 Ibid., p. 25.

97 Ibid., p. 29.

98 Ibid.

99 Ibid.

100 Ibid.

101 Braden, Nate, 'Mutiny on the Sentry', *HistoryNet*, 29 May 2018, https://tinyurl.com/5x62vvxs. Accessed on 28 August 2025.

102 Essen, Michael Fredholm Von, *The Hunt for Storozhevoy: The 1975 Soviet Navy Mutiny in the Baltic*, Helio & Company, 2022, p. 28.

103 Young, Gregory D. and Nate Braden, *The Last Sentry: The True Story That Inspired The Hunt for Red October*, Naval Institute Press, 2005, p. 105.

104 Hagberg, David and Boris Gindin, *Mutiny: The True Events That Inspired The Hunt for Red October*, Forge Books, 2009, p. 292.

105 Young, Gregory D. and Nate Braden, *The Last Sentry: The True Story That Inspired The Hunt for Red October*, Naval Institute Press, 2005, p. 109.

106 Essen, Michael Fredholm Von, *The Hunt for Storozhevoy: The 1975 Soviet Navy Mutiny in the Baltic*, Helio & Company, 2022, p. 35.

107 Young, Gregory D. and Nate Braden, *The Last Sentry: The True Story That Inspired The Hunt for Red October*, Naval Institute Press, 2005, p. 110.

108 Hagberg, David and Boris Gindin, *Mutiny: The True Events That Inspired*

The Hunt for Red October, Forge Books, 2009, p. 315.

109 Young, Gregory D. and Nate Braden, *The Last Sentry: The True Story That Inspired The Hunt for Red October*, Naval Institute Press, 2005, p. 111.

110 Hagberg, David and Boris Gindin, *Mutiny: The True Events That Inspired The Hunt for Red October*, Forge Books, 2009, p. 310.

111 Ibid., p. 312.

112 Ibid., p. 314.

113 Braden, Nate, 'Mutiny on the Sentry', *HistoryNet*, 29 May 2018, https://tinyurl.com/5x62vvxs. Accessed on 28 August 2025.

114 Ibid.

115 Young, Gregory D. and Nate Braden, *The Last Sentry: The True Story That Inspired The Hunt for Red October*, Naval Institute Press, 2005, p. 111.

116 Essen, Michael Fredholm Von, *The Hunt for Storozhevoy: The 1975 Soviet Navy Mutiny in the Baltic*, Helio & Company, 2022, p. 41.

117 Young, Gregory D., 'Mutiny on the *Storozhevoy*: A Case Study of Dissent in the Soviet Navy', *All World Wars*, https://tinyurl.com/yyjwd99c. Accessed on 28 August 2025.

118 Essen, Michael Fredholm Von, *The Hunt for Storozhevoy: The 1975 Soviet Navy Mutiny in the Baltic*, Helio & Company, 2022, p. 33.

119 Young, Gregory D., 'Mutiny on the *Storozhevoy*: A Case Study of Dissent in the Soviet Navy', *All World Wars*, https://tinyurl.com/yyjwd99c. Accessed on 28 August 2025.

120 Essen, Michael Fredholm Von, *The Hunt for Storozhevoy: The 1975 Soviet Navy Mutiny in the Baltic*, Helio & Company, 2022, p. 37.

121 Ibid., p. 38.

122 Anderson, Jack and Dale Van Atta, 'The Incident Behind "Red October"', *The Washington Post*, 25 March 1990, https://tinyurl.com/srmubdtu. Accessed on 28 August 2025.

123 Braden, Nate, 'Mutiny on the Sentry', *HistoryNet*, 29 May 2018, https://tinyurl.com/5x62vvxs. Accessed on 28 August 2025.

Chapter 5: The Frozen Frontier over the Ussuri

1 Carter, James, 'How close, exactly, were Russia and China to nuclear war?', *The China Project*, 03 March 2021, https://tinyurl.com/2x9w8r6p. Accessed on 28 August 2025.

2 Ibid.

3 MacFarquhar, Roderick (ed.), *Cambridge History of China Volume 15: The People's Republic, Part 2: Revolutions within the Chinese Revolution, 1966-1982* , Cambridge University Press, 1991, p. 255.

4 Ryabushkin, Dmitry and Harold Orenstein, *Sino Soviet Border War of 1969: First Clash at Damansky Island*, Helion & Company, 2021, p. 10; Rossisskaya gazeta, 6 October 2011 (No. 5600).

5 Ryabushkin, Dmitry and Harold Orenstein, *Sino Soviet Border War of 1969: First Clash at Damansky Island*, Helion & Company, 2021, p. 7.

6 Ibid., p. 11; Streltsov, D.V. (ed.), *The Territorial Issue in the Afro-Asian World (Территориальный вопрос в афро-азиатском мире [in Russian])*, Aspent Press, Moscow, 2013, p. 100.

7 Gerson, Michael S., 'The Sino-Soviet Border Conflict: Deterrence, Escalation, and the Threat of Nuclear War in 1969', *CAN.org*, p. iii, https://tinyurl.com/4j8czyds. Accessed on 28 August 2025.

8 Gurtov, Melvin and Byong-Moo Hwang, *China under Threat: The Politics of Strategy and Diplomacy*, John Hopkins University Press, 1980, p. 210.

9 Directorate of Intelligence, *Intelligence Memorandum: Military Forces Along the Sino-Soviet Border*, CIA, January 1970, p. 2, https://tinyurl.com/ms7s5wn8. Accessed on 29 August 2025; Board of National Estimates, *Special Memorandum: The Soviet Military Buildup Along the Chinese Border*, CIA, 25 March 1968, p. 12, https://tinyurl.com/5b75mc7y. Accessed on 28 August 2025.

10 Tilly, Charles, 'Reflections on the history of European state-making', *The Formation of National States in Western Europe*, Charles Tilly (ed.), Princeton University Press, New Jersey, 1975. p. 26.

11 Gelman, Harry, 'The Soviet Far East buildup and Soviet risk-taking against China', *Rand*, 1982, p. 12, https://tinyurl.com/nwfjha93. Accessed on 28 August 2025.

12 Kakkar, Ranjana, 'The role of the PLA during the Cultural Revolution', *China Report*, Vol. 13, No. 5, 1977, https://tinyurl.com/6cstb9b5. Accessed on 28 August 2025; see Li and Hao, Wenhua dageming; Harding, Harry, 'Chinese State in Crisis', *The Politics of China Sixty Years of The People's Republic of China*, Roderick MacFarquhar (ed.), Cambridge University Press, 2011, pp. 169–170; MacFarquhar, Roderick and Michael Schoenhals, *Mao's Last Revolution*, Harvard University Press, 2008; Scobell, Andrew, *China's Use of Military Force: Beyond the Great Wall and the Long March*, Cambridge University Press, New York, 2003, pp. 94–11.

13 Harding, Harry, 'The Chinese State in Crisis, 1966-1969', *The Politics of China,* Roderick MacFarquhar (ed.), Cambridge University Press, 2012, p. 169.

14 Fravel, Taylor M., *Strong Borders, Secure Nation: Cooperation and Conflict in China's Territorial Disputes*, Princeton University Press, 2008, p. 210.

15 Rea, Kenneth W., 'Peking and the Brezhnev Doctrine', *Asian Affairs*, Vol. 3,

No.1, September, 1975, pp. 22–30.

16 Fravel, Taylor M., *Strong Borders, Secure Nation: Cooperation and Conflict in China's Territorial Disputes*, Princeton University Press, 2008, p. 208.

17 Meyskens, Covell, *Mao's Third Front: The Militarization of Cold War China*, Cambridge University Press, 2020, p. 150.

18 Fravel, Taylor M., *Strong Borders, Secure Nation: Cooperation and Conflict in China's Territorial Disputes*, Princeton University Press, 2008, p. 203.

19 National Intelligence Estimate, *Warsaw Pact Forces for Operations in Eurasia*, Central Intelligence Agency, Washington, DC, 1971, p. 27, https://tinyurl.com/mryyv3e3. Accessed on 28 August 2025.

20 Fravel, Taylor M., *Strong Borders, Secure Nation: Cooperation and Conflict in China's Territorial Disputes*, Princeton University Press, 2008, p. 204.

21 Ibid., p. 205; Directorate of Intelligence, *Intelligence Memorandum: Military Forces Along the Sino-Soviet Border*, CIA, January 1970, p. 5, https://tinyurl.com/ms7s5wn8. Accessed on 29 August 2025.

22 Fravel, Taylor M., *Strong Borders, Secure Nation: Cooperation and Conflict in China's Territorial Disputes*, Princeton University Press, 2008, p. 204.

23 *The Sino-Soviet Dispute: Keesing's Research Report*, Redwood Press, 1970, p. 209, https://tinyurl.com/3ufascp5. Accessed on 28 August 2025.

24 Fravel, Taylor M., *Strong Borders, Secure Nation: Cooperation and Conflict in China's Territorial Disputes*, Princeton University Press, 2008, p. 209.

25 Goldstein, Lyle, 'Do Nascent WMD Arsenals Deter? The Sino-Soviet Crisis of 1969', *Political Science Quarterly*. Vol. 118, No. 1, 2003, pp. 53–80.

26 Fravel, Taylor M., *Strong Borders, Secure Nation: Cooperation and Conflict in China's Territorial Disputes*, Princeton University Press, 2008, p. 211.

27 Li, Mingjiang, *Mao's China and the Sino-Soviet Split: Ideological Dilemma*, Routledge, 2012, p. 145.

28 Meyskens, Covell, *Mao's Third Front: The Militarization of Cold War China*, Cambridge University Press, 2020, p. 12.

29 Li, Mingjiang, *Mao's China and the Sino-Soviet Split: Ideological Dilemma*, Routledge, 2012, p. 144.

30 It referred to the third strategic industrial and military zone, designed as a backup base deep in China's interior in case of a major war with the United States or the Soviet Union.

31 Carter, James, 'How close, exactly, were Russia and China to nuclear war?', *The China Project*, 3 March 2021, https://tinyurl.com/2x9w8r6p. Accessed on 28 August 2025.

32 Meyskens, Covell, *Mao's Third Front: The Militarization of Cold War China*, Cambridge University Press, 2020, p. 4.

33 Ibid., p. 3; Zhao, Dexin, *Zhonghua renmin gongheguo jingji shi 1967–1984*,

Henan renmin chubanshe, Zhengzhou , 1991, p. 183.

34 Petrov, Vladimir (ed.), *Soviet-Chinese Relations 1945-1970*, Indiana University Press, 1975, p. 324; Goldstein, Lyle J., 'Return to Zhanbao Island: Who Started Shooting and Why it Matters', *The China Quarterly*, No. 168, 2001, pp. 985–997, https://tinyurl.com/mpwx83u9. Accessed on 28 August 2025.

35 Kuisong, Yang, 'The Sino-Soviet Border Clash of 1969: from Zhenbao Island to Sino-American Rapprochement', *Cold War History*, Vol. 1, No. 1, 2000, pp. 21–52, https://tinyurl.com/2ksan6av. Accessed on 28 August 2025.

36 Carter, James, 'How close, exactly, were Russia and China to nuclear war?', *The China Project*, 3 March 2021, https://tinyurl.com/2x9w8r6p. Accessed on 28 August 2025.

37 Gitter, David, '50 Years Later: How the Soviet Union Called China's Bluff in 1969', *CCP Watch*, 1 March 2019, https://tinyurl.com/4z4w8jsm. Accessed on 28 August 2025.

38 Li, Mingjiang, *Mao's China and the Sino-Soviet Split: Ideological Dilemma*, Routledge, 2012, p. 144.

39 Gerson, Michael S., 'The Sino-Soviet Border Conflict: Deterrence, Escalation, and the Threat of Nuclear War in 1969', *CAN.org*, November 2010, p. 21, https://tinyurl.com/4j8czyds. Accessed on 28 August 2025.

40 Fravel, Taylor M., *Strong Borders, Secure Nation: Cooperation and Conflict in China's Territorial Disputes*, Princeton University Press, 2008, p. 212.

41 Gerson, Michael S., 'The Sino-Soviet Border Conflict: Deterrence, Escalation, and the Threat of Nuclear War in 1969', *CAN.org*, November 2010, p. 19, https://tinyurl.com/4j8czyds. Accessed on 28 August 2025.

42 Ibid., p. 21.

43 Ibid., p. 21.

44 Fravel, Taylor M., *Strong Borders, Secure Nation: Cooperation and Conflict in China's Territorial Disputes*, Princeton University Press, 2008, p. 213.

45 Ryabushkin, Dmitry and Harold Orenstein, *Sino Soviet Border War of 1969: First Clash at Damansky Island*, Helion & Company, 2021, p. 20.

46 Fravel, Taylor M., *Strong Borders, Secure Nation: Cooperation and Conflict in China's Territorial Disputes*, Princeton University Press, 2008, p. 212.

47 Ibid., p. 211.

48 Ryabushkin, Dmitry and Harold Orenstein, *The Sino-Soviet Border War: Volume 2: Confrontation at Lake Zhalanashkol*, Helion & Company, 2021, p. 3.

49 Fravel, Taylor M., *Strong Borders, Secure Nation: Cooperation and Conflict in China's Territorial Disputes*, Princeton University Press, 2008, p. 212.

50 Ryabushkin, Dmitry and Harold Orenstein, *Sino Soviet Border War of 1969: First Clash at Damansky Island*, Helion & Company, 2021, p. 20.
51 Ibid.
52 Ibid.
53 Carter, James, 'How close, exactly, were Russia and China to nuclear war?', *The China Project*, 3 March 2021, https://tinyurl.com/2x9w8r6p. Accessed on 28 August 2025.
54 MacFarquhar, Roderick (ed.), *Cambridge History of China Volume 15: The People's Republic, Part 2: Revolutions within the Chinese Revolution, 1966-1982* , Cambridge University Press, 1991, p. 257.
55 Gerson, Michael S., 'The Sino-Soviet Border Conflict: Deterrence, Escalation, and the Threat of Nuclear War in 1969', *CAN.org*, November 2010, p. 3, https://tinyurl.com/4j8czyds. Accessed on 28 August 2025.
56 Ibid.
57 Ryabushkin, Dmitry and Harold Orenstein, *The Sino-Soviet Border War Volume 2: Confrontation at Lake Zhalanashkol*, Helion & Company, 2021, p. 3.
58 Gerson, Michael S., 'The Sino-Soviet Border Conflict: Deterrence, Escalation, and the Threat of Nuclear War in 1969', *CAN.org*, November 2010, p. 26, https://tinyurl.com/4j8czyds. Accessed on 28 August 2025.
59 Ryabushkin, Dmitry and Harold Orenstein, *The Sino-Soviet Border War Volume 2: Confrontation at Lake Zhalanashkol*, Helion & Company, 2021, p. 5.
60 Ibid., p. 6.
61 Ibid., p. 7.
62 Gerson, Michael S., 'The Sino-Soviet Border Conflict: Deterrence, Escalation, and the Threat of Nuclear War in 1969', *CAN.org*, November 2010, p. 26, https://tinyurl.com/4j8czyds. Accessed on 28 August 2025.
63 MacFarquhar, Roderick (ed.), *Cambridge History of China Volume 15: The People's Republic, Part 2: Revolutions within the Chinese Revolution, 1966-1982* , Cambridge University Press, 1991, p. 260.
64 Ryabushkin Dmitry and Harold Orenstein, *The Sino-Soviet Border War Volume 2: Confrontation at Lake Zhalanashkol*, Helion & Company, 2021, p. 9.
65 Gerson, Michael S., 'The Sino-Soviet Border Conflict: Deterrence, Escalation, and the Threat of Nuclear War in 1969', *CAN.org*, November 2010, https://tinyurl.com/4j8czyds, Accessed on 28 August 2025.
66 Ryabushkin Dmitry and Orenstein, Harold, *The Sino-Soviet Border War Volume 2: Confrontation at Lake Zhalanashkol*, Helion&Company, 2021, p. 19.
67 Ibid., p. 10.

68 Ibid.

69 Ryabushkin, Dmitry and Harold Orenstein, *The Sino-Soviet Border War Volume 2: Confrontation at Lake Zhalanashkol*, Helion & Company, 2021, p. 19.

70 MacFarquhar, Roderick (ed.), *Cambridge History of China Volume 15: The People's Republic, Part 2: Revolutions within the Chinese Revolution, 1966–1982*, Cambridge University Press, 1991, p. 260.

71 'Document No. 4: Mao Zedong's Talk at a Meeting of the Central Cultural Revolution Group (Excerpt), 15 March 1969', Cold War International History Project Bulletin, No. 11, Winter 1998, p. 162.

72 Gitter, David, '50 Years Later: How the Soviet Union Called China's Bluff in 1969', *CCP Watch*, 1 March 2019, https://tinyurl.com/4z4w8jsm. Accessed on 28 August 2025.

73 Gerson, Michael S., 'The Sino-Soviet Border Conflict: Deterrence, Escalation, and the Threat of Nuclear War in 1969', *CAN.org*, November 2010, p. iii, https://tinyurl.com/4j8czyds. Accessed on 28 August 2025.

74 Gitter, David, '50 Years Later: How the Soviet Union Called China's Bluff in 1969'. *CCP Watch*, 01 March 2019, https://tinyurl.com/4z4w8jsm. Accessed on 28 August 2025.

75 Ibid.

76 Gerson, Michael S., 'The Sino-Soviet Border Conflict: Deterrence, Escalation, and the Threat of Nuclear War in 1969', *CAN.org*, November 2010, pp. 28–29, https://tinyurl.com/4j8czyds. Accessed on 28 August 2025; Ostermann, Christian F, 'East German Documents in the Sino-Societ Border Conflict 1969 - Document No. 2: Telegram to East German Foreign Ministry from GDR Ambassador to PRC, 2 April 1969', *Cold War International History Project Bulletin*, No. 6/7, Winter 1995, pp. 190–191, https://tinyurl.com/33z42j2t; Kuisong, Yang, 'The Sino-Soviet Border Clash of 1969: from Zhenbao Island to Sino-American Rapprochement', *Cold War History*, Vol. 1 , No. 1, 2000, p. 32, https://tinyurl.com/2ksan6av. Accessed on 28 August 2025.

77 'Soviet Statement of March 29 to the C.P.R.: TASS International Service, March 30, 1969', *Studies in Comparative Communism*, Vol. 2, No. 3–4, 1969, pp. 181–187, https://tinyurl.com/2jwzuhu3. Accessed on 28 August 2025.

78 Directorate of Intelligence, 'Intelligence Report: The Evolution of Soviet Policy in the Sino-Soviet Border Dispute', *Central Intelligence Agency*, 1970, p. 53, https://tinyurl.com/mryypz2v. Accessed on 28 August 2025.

79 Ibid., pp. 54–60.

80 Gerson, Michael S., 'The Sino-Soviet Border Conflict: Deterrence, Escalation, and the Threat of Nuclear War in 1969', *CAN.org*, November

2010, p. 41, https://tinyurl.com/4j8czyds. Accessed on 28 August 2025.

81 Lüthi, Lorenz, 'Restoring Chaos to History: Sino-Soviet-American Relations, 1969', *The China Quarterly*. No. 210, 2012, p. 389, https://tinyurl.com/46wjva2c. Accessed on 28 August 2025.

82 Gitter, David, '50 Years Later: How the Soviet Union Called China's Bluff in 1969', *CCP Watch*, 1 March 2019, https://tinyurl.com/4z4w8jsm. Accessed on 28 August 2025.

83 *Office of the Historian*, 'Memorandum of Conversation', https://tinyurl.com/4986yw79. Accessed on 28 August 2025.

84 Ibid.; Ryabushkin Dmitry and Harold Orenstein, *The Sino-Soviet Border War Volume 2: Confrontation at Lake Zhalanashkol*, Helion & Company, 2021, p. 51.

85 *Office of the Historian*, 'Washington Special Actions Group Report', https://tinyurl.com/3yu28447. Accessed on 28 August 2025.

86 Gerson, Michael S., 'The Sino-Soviet Border Conflict: Deterrence, Escalation, and the Threat of Nuclear War in 1969', *CAN.org*, November 2010, p. 32, https://tinyurl.com/4j8czyds. Accessed on 28 August 2025.

87 Ibid., p. 34.

88 Roberts, Chalmers M., 'Russia Reported Eyeing Strikes at China A-Sites', *The Washington Post*, 28 August 1969, https://tinyurl.com/h87fzdva. Accessed on 28 August 2025; Gerson, Michael S., 'The Sino-Soviet Border Conflict: Deterrence, Escalation, and the Threat of Nuclear War in 1969', *CAN.org*, November 2010, https://tinyurl.com/4j8czyds. Accessed on 28 August 2025.

89 Gerson, Michael S., 'The Sino-Soviet Border Conflict: Deterrence, Escalation, and the Threat of Nuclear War in 1969', *CAN.org*, November 2010, p. 41, https://tinyurl.com/4j8czyds. Accessed on 28 August 2025.

90 Carter, James, 'How close, exactly, were Russia and China to nuclear war?', *The China Project*, 3 March 2021, https://tinyurl.com/2x9w8r6p. Accessed on 28 August 2025.

91 Gerson, Michael S., 'The Sino-Soviet Border Conflict: Deterrence, Escalation, and the Threat of Nuclear War in 1969', *CAN.org*, November 2010, p. 41, https://tinyurl.com/4j8czyds. Accessed on 28 August 2025.

92 Directorate of Intelligence, *Intelligence Memorandum: Indo-Soviet Relations*, Central Intelligence Agency, 1972, https://tinyurl.com/mry6np78. Accessed on 28 August 2025.

93 Gerson, Michael S., 'The Sino-Soviet Border Conflict: Deterrence, Escalation, and the Threat of Nuclear War in 1969', *CAN.org*, November 2010, pp. 40–46, https://tinyurl.com/4j8czyds. Accessed on 28 August 2025; Gitter, David, '50 Years Later: How the Soviet Union Called China's

Bluff in 1969', *CCP Watch*, 1 March 2019, https://tinyurl.com/4z4w8jsm. Accessed on 28 August 2025.

94 Ryabushkin, Dmitry, and Harold Orenstein, *The Sino-Soviet Border War: Volume 2: Confrontation at Lake Zhalanashkol*, Helion & Company, 2021, p. 52.

95 Ibid.

96 Yixian, Xie (ed.), *Zhongguo dangdai waijiao shi, 1949-2001 [China's Contemporary Foreign Affairs History, 1949-2001]*, China Youth Press, Beijing, 2002, pp. 246–247.

97 Gerson, Michael S., 'The Sino-Soviet Border Conflict: Deterrence, Escalation, and the Threat of Nuclear War in 1969', *CAN.org*, November 2010, p. 46. https://tinyurl.com/4j8czyds. Accessed on 28 August 2025.

98 Ibid., p. 47.

99 Ibid., p. 48.

100 Ibid.

101 Ibid., p. 49.

102 Ibid.

103 Ping Li and Ma Zhisun (eds.), *Zhou Enlai nianpu (1949-1976, xia jua) [A Chronicle of Zhou Enlai (1949-1976, Part II)]*, Central Literary Press, Beijing, 1997, pp. 323–324.

104 Yunsheng, Zhang, *A Firsthand Account of Maojiawan: The Memoirs of Lin Biao's Secretary*, Chunqiu Publishing House, Beijing, 1989, pp. 307–308.

105 Ibid.

106 Ibid., pp. 319–320.

107 Gerson, Michael S., 'The Sino-Soviet Border Conflict: Deterrence, Escalation, and the Threat of Nuclear War in 1969', *CAN.org*, November 2010, https://tinyurl.com/4j8czyds. Accessed on 28 August 2025.

108 Yunsheng, Zhang, *A Firsthand Account of Maojiawan: The Memoirs of Lin Biao's Secretary*, p. 317.

109 Ibid., p. 318.

110 Brezhnev, A.A., *Notes from China, Diplomats Remember*, Nauchnaia Kniga, Moscow, 1997, p. 350.

111 Gitter, David, '50 Years Later: How the Soviet Union Called China's Bluff in 1969'. *CCP Watch*, 1 March 2019, https://tinyurl.com/4z4w8jsm. Accessed on 28 August 2025; Gerson, Michael S., 'The Sino-Soviet Border Conflict: Deterrence, Escalation, and the Threat of Nuclear War in 1969', *CAN.org*, November 2010, https://tinyurl.com/4j8czyds. Accessed on 28 August 2025.

Chapter 6: Operation Able Archer: The Military Exercise That Almost Started World War III

1 Mahan, Erin R., *Harold Brown 1977–1981, Secretaries of Defense Historical Series*, Volume IX, Office of the Secretary of Defense, Washington, DC, p. 439, https://tinyurl.com/56kv9w42. Accessed on 28 August 2025.

2 Garland, Andrew R., '1983: The most dangerous year', Master's Thesis, University of Nevada, Las Vegas, 2011, p. 5.

3 Uenuma, Francine, 'The 1983 Military Drill That Nearly Sparked Nuclear War With the Soviets', *Smithsonian Magazine*, 27 April 2022, https://tinyurl.com/p45pbxss. Accessed on 28 August 2025.

4 *Atomic Heritage Foundation*, 'Nucelar Close Calls: Able Archer 83', 15 June 2018, https://tinyurl.com/5n8sc337. Accessed on 28 August 2025.

5 Uenuma, Francine, 'The 1983 Military Drill That Nearly Sparked Nuclear War With the Soviets', *Smithsonian Magazine*, 27 April, 2022, https://tinyurl.com/p45pbxss. Accessed on 28 August 2025.

6 Downing, Taylor, *1983: Reagan, Andropov, and a World on the Brink*, Da Capo Press, 2018, p. 52.

7 Ibid., p. 53.

8 Ibid., p. 55.

9 Ibid., p. 108.

10 History.com Editors, 'Reagan refers to U.S.S.R. as "evil empire," again', *History.com,* 16 November 2009, https://tinyurl.com/3v4td4an. Accessed on 28 August 2025.

11 Uenuma, Francine, 'The 1983 Military Drill That Nearly Sparked Nuclear War With the Soviets', *Smithsonian Magazine*, 27 April 2022, https://tinyurl.com/p45pbxss. Accessed on 28 August 2025.

12 Vistica, Gregory L., *Fall from Glory: The Men Who Sank the U.S. Navy*, Simon & Schuster, New York, 1996, pp. 105–108, 116–118, and 129–135.

13 Ibid., pp. 131–132.

14 Fischer, Benjamin B., *A Cold War Conundrum: The 1983 Soviet War Scare*, George Washington University Press, p. 7.

15 Ambinder, Marc, *The Brink: President Reagan and the Nuclear War Scare of 1983*, Simon and Schuster, 2018, p. 131.

16 Ibid., p. 132.

17 Ibid., p. 133.

18 Ibid., p. 134.

19 Ibid.

20 Director of Central Intelligence, 'Soviet Naval Strategy and Programs', *National Intelligence Estimate NIE 11-15/82D*, 1983, pp. 18–19.

21 Command History Division Office of the Joint Secretary, 'PROMULGATION OF USCINCPAC COMMAND HISTORY 1984', 1984, https://tinyurl.com/2s4ytydw. Accessed on 28 August 2025, p. 396.
22 Jones, Nates, 'Countdown to declassification: Finding answers to a 1983 nuclear war scare', *Bulletin of the Atomic Scientists*, Vol. 69, No. 6, 1 November 2013, https://tinyurl.com/mvv4rw7d. Accessed on 28 August 2025.
23 Uenuma, Francine, 'The 1983 Military Drill That Nearly Sparked Nuclear War With the Soviets', *Smithsonian Magazine*, 27 April 2022, https://tinyurl.com/p45pbxss. Accessed on 28 August 2025.
24 Ambinder, Marc, *The Brink: President Reagan and the Nuclear War Scare of 1983*, Simon & Schuster, 2018, p. 167.
25 Downing, Taylor, *1983: Reagan, Andropov, and a World on the Brink*, De Capo Pr, 2018, p. 149.
26 Ibid., p. 150.
27 Ibid., p. 158.
28 Ibid., p. 157.
29 Ibid., p. 161.
30 Ibid., p. 157.
31 Ibid., p. 163.
32 Ibid., p. 164.
33 Ibid., p. 165.
34 Ibid., p. 166
35 Ibid., p. 167.
36 Ambinder, Marc, *The Brink: President Reagan and the Nuclear War Scare of 1983*, Simon & Schuster, 2018, p. 168.
37 Jones, Nate and David E. Hoffman, 'Newly Released documents shed light on 1983 nuclear war scare with Soviets', 1 November 2013, *The Washington Post*, 17 February 2021, https://tinyurl.com/yr4rpuxm. Accessed on 28 August 2025.
38 Hoffman, David, 'I Had a Funny Feeling in My Gut', *Washington Post*, 10 February 1999, https://tinyurl.com/539hafyw. Accessed on 28 August 2025.
39 *Atomic Heritage Foundation*, 'Nucelar Close Calls: Able Archer 83', 15 June 2018, https://tinyurl.com/5n8sc337. Accessed on 28 August 2025.
40 President's Foreign Intelligence Advisory Board, *The Soviet War Scare*, 15 February 1990, https://tinyurl.com/sdkamxjx. Accessed on 28 August 2025, p. 53.
41 Ambinder, Marc, *The Brink: President Reagan and the Nuclear War Scare of 1983*, Simon & Schuster, 2018, p. 60.
42 Hoffman, David, 'In 1983 "war scare", Soviet Leadership feared nuclear

surprise attack by U.S.', *The Washington Post*, 24 October 2015, https://tinyurl.com/3c6y83dk. Accessed on 28 August 2025.

43 *Atomic Heritage Foundation*, 'Nuclear Close Calls: Able Archer 83', 15 June 2018, https://tinyurl.com/5n8sc337. Accessed on 28 August 2025.

44 Fischer, Benjamin B., *A Cold War Conundrum: The 1983 Soviet War Scare*, Central Intelligence Agency, p. 22.

45 President's Foreign Intelligence Advisory Board, *The Soviet War Scare*, 15 February 1990, https://tinyurl.com/sdkamxjx. Accessed on 28 August 2025, p. 56.

46 Committee for State Security (KGB), 'Indicators to Recognize Adversarial Preparations for a Surprise Nuclear Missile Attack', *Wilson Center*, 26 November 1984, https://tinyurl.com/bdz7327a. Accessed on 28 August 2025.

47 Andrew, Christopher and Oleg Gordievsky, *Comrade Kryuchkov's Instructions: Top Secret Files on KGB Foreign Operations, 1975-1985*, Stanford University Press, 1994, p. 75.

48 Downing, Taylor, *1983: Reagan, Andropov, and a World on the Brink*, De Capo Pr, 2018, p. 196.

49 Ambinder, Marc, *The Brink: President Reagan and the Nuclear War Scare of 1983*, Simon & Schuster, 2018, p. 181.

50 Downing, Taylor, *1983: Reagan, Andropov, and a World on the Brink*, De Capo Pr, 2018, p. 197.

51 Hoffman, David, 'I Had a Funny Feeling in My Gut', *Washington Post*, 10 February 1999, https://tinyurl.com/539hafyw. Accessed on 28 August 2025.

52 Ibid.

53 Downing, Taylor, *1983: Reagan, Andropov, and a World on the Brink*, De Capo Pr, 2018, p. 198.

54 Ambinder, Marc, *The Brink: President Reagan and the Nuclear War Scare of 1983*, Simon & Schuster, 2018, p. 183.

55 Hoffman, David, 'I Had a Funny Feeling in My Gut', *The Washington Post*, 10 February 1999, https://tinyurl.com/539hafyw. Accessed on 28 August 2025.

56 Downing, Taylor, *1983: Reagan, Andropov, and a World on the Brink*, De Capo Pr, 2018, p. 199.

57 Ambinder, Marc, *The Brink: President Reagan and the Nuclear War Scare of 1983*, Simon & Schuster, 2018, p. 184.

58 Hoffman, David, 'I Had a Funny Feeling in My Gut', *The Washington Post*, 10 February 1999, https://tinyurl.com/539hafyw. Accessed on 28 August 2025.

59 *Center For Arms Control and Non-Proliferation*, 'The Soviet False Alarm

Incident and Able Archer 83', 14 October 2022, https://tinyurl.com/y6xhu5yy. Accessed on 28 August 2025.

60 *Atomic Heritage Foundation*, 'Nucelar Close Calls: Able Archer 83', 15 June 2018, https://tinyurl.com/5n8sc337. Accessed on 28 August 2025.

61 Jones, Nate, 'Countdown to declassification: Finding answers to a 1983 nuclear war scare', *Bulletin of the Atomic Scientists*, Vol. 69, No. 6, 1 November 2013. https://tinyurl.com/mvv4rw7d. Accessed on 28 August 2025.

62 Ambinder, Marc, *The Brink: President Reagan and the Nuclear War Scare of 1983*, Simon & Schuster, 2018, p. 51.

63 Newdick, Thomas, 'New Docs Show 1983 NATO Exercise Led to the Soviets Arming 100 Jets For Nuclear War', *TWZ*, 18 February 2021, https://tinyurl.com/yc7c25rb. Accessed on 28 August 2025.

64 Dibb, Paul, '1983: on the brink (part 1)', *The Strategist*, 9 October 2013, https://tinyurl.com/3hnu4rdv. Accessed on 28 August 2025.

65 Newdick, Thomas, 'New Docs Show 1983 NATO Exercise Led to the Soviets Arming 100 Jets For Nuclear War', *TWZ*, 18 February 2021, https://tinyurl.com/yc7c25rb. Accessed on 28 August 2025.

66 *Atomic Heritage Foundation*, 'Nucelar Close Calls: Able Archer 83', 15 June 2018, https://tinyurl.com/5n8sc337. Accessed on 28 August 2025.

67 Oberdorfer, D., 'Unpublished interview with former Soviet Head of General Staff Marshal Sergei Akhromeyev', 10 January 1990, Don Oberdorfer Papers 1983–1990, Series 1, Soviet Interviews, Mudd Manuscript Library, Princeton University.

68 Downing, Taylor, *1983: Reagan, Andropov, and a World on the Brink*, De Capo Pr, 2018, p. 224.

69 Jones, Nate, 'Countdown to declassification: Finding answers to a 1983 nuclear war scare', *Bulletin of the Atomic Scientists*, Vol. 69, No. 6, 1 November 2013, https://tinyurl.com/mvv4rw7d. Accessed on 28 August 2025.

70 Jones, Nate, 'The 1983 War Scare: "The Last Paroxysm" of the Cold War Part 1', *The National Security Archive*, 21 May 2013, https://tinyurl.com/49t6xjtv. Accessed on 28 August 2025.

71 US Air Force, *Exercise Able Archer 83, SAC ADVON, After Action Report*, Seventh Air Division, Ramstein Air Base, Secret NOFORN (No Foreign Nationals), FIOA release, 1983available at National Security Archive.

72 Jones, Nate, *Able Archer 83*, The New Press, 2016, p. 38.

73 Downing, Taylor, *1983: Reagan, Andropov, and a World on the Brink*, De Capo Pr, 2018, p. 227.

74 Ambinder, Marc, *The Brink: President Reagan and the Nuclear War Scare of*

1983, Simon & Schuster, 2018, p. 196.

75 Ibid., p. 195.

76 Ibid., p. 196.

77 *Atomic Heritage Foundation*, 'Nucelar Close Calls: Able Archer 83', 15 June 2018, https://tinyurl.com/5n8sc337. Accessed on 28 August 2025.

78 Uenuma, Francine, 'The 1983 Military Drill That Nearly Sparked Nuclear War With the Soviets', *Smithsonian Magazine*, 27 April 2022, https://tinyurl.com/p45pbxss. Accessed on 28 August 2025.

79 Downing, Taylor, *1983: Reagan, Andropov, and a World on the Brink*, De Capo Pr, 2018, p. 237.

80 Ibid., p. 230.

81 Ibid., p. 231.

82 Hoffman, David, 'In 1983 "war scare", Soviet Leadership feared nuclear surprise attack by U.S.', *The Washington Post*, 24 October 2015, https://tinyurl.com/3c6y83dk. Accessed on 28 August 2015.

83 Newdick, Thomas, 'New Docs Show 1983 NATO Exercise Led to the Soviets Arming 100 Jets For Nuclear War', *TWZ*, 18 February 2021, https://tinyurl.com/yc7c25rb. Accessed on 28 August 2025.

84 Uenuma, Francine, 'The 1983 Military Drill That Nearly Sparked Nuclear War With the Soviets', *Smithsonian Magazine*, 27 April 2022, https://tinyurl.com/p45pbxss. Accessed on 28 August 2025.

85 President's Foreign Intelligence Advisory Board, *The Soviet War Scare*, 15 February 1990, https://tinyurl.com/sdkamxjx. Accessed on 28 August 2025, p. 51.

86 Andrew, Christopher and Oleg Gordievsky, *Comrade Kryuchkov's Instructions: Top Secret Files on KGB Foreign Operations, 1975-1985*, Stanford University Press, 1994.

87 Meyer, Herbert, 'Why is the world so dangerous?', Central Intelligence Agency memo for the director and deputy director, 1983, https://tinyurl.com/y8huxr2h. Accessed on 28 August 2025.

88 Jones, Nate, 'Countdown to declassification: Finding answers to a 1983 nuclear war scare', *Bulletin of the Atomic Scientists*, Vol. 69, No. 6, 1 November 2013, https://tinyurl.com/mvv4rw7d. Accessed on 28 August 2025.

89 Downing, Taylor, *1983: Reagan, Andropov, and a World on the Brink*, De Capo Pr, 2018, p. 238.

90 Ibid., p. 242.

91 Ibid., p. 245.

92 Ibid., p. 238.

93 Ambinder, Marc, *The Brink: President Reagan and the Nuclear War Scare of*

1983, Simon & Schuster, 2018, p. 203.

94 Newdick, Thomas, 'New Docs Show 1983 NATO Exercise Led to the Soviets Arming 100 Jets For Nuclear War', *TWZ*, 18 February 2021, https://tinyurl.com/yc7c25rb. Accessed on 28 August 2025.

95 Jones, Nate and David Hoffman, 'Newly Released documents shed light on 1983 nuclear war scare with Soviets', *The Washington Post*, 17 February 2021, https://tinyurl.com/3c5bm4ah. Accessed on 28 August 2025.

96 *National Security Archive*, Able Archer War Scare "Potentially Disastrous"', 17 February 2021, https://tinyurl.com/25nzt72n. Accessed on 28 August 2025.

97 Downing, Taylor, *1983: Reagan, Andropov, and a World on the Brink*, De Capo Pr, 2018, p. 248.

98 Jones, Nate and David Hoffman, 'Newly Released documents shed light on 1983 nuclear war scare with Soviets', *The Washington Post*, 17 February 2021, https://tinyurl.com/3c5bm4ah. Accessed on 28 August 2025.

99 Newdick, Thomas, 'New Docs Show 1983 NATO Exercise Led to the Soviets Arming 100 Jets For Nuclear War', *TWZ*, 18 February 2021, https://tinyurl.com/yc7c25rb. Accessed on 28 August 2025.

100 Ibid.

101 Downing, Taylor, *1983: Reagan, Andropov, and a World on the Brink*, De Capo Pr, 2018, p. 244.

102 Ibid., p. 239.

103 Ibid., p. 244.

104 The Soviet War Scare. President's Foreiqn Intelligence Advisory Board, p. 51.

105 Downing, Taylor, *1983: Reagan, Andropov, and a World on the Brink*, De Capo Pr, 2018, p. 246.

106 'The Soviet Side of the 1983 War Scare', *History News Network*, https://tinyurl.com/yrphretx. Accessed on 28 August 2025.

107 The Director of Central Intelligence, https://tinyurl.com/4sapx9xx. Accessed on 28 August 2025.

108 *National Security Archive*, Able Archer War Scare "Potentially Disastrous"', 17 February 2021, https://tinyurl.com/25nzt72n. Accessed on 28 August 2025.

109 Downing, Taylor, *1983: Reagan, Andropov, and a World on the Brink*, De Capo Pr, 2018, p. 253.

110 Ambinder, Marc, *The Brink: President Reagan and the Nuclear War Scare of 1983*, Simon & Schuster, 2018, p. 62.

111 Macintyre, Ben, *The Spy and The Traitor: The Greatest Espionage Story of the Cold War*, Crown, 2018, p. 24.

112 *Atomic Heritage Foundation*, 'Nucelar Close Calls: Able Archer 83', 15 June 2018, https://tinyurl.com/5n8sc337. Accessed on 28 August 2025.

113 Macintyre, Ben, *The Spy and The Traitor: The Greatest Espionage Story of the Cold War*, Crown, 2018, p. 153.

114 President's Foreign Intelligence Advisory Board, *The Soviet War Scare*, 15 February 1990, p. 22, https://tinyurl.com/sdkamxjx. Accessed on 28 August 2025.

115 Ibid., p. 23.

116 Ambinder, Marc, *The Brink: President Reagan and the Nuclear War Scare of 1983*, Simon & Schuster, 2018, p. 117.

117 Macintyre, Ben, *The Spy and The Traitor: The Greatest Espionage Story of the Cold War*, Crown, 2018, p. 215.

118 *Atomic Heritage Foundation*, 'Nucelar Close Calls: Able Archer 83', 15 June 2018, https://tinyurl.com/5n8sc337. Accessed on 28 August 2025.

119 Jones, Nate, 'Countdown to declassification: Finding answers to a 1983 nuclear war scare', *Bulletin of the Atomic Scientists*, Vol. 69, No. 6, 1 November 2013, https://tinyurl.com/mvv4rw7d. Accessed on 28 August 2025.

120 Jones, Nate, 'The 1983 War Scare: "The Last Paroxysm" of the Cold War Part 1', *The National Security Archive,*16 May 2013, https://tinyurl.com/yehx2pe7. Accessed on 28 August 2025.

121 Jones, Nate, 'Countdown to declassification: Finding answers to a 1983 nuclear war scare', *Bulletin of Atomic Scientists*, Vol. 69, No. 6, 13 November 2013, https://tinyurl.com/4x385x22. Accessed on 28 August 2025, pp. 47–57.

122 Downing, Taylor, *1983: Reagan, Andropov, and a World on the Brink*, De Capo Pr, 2018, p. 256.

123 Ibid., p. 255.

124 Ibid., p. 259.

125 Uenuma, Francine, 'The 1983 Military Drill That Nearly Sparked Nuclear War With the Soviets', *Smithsonian Magazine*, 27 April 2022, https://tinyurl.com/p45pbxss. Accessed on 28 August 2025.

126 Fischer, Benjamin B., *A Cold War Conundrum: The 1983 Soviet War Scare,* George Washington University Press, p. 2.

127 Massie, Suzanne, *Trust but Verify: Ronald Reagan, and Me,* Authors Publishing, Maine, 2013.

128 Andrew, Christopher and Oleg Gordievsky, '*MORE 'INSTRUCTIONS FROM THE CENTRE': Top Secret Files on KGB Global Operations, 1975-1985'*, Routledge, 1992, p. 1.

Chapter 7: One Minute to Accuracy: The Silent Strike on Yamamoto

1 Davis, Burke, *Get Yamamoto*, Random House, 1969, p. 12.
2 Glines, Carroll, *Attack on Yamamoto*, Schiffer Military, 1993, p. 1.
3 Ibid. p. 13.
4 Davis, Burke, *Get Yamamoto*, Random House, 1969, p. 3.
5 Stempel, Jim, 'Operation Vengeance – Inside the Improbable U.S. Mission to Kill Japan's Admiral Yamamoto', *Military History Now*, 24 October 2020, https://tinyurl.com/2masrp3y. Accessed on 28 August 2025.
6 Lehr, Dick, *Dead Reckoning: The Story of How Johnny Mitchell and His Fighter Pilots Took On Admiral Yamamoto and Avenged Pearl Harbor*, HarperCollins, 2020, p. 157.
7 Stempel, Jim, 'Operation Vengeance – Inside the Improbable U.S. Mission to Kill Japan's Admiral Yamamoto, *Military History Now*, 24 October 2020, https://tinyurl.com/2masrp3y. Accessed on 28 August 2025.
8 Lehr, Dick, *Dead Reckoning: The Story of How Johnny Mitchell and His Fighter Pilots Took On Admiral Yamamoto and Avenged Pearl Harbor*, HarperCollins, 2020, p. 158.
9 Davis, Burke, *Get Yamamoto*, Random House, 1969, p. 4.
10 Sheppard, Si, *We Killed Yamamoto: The long-range P-38 assassination of the man behind Pearl Harbor Bougainville 1943*, Osprey Publishing, 2020, p. 27.
11 Davis, Burke, *Get Yamamoto*, Random House, 1969, p. 5.
12 Cox, Samuel J., 'H-018-2: Operation Vengeance – Admiral Yamamoto Shot Down, 18 April 1943', *Naval History and Heritage Command*, April 2018, https://tinyurl.com/4pj8jxhu. Accessed on 28 August 2025.
13 Glines, Carroll, *Attack on Yamamoto*, Schiffer Military, 1993, p. 4.
14 Davis, Burke, *Get Yamamoto*, Random House, 1969, p. 6.
15 Ibid., p. 7.
16 Glines, Carroll, *Attack on Yamamoto*, Schiffer Military, 1993, p. 4.
17 Lehr, Dick, *Dead Reckoning: The Story of How Johnny Mitchell and His Fighter Pilots Took On Admiral Yamamoto and Avenged Pearl Harbor*, HarperCollins, 2020, p. 160.
18 Davis, Burke, *Get Yamamoto*, Random House, 1969, p. 6.
19 Davis, Donald, *Lightning Strike: The Secret Mission to Kill Admiral Yamamoto and Avenge Pearl Harbor*, St. Martin's Griffin, 2006, p. 73.
20 Sheppard, Si, *We Killed Yamamoto: The long-range P-38 assassination of the man behind Pearl Harbor Bougainville 1943*, Osprey Publishing, 2020, p. 12.
21 Layton, Edwin, *And I Was There: Breaking the Secrets – Pearl Harbor and Midway*, Konecky&Konecky, 2001, pp. 430, 438.

22 Stempel, Jim, 'Operation Vengeance – Inside the Improbable U.S. Mission to Kill Japan's Admiral Yamamoto', *Military History Now*, 24 October 2020, https://tinyurl.com/2masrp3y. Accessed on 28 August 2025.

23 Davis, Donald, *Lightning Strike: The Secret Mission to Kill Admiral Yamamoto and Avenge Pearl Harbor*, St. Martin's Griffin, 2006, p. 37.

24 Stille, Mark, and Adam Hook, *Yamamoto Isoroku*, Osprey Publishing, 2012, p. 7.

25 Glines, Carroll, *Attack on Yamamoto*, Schiffer Military, 1993, p. 43.

26 Hampton, Dan, *Operation Vengeance: The Astonishing Aerial Ambush That Changed World War II*, William Morrow, 2020, p. 22.

27 Glines, Carroll, *Attack on Yamamoto*, Schiffer Military, 1993, p. 43.

28 Davis, Donald, *Lightning Strike: The Secret Mission to Kill Admiral Yamamoto and Avenge Pearl Harbor*, St. Martin's Griffin, 2006, p. 39.

29 Ibid., p. 40.

30 Ibid., p. 43.

31 Glines, Carroll, *Attack on Yamamoto*, Schiffer Military, 1993, p. 44.

32 Davis, Donald, *Lightning Strike: The Secret Mission to Kill Admiral Yamamoto and Avenge Pearl Harbor*, St. Martin's Griffin, 2006, p. 2.

33 Ibid., p. 43.

34 Lehr, Dick, *Dead Reckoning: The Story of How Johnny Mitchell and His Fighter Pilots Took On Admiral Yamamoto and Avenged Pearl Harbour*, HarperCollins, 2020, p. 34.

35 Ibid., p. 52.

36 Davis, Donald, *Lightning Strike: The Secret Mission to Kill Admiral Yamamoto and Avenge Pearl Harbor*, St. Martin's Griffin, 2006, p. 47.

37 Lehr, Dick, *Dead Reckoning: The Story of How Johnny Mitchell and His Fighter Pilots Took On Admiral Yamamoto and Avenged Pearl Harbor*, HarperCollins, 2020, p. 52.

38 Davis, Donald, *Lightning Strike: The Secret Mission to Kill Admiral Yamamoto and Avenge Pearl Harbor*, St. Martin's Griffin, 2006, p. 58.

39 Davis, Burke, *Get Yamamoto*, Random House, 1969, p. 117.

40 Glines, Carroll, *Attack on Yamamoto*, Schiffer Military, 1993, p. 5.

41 Ibid., p. 12.

42 Ibid., p. 28.

43 Ibid.

44 Ibid., p. 29.

45 Davis, Burke, *Get Yamamoto*, Random House, 1969, p. 120.

46 Lehr, Dick, *Dead Reckoning: The Story of How Johnny Mitchell and His Fighter Pilots Took On Admiral Yamamoto and Avenged Pearl Harbor*, HarperCollins, 2020, p. 165.

47 Ibid., p. 170.
48 Davis, Donald, *Lightning Strike: The Secret Mission to Kill Admiral Yamamoto and Avenge Pearl Harbor*, St. Martin's Griffin, 2006, p. 233.
49 Glines, Carroll, *Attack on Yamamoto*, Schiffer Military, 1993, p. 36.
50 Ibid., p. 37.
51 Lehr, Dick, *Dead Reckoning: The Story of How Johnny Mitchell and His Fighter Pilots Took On Admiral Yamamoto and Avenged Pearl Harbor*, HarperCollins, 2020, p. 173.
52 Davis, Donald, *Lightning Strike: The Secret Mission to Kill Admiral Yamamoto and Avenge Pearl Harbor*, St. Martin's Griffin, 2006, p. 247.
53 Davis, Burke, *Get Yamamoto*, Random House, 1969, p. 116.
54 Sheppard, Si, *We Killed Yamamoto: The long-range P-38 assassination of the man behind Pearl Harbor Bougainville 1943*, Osprey Publishing, 2020, p. 38.
55 Davis, Burke, *Get Yamamoto*, Random House, 1969, p. 125.
56 Hampton, Dan, *Operation Vengeance: The Astonishing Aerial Ambush That Changed World War II*, William Morrow, 2020, p. 110.
57 Sheppard, Si, *We Killed Yamamoto: The long-range P-38 assassination of the man behind Pearl Harbor Bougainville 1943*, Osprey Publishing, 2020, p. 39.
58 Ibid.
59 Glines, Carroll, *Attack on Yamamoto*, Schiffer Military, 1993, p. 32.
60 Ibid., p. 10.
61 Ibid., p. 2.
62 Davis, Donald, *Lightning Strike: The Secret Mission to Kill Admiral Yamamoto and Avenge Pearl Harbor*, St. Martin's Griffin, 2006, p. 232.
63 Davis, Burke, *Get Yamamoto*, Random House, 1969, p. 76.
64 Davis, Donald, *Lightning Strike: The Secret Mission to Kill Admiral Yamamoto and Avenge Pearl Harbor*, St. Martin's Griffin, 2006, p. 238.
65 Sheppard, Si, *We Killed Yamamoto: The long-range P-38 assassination of the man behind Pearl Harbor Bougainville 1943*, Osprey Publishing, 2020, p. 40.
66 Lehr, Dick, *Dead Reckoning: The Story of How Johnny Mitchell and His Fighter Pilots Took On Admiral Yamamoto and Avenged Pearl Harbor*, HarperCollins, 2020, p. 174.
67 Davis, Burke, *Get Yamamoto*, Random House, 1969, p. 137.
68 Ibid., p. 138.
69 Sheppard, Si, *We Killed Yamamoto: The long-range P-38 assassination of the man behind Pearl Harbor Bougainville 1943*, Osprey Publishing, 2020, p. 40.
70 Lehr, Dick, *Dead Reckoning: The Story of How Johnny Mitchell and His Fighter Pilots Took On Admiral Yamamoto and Avenged Pearl Harbor*, HarperCollins, 2020, p. 174.
71 Sheppard, Si, *We Killed Yamamoto: The long-range P-38 assassination of the*

man behind Pearl Harbor Bougainville 1943, Osprey Publishing, 2020, p. 42.
72 Ibid.
73 Davis, Donald, *Lightning Strike: The Secret Mission to Kill Admiral Yamamoto and Avenge Pearl Harbor*, St. Martin's Griffin, 2006, p. 250.
74 Davis, Burke, *Get Yamamoto*, Random House, 1969, p. 141.
75 Sheppard, Si, *We Killed Yamamoto: The long-range P-38 assassination of the man behind Pearl Harbor Bougainville 1943*, Osprey Publishing, 2020, p. 42.
76 Davis, Donald, *Lightning Strike: The Secret Mission to Kill Admiral Yamamoto and Avenge Pearl Harbor*, St. Martin's Griffin, 2006, p. 250.
77 Lehr, Dick, *Dead Reckoning: The Story of How Johnny Mitchell and His Fighter Pilots Took On Admiral Yamamoto and Avenged Pearl Harbor*, HarperCollins, 2020, p. 175.
78 Davis, Burke, *Get Yamamoto*, Random House, 1969, p. 141.
79 Ibid., p. 142.
80 Ibid.
81 Ibid., p. 144.
82 Ibid., p. 106.
83 Lehr, Dick, *Dead Reckoning: The Story of How Johnny Mitchell and His Fighter Pilots Took On Admiral Yamamoto and Avenged Pearl Harbor*, HarperCollins, 2020, p. 14.
84 Davis, Donald, *Lightning Strike: The Secret Mission to Kill Admiral Yamamoto and Avenge Pearl Harbor*, St. Martin's Griffin, 2006, p. 240.
85 Davis, Burke, *Get Yamamoto*, Random House, 1969, p. 147.
86 Davis, Donald, *Lightning Strike: The Secret Mission to Kill Admiral Yamamoto and Avenge Pearl Harbor*, St. Martin's Griffin, 2006, p. 248.
87 Davis, Burke, *Get Yamamoto*, Random House, 1969, p. 147.
88 Lehr, Dick, *Dead Reckoning: The Story of How Johnny Mitchell and His Fighter Pilots Took On Admiral Yamamoto and Avenged Pearl Harbor*, HarperCollins, 2020, p. 176.
89 Davis, Donald, *Lightning Strike: The Secret Mission to Kill Admiral Yamamoto and Avenge Pearl Harbor*, St. Martin's Griffin, 2006, p. 249.
90 Hampton, Dan, *Operation Vengeance: The Astonishing Aerial Ambush That Changed World War II*, William Morrow, 2020, p. 139.
91 Davis, Donald, *Lightning Strike: The Secret Mission to Kill Admiral Yamamoto and Avenge Pearl Harbor*, St. Martin's Griffin, 2006, p. 249.
92 Glines, Carroll, *Attack on Yamamoto*, Schiffer Military, 1993, p. 96.
93 Lehr, Dick, *Dead Reckoning: The Story of How Johnny Mitchell and His Fighter Pilots Took On Admiral Yamamoto and Avenged Pearl Harbor*, HarperCollins, 2020, p. 176.
94 Davis, Donald, *Lightning Strike: The Secret Mission to Kill Admiral*

Yamamoto and Avenge Pearl Harbor, St. Martin's Griffin, 2006, p. 239.
95 Ibid., p. 249.
96 Lehr, Dick, *Dead Reckoning: The Story of How Johnny Mitchell and His Fighter Pilots Took On Admiral Yamamoto and Avenged Pearl Harbor*, HarperCollins, 2020, p. 176.
97 Davis, Burke, *Get Yamamoto*, Random House, 1969, p. 147.
98 Sheppard, Si, *We Killed Yamamoto: The long-range P-38 assassination of the man behind Pearl Harbor Bougainville 1943*, Osprey Publishing, 2020, p. 47.
99 Ibid., p. 48.
100 Davis, Burke, *Get Yamamoto*, Random House, 1969, p. 149.
101 Davis, Donald, *Lightning Strike: The Secret Mission to Kill Admiral Yamamoto and Avenge Pearl Harbor*, St. Martin's Griffin, 2006, p. 253.
102 Davis, Burke, *Get Yamamoto*, Random House, 1969, p. 150.
103 Ibid., p. 151.
104 Hampton, Dan, *Operation Vengeance: The Astonishing Aerial Ambush That Changed World War II*, William Morrow, 2020, p. 12.
105 Davis, Burke, *Get Yamamoto*, Random House, 1969, p. 145.
106 Ibid., p. 145.
107 Ibid., p. 151.
108 Davis, Donald, *Lightning Strike: The Secret Mission to Kill Admiral Yamamoto and Avenge Pearl Harbor*, St. Martin's Griffin, 2006, p. 251.
109 Davis, Burke, *Get Yamamoto*, Random House, 1969, p. 149.
110 Lehr, Dick, *Dead Reckoning: The Story of How Johnny Mitchell and His Fighter Pilots Took On Admiral Yamamoto and Avenged Pearl Harbor*, HarperCollins, 2020, p. 180.
111 Sheppard, Si, *We Killed Yamamoto: The long-range P-38 assassination of the man behind Pearl Harbor Bougainville 1943*, Osprey Publishing, 2020, p. 48.
112 Davis, Burke, *Get Yamamoto*, Random House, 1969, p. 152.
113 Hampton, Dan, *Operation Vengeance: The Astonishing Aerial Ambush That Changed World War II*, William Morrow, 2020, p. 14.
114 Davis, Burke, *Get Yamamoto*, Random House, 1969, p. 152.
115 Ibid.
116 Ibid.
117 Davis, Donald, *Lightning Strike: The Secret Mission to Kill Admiral Yamamoto and Avenge Pearl Harbor*, St. Martin's Griffin, 2006, p. 254.
118 Glines, Carroll, *Attack on Yamamoto*, Schiffer Military, 1993, p. 61.
119 Davis, Burke, *Get Yamamoto*, Random House, 1969, p. 153.
120 Glines, Carroll, *Attack on Yamamoto*, Schiffer Military, 1993, p. x.
121 Ibid.
122 Lehr, Dick, *Dead Reckoning: The Story of How Johnny Mitchell and His*

Fighter Pilots Took On Admiral Yamamoto and Avenged Pearl Harbor, HarperCollins, 2020, p. 182.

123 Davis, Donald, *Lightning Strike: The Secret Mission to Kill Admiral Yamamoto and Avenge Pearl Harbor*, St. Martin's Griffin, 2006, p. 285.

124 Ibid., p. 285.

125 Davis, Burke, *Get Yamamoto*, Random House, 1969, p. 157.

126 Glines, Carroll, *Attack on Yamamoto*, Schiffer Military, 1993, p. 96.

127 Sheppard, Si, *We Killed Yamamoto: The long-range P-38 assassination of the man behind Pearl Harbor Bougainville 1943*, Osprey Publishing, 2020, p. 60.

128 Davis, Burke, *Get Yamamoto*, Random House, 1969, p. 161.

129 Sheppard, Si, *We Killed Yamamoto: The long-range P-38 assassination of the man behind Pearl Harbor Bougainville 1943*, Osprey Publishing, 2020, p. 60.

130 Hampton, Dan, *Operation Vengeance: The Astonishing Aerial Ambush That Changed World War II*, William Morrow, 2020, p. 149.

131 Lehr, Dick, *Dead Reckoning: The Story of How Johnny Mitchell and His Fighter Pilots Took On Admiral Yamamoto and Avenged Pearl Harbor*, HarperCollins, 2020, p. 183.

132 Ibid., p. 184.

133 Glines, Carroll, *Attack on Yamamoto*, Schiffer Military, 1993, p. 204.

134 Davis, Burke, *Get Yamamoto*, Random House, 1969, p. 191.

135 Hampton, Dan, *Operation Vengeance: The Astonishing Aerial Ambush That Changed World War II*, William Morrow, 2020, p. 158.

136 Glines, Carroll, *Attack on Yamamoto*, Schiffer Military, 1993, p. 96.

137 Davis, Donald, *Lightning Strike: The Secret Mission to Kill Admiral Yamamoto and Avenge Pearl Harbor*, St. Martin's Griffin, 2006, p. 270.

138 Davis, Burke, *Get Yamamoto*, Random House, 1969, p. 167.

139 Ibid.

140 Ibid.

141 Glines, Carroll, *Attack on Yamamoto*, Schiffer Military, 1993, p. 71.

142 Davis, Burke, *Get Yamamoto*, Random House, 1969, p. 170.

143 Sheppard, Si, *We Killed Yamamoto: The long-range P-38 assassination of the man behind Pearl Harbor Bougainville 1943*, Osprey Publishing, 2020, p. 53.

144 Davis, Burke, *Get Yamamoto*, Random House, 1969, p. 168.

145 Glines, Carroll, *Attack on Yamamoto*, Schiffer Military, 1993, p. 72.

146 Ibid., p. 102.

147 Davis, Donald, *Lightning Strike: The Secret Mission to Kill Admiral Yamamoto and Avenge Pearl Harbor*, St. Martin's Griffin, 2006, p. 270.

148 Sheppard, Si, *We Killed Yamamoto: The long-range P-38 assassination of the man behind Pearl Harbor Bougainville 1943*, Osprey Publishing, 2020, p. 53.

149 Davis, Burke, *Get Yamamoto*, Random House, 1969, p. 172.

150 Ibid., p. 177.
151 Ibid., p. 178.
152 Sheppard, Si, *We Killed Yamamoto: The long-range P-38 assassination of the man behind Pearl Harbor Bougainville 1943*, Osprey Publishing, 2020, p. 63.
153 Davis, Burke, *Get Yamamoto*, Random House, 1969, p. 182.
154 Ibid., p. 182.
155 Ibid., p. 178.
156 Ibid., p. 179.
157 Glines, Carroll, *Attack on Yamamoto*, Schiffer Military, 1993, p. 91.
158 Lehr, Dick, *Dead Reckoning: The Story of How Johnny Mitchell and His Fighter Pilots Took On Admiral Yamamoto and Avenged Pearl Harbor*, HarperCollins, 2020, p. 187.
159 Davis, Burke, *Get Yamamoto*, Random House, 1969, p. 179.
160 Ibid., p. 188.
161 Ibid.
162 Lehr, Dick, *Dead Reckoning: The Story of How Johnny Mitchell and His Fighter Pilots Took On Admiral Yamamoto and Avenged Pearl Harbor*, HarperCollins, 2020, p. 186.
163 Davis, Burke, *Get Yamamoto*, Random House, 1969, p. 200.
164 Glines, Carroll, *Attack on Yamamoto*, Schiffer Military, 1993, p. 103.
165 Davis, Burke, *Get Yamamoto*, Random House, 1969, p. 210.
166 Ibid., p. 211.
167 Ibid., p. 207.
168 Davis, Donald, *Lightning Strike: The Secret Mission to Kill Admiral Yamamoto and Avenge Pearl Harbor*, St. Martin's Griffin, 2006, p. 295.
169 Davis, Burke, *Get Yamamoto*, Random House, 1969, p. 206.
170 Sheppard, Si, *We Killed Yamamoto: The long-range P-38 assassination of the man behind Pearl Harbor Bougainville 1943*, Osprey Publishing, 2020, p. 74.

Glossary

APC: Armoured personnel carrier

B5N aircraft: The Nakajima B5N was a crucial Japanese carrier-based torpedo bomber used throughout World War II.

Blenheim medium bombers: The Bristol Blenheim British medium bomber designed and built by the Bristol Aeroplane Company, used extensively in the first two years of the Second World War.

Cape Spada action: The naval battle of Cape Spada was fought on 19 July 1940 during World War II in the Mediterranean Sea off the coast of Crete. The battle involved HMAS *Sydney* and two Italian light cruisers, *Bartolomeo Colleoni* and *Giovanni delle Bande Nere*. HMAS *Sydney* sunk the *Bartolomeo Colleoni* and damaged the *Giovanni delle Bande Nere*.

Carley float: A type of life raft used on ships during World War I and World War II

Carnarvon: The HMS *Carnarvon Bay* was a Bay-class anti-aircraft frigate of the British Royal Navy.

Catalina: The Consolidated Model 28, more commonly known as the PBY Catalina (US Navy designation), is a flying boat and amphibious aircraft designed by Consolidated Aircraft.

CIA (Central Intelligence Agency): The civilian foreign intelligence service of the US government

CLH: Calcutta Light Horse Regiment

DIA (Defense Intelligence Agency): The government agency that provides military intelligence to the US Department of Defense and the military

DNOWA: District Naval Officer Western Australia

FECB (Far East Combined Bureau): An outstation of the British Intelligence Services which was established to monitor Japanese, Chinese and Russian intelligence and radio traffic

FRUMEL: Fleet Radio Unit, Melbourne

FRUPAC: Fleet Radio Unit, Pacific

Fulmar fighter: A British carrier-borne reconnaissance fighter aircraft

GRU: A powerful and secretive organization that conducted intelligence gathering, analysis and clandestine operations. It was known for creating the Spetsnaz special forces.

Grumman Wildcat: The Grumman F4F Wildcat is an American carrier-based fighter aircraft that entered service in 1940 with the United States Navy and the British Royal Navy.

Hurricane fighter aircraft: The Hawker Hurricane is a British single-seat fighter aircraft of the 1930s–40s, designed and built by Hawker Aircraft Ltd for the Royal Air Force.

ICBM: Intercontinental ballistic missile

IGHQ-Army/Navy Intelligence section: The top-level command for the armed forces of a country. It is where the military intelligence agencies (army and navy) are likely coordinated.

JN25B message: A Japanese naval code used during World War II

KGB (Komitet Gosudarstvennoy Bezopasnosti): The main security and intelligence agency of the Soviet Union from 1954 to 1991

Kidō Butai: The First Air Fleet was also known as the Kidō Butai ('Mobile Force'). It consisted of a combined carrier battle group comprising most of the aircraft carriers and carrier air groups of the Imperial Japanese Navy.

Kokutai 204: The land-based air group of the Imperial Japanese Navy Air Service during World War II

Kriegsmarine: The name for the German Navy from 1935 to 1945

Military backwater: A remote or underdeveloped area of little strategic importance that is still used by the military for training, storage, or other support activities

NSA (National Security Agency): The agency responsible for global monitoring, collection and processing of data for intelligence and counterintelligence purposes

Oberleutenat zur See: An officer rank in the German Navy, equivalent to a sub-lieutenant in the Royal Navy

Perth-class: The modified Leander-class light cruisers that served in the Royal Australian Navy

Pincer movement: A military tactic where forces simultaneously attack an enemy from two or more directions, converging to surround and overwhelm them

PLA: People's Liberation Army

President's Daily Brief: A top-secret document produced and given to the president of the United States every morning. It includes highly classified intelligence analysis and information. The PDB is produced by the director of national intelligence.

R-class battleships: The R-class consisted of five Dreadnought battleships built for the Royal Navy in the 1910s (see also, Revenge-class battleships).

Revenge-class battleships: The Revenge-class—sometimes referred to as the Royal Sovereign-class or the R-class—consisted of five Dreadnought battleships built for the Royal Navy in the 1910s.

Royal Indian Navy W7T and Cypher Office: This was the department responsible for cryptography, code breaking and secure communication. It was crucial for intelligence gathering, operational security, and communication with other naval forces.

SIGINT (signals intelligence): A form of intelligence gathering that involves intercepting and analysing electronic signals, including communications and non-communications signals

SOE: Special operations executive

Swordfish biplanes: The Fairey Swordfish is a torpedo bomber.

The Zero fighter: The Mitsubishi A6M 'Zero' is a long-range carrier-capable fighter aircraft formerly manufactured by Mitsubishi Aircraft Company. It was operated by the Imperial Japanese Navy from 1940 to 1945.

Two batteries of light howitzers: A battery of light howitzers typically consists of multiple howitzers—usually six—along with supporting personnel and equipment.

WEC: The British Wireless Experimental Centre (WEC) was the SIGINT hub during World War II which was primarily responsible for intercepting and analysing Japanese military communications.

Index